THE CHALET SCHOOL REVISITED

Edited by

ROSEMARY AUCHMUTY &
JULIET GOSLING

Bettany Press
1994

First published by Bettany Press 1994
52 Warham Road, London N4 1AT

© Bettany Press 1994

British Library Cataloguing in Publication Data
A catalogue record for this book is available
from the British Library

This book is sold subject to the condition that it shall not, by way of trade or otherwise, be lent, re-sold, hired out, or otherwise circulated without the Publisher's prior consent in any form of binding or cover other than that in which it is published and without a similar condition including this condition being imposed on the subsequent purchaser.
All rights reserved

ISBN 0 9524680 0 X

Design & DTP by Green Gosling, London
Printed and bound in Great Britain by
Dramrite Lithosphere, Southwark,
London SE1 3UW

CONTENTS

Notes on Contributors	iv
List of Illustrations	vii
Acknowledgements	viii
Introduction ROSEMARY AUCHMUTY AND JULIET GOSLING	1
In Search of Elinor HELEN MCCLELLAND	29
Excitements for the Chalet Fans POLLY GOERRES	67
The Literary Context SHEILA RAY	97
"School with bells on!" The school at the Chalet and beyond JULIET GOSLING	139
The Chalet School Guides. Girls' Organisations and Girls' School Stories ROSEMARY AUCHMUTY	173
My God, It's the Head! JUDITH HUMPHREY	213
The Series Factor SUE SIMS	253
Confessions of a Chalet School Collector GILL BILSKI	283
Images of the Chalet School. Dust Wrappers, Covers and Illustrations CLARISSA CRIDLAND	309
Books by Elinor M. Brent-Dyer	323
Price Guide to books by Elinor M. Brent-Dyer GILL BILSKI	327

NOTES ON CONTRIBUTORS

Rosemary Auchmuty was born in Egypt in 1950 to an American mother and Irish father, and grew up in Australia. She was educated at Newcastle Girls' High School (where she became School Captain) and the Australian National University (from which she obtained a Ph.D. in history in 1975). She moved to London in 1978, and now teaches law and women's studies at the University of Westminster. She has published two school textbooks and many articles on women's history, and contributed two chapters to the Lesbian History Group's book, *Not a Passing Phase* (Women's Press, 1989). She has also published a number of short stories. An avid reader of girls' school stories since the age of nine, in 1992 her study of girls' school stories, *A World of Girls*, was published by the Women's Press.

Gill Bilski was born in Middlesex in 1956 and became an avid reader of the Chalet School books at the age of 10. Married with two daughters (neither of whom read the Chalet School!), she is a leading seller of second-hand children's books and a Committee member of Friends of the Chalet School. She also runs a large Guide company, and in her very limited spare time enjoys watching Australian soap operas, listening to cricket on the radio, making tapestries and of course reading!

Clarissa Cridland was born in Guildford in 1955. She attended two boarding schools, neither of which was anything like the Chalet School. On leaving school she spent a year in Paris followed by a year's teacher training, but soon found that her real vocation lay in publishing. For the past 17 years she has worked for a variety of companies, ending as the director responsible for rights and contracts at Pan Macmillan Children's Books before going freelance in 1994. A voracious Chalet School reader from the age of ten, the books remain her favourites today, although she also collects other children's books. She now lives in Somerset with Friends of the Chalet School founder Ann Mackie-Hunter.

Polly Goerres was born in Leamington Spa in 1963 and educated at the King's High School for Girls, Warwick and the University of Sheffield. A Brent-Dyer fan from the age of ten, she wrote an undergraduate dissertation on the Chalet School series, and even spent her honeymoon in Pertisau am Achensee. Although presently working for Jaguar cars, much of Polly's time is devoted to her work as a Committee member of Friends of the Chalet School. She also enjoys travelling all over the country to watch football, (sometimes accompanied by a talking donkey) and to search for *The School by the River*.

Juliet Gosling was born in Essex in 1962 and attended Colchester County High School for Girls. Although her happiest day at school was the one when she left, she has spent the last six years studying girls' school stories. In 1992 she was awarded an M. A. by the University of East London for her thesis on representations of girls and women in the Chalet School. She is currently researching the reasons for the popularity of girls' school stories for a Ph.D. in Communication and Image Studies at the University of Kent at Canterbury, and hopes to present her findings as a multi-media hypertext. A journalist by profession, she has worked extensively in the media.

Judith Humphrey was born in Wales in 1947 and spent the 1960s at a girls' grammar school. She loved school, both for the intellectual stimulation and for the friendships with girls and staff, and ended as Head Girl. It seemed natural for her to continue into teaching (although teaching French in the local comprehensive is a somewhat different experience!). When her children were small, she was also involved in Development Education and in writing French courses for the Longman Group. A committed and practising Christian, she discovered feminism 12 years ago; since then she has rediscovered the Chalet School books which she collected avidly in her youth. She believes that the books celebrate female autonomy and female friendship, and is currently developing her analysis into a Ph.D. for the Open University.

Helen McClelland was born and educated in Scotland, migrating southwards in the late 1940s to pursue her musical studies in London and Paris. As a busy professional cellist she has played at concerts in many parts of the world, and currently teaches at the Royal College of Music in Manchester. Her love of writing dates from around the age of eight, but it was not until the 1970s that her special interest in the phenomenom of "Chaletomania" led to the writing of *Behind the Chalet School* — her biography of Elinor M. Brent-Dyer — and her two other Chalet books. She is married to pianist Alexander Kelly, has two daughters, and adopted the name Helen McClelland from her maternal grandmother.

Sheila Ray graduated from the University of Leeds in 1951, trained as a librarian and then specialised in work with children and young people. From 1968 she taught at the City of Birmingham Polytechnic, and since taking early retirement in 1983 she has lectured in children's literature and school librarianship as a freelance. She has been British associate editor for *Bookbird* (1973-93) and assistant editor of *Children's Literature Abstracts* (1973-91), and is currently editor of the *School Librarian* and a contributor to and book reviewer for a variety of librarianship and children's literature journals. An honorary fellow of the Library Association, in 1980 she was awarded an M.Phil. for her thesis on Enid Blyton, published as *The Blyton Phenomenom* (1982).

Sue Sims was born in London in 1952 and read English at Oxford. She then taught in various comprehensive and grammar schools, including King Edward's High School for Girls in Birmingham which had about 50 Brent-Dyers including *A Quintette in Queensland* and the original *Chalet School and Rosalie* (a private arrangement with the librarian means it no longer has either). She paused her career to produce three boys (with the co-operation of her husband, Paul) and now teaches A-level English part-time at Brockenhurst College of Further Education. She also co-produces *Folly,* a magazine devoted to the lighter type of children's literature, with Belinda Copson.

LIST OF ILLUSTRATIONS

The Chalet Girls' Cook Book; Helen McClelland's The Chalet School Companion and Elinor M. Brent-Dyer's Chalet School	28
The original dust wrappers of the first six books, published by Chambers and illustrated by Nina K. Brisley	172
The Chalet School and Barbara and The Chalet School Goes to It; first and paperback editions	252
First and paperback editions of The Coming of Age of the Chalet School, The Chalet School and Richenda, Trials for the Chalet School and Theodora and the Chalet School	282
First, subsequent and paperback editions of Three Go to the Chalet School and The Chalet School and the Island	322

ACKNOWLEDGEMENTS

Many people have assisted in the preparation of *The Chalet School Revisited*. All the contributors did much more than simply produce their own articles: they helped in a variety of ways, from checking each other's chapters for accuracy to obtaining permissions to use copyright material, from drawing up contracts to copying and sending out flyers. For all these efforts, the editors are very appreciative.

We especially wish to thank Chloe Rutherford and HarperCollins Armada for permission to quote and reproduce illustrations from the works of Elinor Brent-Dyer.

Our heartfelt thanks go to Joy Wotton, who copyedited the manuscript with dedication and enthusiasm, and to Alan Slingsby for typesetting training and support. Their professional skills ensured a truly professional product.

We are grateful to all those Friends of the Chalet School who gave assistance with the processing of orders and sales and the storage and mailing out of the books, and to everyone who sent in their orders so promptly, often with encouraging messages of support, so that we knew how many books we could afford to print.

Finally, we thank Sibyl Grundberg and Nick Green for their unfailing support and patience.

The editors hope that you think our efforts have been worthwhile, and that you enjoy this book.

Rosemary Auchmuty & Juliet Gosling, London 1994

INTRODUCTION

ROSEMARY AUCHMUTY & JULIET GOSLING

THE *Chalet School Revisited* has been written to mark the centenary of the birth of Elinor M. Brent-Dyer, author of the Chalet School series. Brent-Dyer's books, so long disregarded by the critics, are now being rehabilitated, and her achievement is beginning to receive the appreciation so long overdue. The achievement is, indeed, remarkable. Elinor Brent-Dyer published no fewer than 100 books; of these, 59 made up the Chalet School series, the longest series for girls ever written and only the second longest in juvenile fiction (after the Biggles series). Some of her books have been more or less continuously in print since they were written, and by 1995 the entire Chalet School series will have been reissued in paperback, courtesy of HarperCollins Armada. While these paperbacks sell upwards of 100,000 copies every year, second-hand hardback copies change hands for £50 or even £100; some very rare titles, such as *The School by the River*, are in effect priceless. A score of major dealers in children's fiction, and numerous smaller ones, now cater to the demands of hundreds of collectors, many of whom value the works of Brent-Dyer above all other children's books. In her lifetime, Brent-Dyer had a fan club with nearly 4,000 members world-wide; today, the Friends of the Chalet School — with more than 800 members — is the largest of several organisations devoted to the appreciation of girls' school stories and their authors.[1]

We should bear this achievement in mind whenever we are tempted to apologise for our interest in such a "low" form of literature — for the fact that we continue to read and enjoy the Chalet School books. For a start, we should remember that we are not alone. Elinor Brent-Dyer deserves serious critical attention not simply because she is clearly a significant social phenomenon, but because she has given us and thousands of others so much pleasure. And we should be clear in our minds that what we like is just as important as what other people like, and a great deal more important than what other people think we should like.

THE SCHOOL STORY AS A LITERARY GENRE

When Elinor Brent-Dyer embarked upon a writing career with *Gerry Goes to School*, her decision to write a school story was an obvious choice to make. In 1922 there was a strong demand for girls' school stories. Publishers were only too eager to sign up new authors, and girls (and their mentors) could hardly get enough of them. It was a genre eminently suited to women who, like Brent-Dyer, spent a good deal of time with girls and knew what girls enjoyed, in a world where girls were still educated separately from boys and enjoyed separate leisure interests. For this reason not only Brent-Dyer but also her heroine Jo Bettany began their writing careers as authors of girls' school stories.

That the genre was in its heyday from the 1920s to the 1950s in Britain is well-known to many adult fans, but it is a point worth making when we consider how different was the situation in, say, the 1960s, or the 1860s, or even today. A woman bent on earning her living as a writer would not now be advised to write a school story. Despite the relatively recent example of Antonia Forest and the contemporary success of Anne Digby and others, who have proved the existence of a continuing market, the modern writer would almost certainly experience difficulty in finding a publisher for a new girls' school story.[2] It is not that the girls of today won't read them — sales figures for reprints of the Chalet School books alone belie this suggestion; rather, the critics and editors don't like them. They associate school stories with all that is elitist, outdated and formulaic in children's literature. The values for which the books were welcomed between the wars have become the grounds on which they are now condemned.

The main outline of the history of girls' school stories is now well established, after decades of contemptuous neglect. The first well-known exponent was L. T. (Elisabeth Thomasina) Meade (1854-1914), who published *A World of Girls* in 1886, one of more than 300 novels for young people of which several had boarding school settings. But the girls' school story did not develop into a separate genre until the beginning of the 20th century, with the publication of Angela Brazil's first school story, *The Fortunes of Philippa*, in 1906. These later stories were characterised not simply by their school setting — usually but not always boarding — but also by their almost exclusively female cast of characters, their "optimism about the female state"[3] and their female authorship. Brazil, who continued to publish school stories until shortly before her death in 1947, is regarded as one of the three great writers of girls' school stories, together with Dorita Fairlie Bruce (1885-1970) and Elinor M. Brent-Dyer (1894-1969). To this group many would add the name of Elsie Jeanette Oxenham (1880-1960).[4]

Dorita Fairlie Bruce wrote 39 novels between 1920 and 1961, of which the Dimsie, Nancy (St Bride's and Maudsley) and Springdale series are the best-known. Elsie Oxenham wrote over 90 novels between 1907 and 1959, of which the Abbey series (38 books in all) are by far the most famous. But Elinor Brent-Dyer outdid them all.

Girls' school stories retained their popularity through and after the Second World War, thanks in part to the contributions of the prolific children's writer Enid Blyton (1897-1968); her Naughtiest Girl (1940-4), St Clare's (1941-5) and Malory Towers (1946-51) series are probably the most widely read school stories ever written. But no authors appeared after the 1940s who could rival Blyton's popularity, and from that time on school stories began to borrow heavily from the mystery and crime genres also popular at the time — an influence which is apparent in the later work of Dorita Fairlie Bruce (for example, the books set during the Second World War) and Elinor Brent-Dyer (the Fardingales and Chudleigh Hold series).

By the mid-1960s, popular writers for girls had largely ceased to write in the school-story genre. Carpenter and Prichard state that "The 1950s saw the beginning of a general improvement in British children's fiction, leading to a decline in the number of books written specifically for girls"[5], and it is probable that the reduction in the number of girls' school stories being published reflected this trend towards publishing books that would appeal to both sexes. The belief that publishing books for girls alone was undesirable persisted into the 1970s. Cadogan and Craig wrote in their introduction to *You're a Brick, Angela! A New Look at Girls' Fiction 1839-1975* (1976):

At the present time girls' fiction appears almost redundant as a genre: the most interesting work which is being produced is capable of appreciation by anyone. Classification along rigid sexually-determined lines is, or should be, no longer valid.[6]

Another reason for the decline of the girls' school story was the frequently expressed preference of critics in the later 20th century for "realism" in children's books. In the mid-1970s Robert Leeson, then literary editor of the *Morning Star*, having first dismissed the Chalet School series as "sentimentally escapist", wrote with satisfaction that there was:

> a slowly increasing number of stories featuring the ordinary day school in an industrial town as the well realised, unselfconscious background to drama and comedy. The modern school story must essentially come to grips with the life of working-class children and their home background.[7]

Yet other critics criticised girls' school stories as realistic representations of a particular lifestyle — one that they deplored. As Gill Frith put it in "'The Time of Your Life': The Meaning of the School Story": "Exclusive, expensive and enclosed, they represent a sealed, rigidly hierarchical world in which 'normality' is white and middle-class".[8] As politicians and educationists sought to ensure greater equality of opportunity in education in the 1960s, stories which portrayed private boarding-schools in a positive light were increasingly seen as undesirable.

A further reason that girls' school stories largely ceased publication in the mid-1960s may have been the increasing hostility towards Enid Blyton, who with Brent-Dyer was the most popular of the post-war girls' school-story writers and was therefore closely identified with the genre. Blyton became a focus of antagonism from librarians and educationists like Colin Welch who claimed that her books were mediocre, had a limited vocabulary and upheld class distinctions. This received enormous coverage in the national press.[9]

One girls' boarding school-story series which is currently in production is Anne Digby's Trebizon series, which began in 1978 with *First Term at Trebizon* and now numbers 14 books. This series does indeed concentrate on "realism", with its foregrounding of a contemporary girls' public-school setting, male masters and boyfriends. In this it differs fundamentally from its predecessors, and it is doubtful whether it can be considered part of the same genre.

However, despite the fact that the majority of authors ceased to write school stories, and that books by lesser-known authors quickly went out of print, girls' school stories have continued to attract successive generations of readers. Brazil's books were still appearing in paperback in the 1970s, Dorita Fairlie Bruce's Dimsie books were reissued in hardback in 1983-4, and Blyton's school series and Brent-Dyer's Chalet School books have remained almost constantly in print. The books are not only bought by children; a significant minority of both purchasers and readers are adults, as are the great majority of subscribers to the fanzines.

THE CHALET SCHOOL STORY

In 1922, when Brent-Dyer set out on her long writing career, she was entering into a distinguished field. Her first attempt, *Gerry Goes to School,* is nothing special as a novel, as Brent-Dyer herself admitted in later years, though it was certainly not bad for a first effort. Still, in a decade in which some of the greatest examples of girls' school stories were published — among them Oxenham's very finest work, including most of her school stories, and Dorita Fairlie Bruce's first seven Dimsie books — Brent-Dyer's output would hardly have excited any attention, were it not for her happy inspiration, following a holiday in the Austrian Tyrol in 1924, to write a series about a school set in this picturesque and unusual location.

In May 1994, a group of Chalet fans led by Daphne Barfoot, and including the editors of this book, returned to the site of Elinor Brent-Dyer's Tyrolean holiday 70 years before and retraced the fictitious footsteps of the Chaletians of those early books. It was not the first time that many of us had been there, since Pertisau-am-Achensee (Brent-Dyer's "Briesau-am-Tiernsee") has long held an attraction for Chalet fans since the secret of its location was revealed in a *Chalet Club News Letter* in the 1960s. But in this centenary year of Brent-Dyer's birth it held a special significance. Thanks to other centenary events held earlier in the year, including the big celebration weekend in Hereford described by Polly Goerres in her chapter in this book, we were already steeped in Chaletiana; and, despite tourism, the Achensee is not so changed that we were unable to imagine the impact of the setting upon the young author in 1924, nor to understand how it inspired a whole series of books, which in turn have enchanted generations of readers.

In *The School at the Chalet* (1925), 24-year-old Madge Bettany travels to the Tyrol to open a school. She needs to earn a living to support herself and her 12-year-old sister, Jo, and Austria is chosen for its cheapness and the Alpine climate, since Jo's "health had been a constant worry to those who had charge of her".[10] Their parents are dead, and Madge's twin brother, Dick, is about to return to his job in India where they were all born. The school opens with 3 pupils; by the end of the first term there are 18, and by the start of the second, 33. (At its largest, many years later in Switzerland, there are over 400.) Madge's teaching career is short-lived, as she becomes engaged at the end of the second book in the series and marries at the end of the third, *The Princess of the Chalet School* (1927), whereupon she retires from teaching. This was, of course, the norm at the time, when women were expected to choose between marriage and a career, and many schools operated a marriage bar.

Madge's husband, Jem Russell, is a doctor who has come to the Tyrol to set up a sanatorium for TB sufferers, and so at first they remain close to the school, both geographically and emotionally. Later, however, when Jo becomes an adult, Madge is mentioned much less frequently, and in the 21st book, *The Chalet School and the Island* (1950), she travels to Canada with her family for an extended stay. By the 30th book, *The Chalet School and Barbara* (1954), this separation has become permanent: Jem remains Head of the Sanatorium in England, where it had relocated during the war years, while the school moves to Switzerland. Madge reappears periodically as a visitor, and is said to retain a financial interest in the school, but from the time she is married she never enjoys the ongoing relationship with the school that Jo does.

Jo is at the centre of the books. For the first 11 she is a pupil at the school, becoming Head Girl in the 7th, *The Chalet School and Jo* (1931). In the 12th book, *Jo Returns to the Chalet School* (1936), she returns temporarily to teach, and in the 14th, *The

Chalet School in Exile (1940), she marries a colleague of Jem Russell, Jack Maynard, who is also a brother of a former mistress at the school. Because of the links between the school and the sanatorium, Jack never works far from the school, and so Jo is able to remain associated with it throughout the series.

> Jo's a married lady and a proud mamma of many [11 eventually], and yet, in one sense, she's a much a part of the school as ever she was when she was Head Girl — or a sickening little nuisance of a Middle, for that matter. In my opinion, she'll still belong when she's a doddering old woman of ninety-odd, telling her great-great-grandchildren all about her evil doings at school![11]

This identification of Jo with the Chalet School becomes complete when the school moves to the Bernese Oberland and Jo and her husband, who is to head a new branch of the sanatorium there, buy a house next door to the school.

There is evidence to suggest that Brent-Dyer's publishers, W. and R. Chambers of Edinburgh, wished to end the series after *Jo Returns to the Chalet School* (1936), both on financial grounds and because "there are now 12 [books] and that is enough".[12] This was perhaps not surprising, given that this was a series of school stories whose central character, Jo, had now left school. True, she returned to the school in the 12th book after leaving, to help the staff out during a bout of illness, but this was an artificial device to keep her there which could not be indefinitely maintained.

Yet the series continued for another 47 books and 34 years. Brent-Dyer was able to go on writing Chalet School stories to the end of her life because of her skill in developing the series and repositioning it whenever necessary. Following her publisher's warnings, she made some major changes to the series in her 13th book, *The New Chalet School* (1938). She replaced the shadowy Headmistress, Mademoiselle Lepattre, who had taken over after Madge's marriage, with Miss Annersley, a far more convincing figure, who steps in when Mademoiselle becomes ill (and eventually dies) and remains Headmistress for the rest of the series. She killed off the Robin's father, always an anachronism since his daughter was being brought up by the Russells. New staff and girls are introduced by merging the Chalet School with a neighbouring school, and Joey's future position as an author and helpmate to the school is established.

By the time Brent-Dyer wrote the next book, *The Chalet School in Exile* (1940), events in Europe had forced her to change the series again. Austria was annexed by the Nazis in 1938, and England went to war in the following year. In the course of this book the school is relocated from Austria to Guernsey, and this is dramatised around Joey and Robin's flight from the Nazis, bringing in adventure elements which would be topical at the time and remain exciting today. Joey becomes engaged while in Austria, and after a ten-month gap in proceedings in the middle of the book (the only occasion when a single book does not follow a continuous time period) she is married, and later gives birth to triplet daughters.

Jack Maynard, Jo's husband, had been a minor character in the series since the sanatorium opened, but had never been suggested as a suitor for Joey before this book. However, because men play only a minor role in the series anyway, Brent-Dyer was able to write quite convincingly that "for the past two years [he] had been quite decided about what she meant to him"[13]; and as men were expected to take the active role in relationships, perhaps the engagement is not unexpected after this. Robin, a romanticised character who has remained a "small girl" since she was introduced to the series, and who would have looked increasingly out of place in the late 1930s, is also transformed into a normal teenager. War thus provided a reason for Joey and Robin to grow up, in Jo's case signified by the trappings of marriage and children, in Robin's by the loss of the prefix "the" from her name and by improvements in her health, which were essential for the series to retain its credibility.

Unfortunately, the Channel Islands, which Brent-Dyer had chosen for her new setting, came under attack by Germany in the early days of the war, and by the 15th book, *The Chalet School Goes to It* (1940), the school has moved again, this time to the Welsh border in Herefordshire, where Brent-Dyer was now living. Once again she capitalised on the opportunities this offered the plot, and dramatised the move with a U-boat attack on the boat carrying Joey and her triplet babies to the mainland. After the war ended in 1945, there was a four-year gap in the series when it was possible that the publishers again wished to finish it, but in 1949 Brent-Dyer produced the twentieth book in the series, *Three Go to the Chalet School*. Of the three new characters mentioned in the title, one, Mary-Lou Trelawney, was to take over many of the schoolgirl Joey's characteristics and importance within the school.

Three Go to the Chalet School was acknowledged to take place some years after the last published book, *Jo to the Rescue* (1945), though in between came the three *Chalet Annuals* (the second and third of which contained the full text of *Tom Tackles the Chalet School*, not published in book form until 1955). Into this gap falls also, as far as the chronology of the series is concerned, the unnumbered Chalet book, *The Chalet School and Rosalie*, published (in soft cover only) in 1951. The time lapse allowed the triplets to reach school age and many of the old characters to be dispensed with; Robin, for example, is now at Oxford. Others have altered subtly in relative age to suit the demands of the plot. It also allowed new characters to be introduced into the series without using the plot device of the "new girl", together with suitable "back-stories" which helped to drive the plot of this and successive books. For example, Joey's youngest triplet Margot, previously depicted as perfectly healthy, is now described as delicate, enabling Madge and Jem to take her with them to the better climate of Canada (*The Chalet School and the Island*, 1950). A more complex back-story underlies the appointment of Peggy Bettany — Dick's eldest girl — as head girl (*Peggy of the Chalet School*, 1950), for the expressed reason that a member of "Special Sixth" had previously made a poor job of the post; this causes a member of the current Special Sixth, a new character Eilunedd, to bear a grudge, as she had a "history" of doing. Successful as these devices were in repositioning the series, they have since caused endless headaches to fans bent on establishing the "true" history of the school, since they often failed to fit into any rational chronology.

Although many of the new characters seemed to be popular with readers — Mary-Lou and the triplets were to be central to most of the succeeding books — the school relocated again in *The Chalet School and the Island* (1950), this time to a small island, "St Briavel's", off the coast of south Wales. This setting allowed for a variety of new interests, among them boating, swimming, water pageants and bird-watching, and water-associated incidents, such as a shipwreck and a near drowning. Prudently, Brent-Dyer invented a reason for the school's removal — bad drains in the old building — which would allow her to send it back to Herefordshire if necessary. But by the following book, *Peggy of the Chalet School* (1950), the school had become established on the island so, due to subsidence in her own house, Joey is made to move to the mainland across the water from the island.

In 1952, with *The Wrong Chalet School*, Brent-Dyer began to set the scene for the school's final relocation to Switzerland, with references to the establishment of a Swiss finishing branch. By the next book, *Shocks for the Chalet School* (1952), this branch is in operation, and it is the subject of the following book, *The Chalet School in the Oberland* (1952). (This is the only book in the series which focuses on the finishing branch. By common consent it is regarded as one of Brent-Dyer's least successful tales, and this may explain why she produced no more with this setting.) *Shocks for the Chalet School* also introduces foreign girls again — the "English" school had been predominantly British during the war and immediately afterwards, for obvious reasons — and since some of these are related to former pupils, new links with earlier books in the series are forged. The 27th book in the series, *Bride Leads the Chalet School* (1953), is still set on the island, but the school has merged again, this time with another "Chalet School" founded on very different principles, thus providing a fresh supply of characters and a variation on a classic plot line which Brent-Dyer used no fewer than three times in the course of the Chalet School series.[14]

By the 28th book, *Changes for the Chalet School*

(1953), it has been decided to move the bulk of the school to the Swiss Oberland, and by the 30th, *The Chalet School and Barbara* (1954), this has become a reality. Again, Brent-Dyer leaves part of the school behind as an "English" branch (actually Welsh) on a mainland site near the island, which could have functioned as yet another setting for the series. In fact she never used it, Switzerland proving a much more attractive location for the postwar reader.

In the 29th book, *Joey Goes to the Oberland* (1954), Jo and Jack also move to the Oberland. Brent-Dyer had experimented with removing Joey from the series, sending her to Canada with her family for a year in *The Wrong Chalet School*, but after the move to Switzerland she remains next door to the school until the end of the series. The link between school and sanatorium, broken while the school was on the island, is also resumed.

The Chalet School continues in its Oberland setting for another 27 books, written over 16 years (*Prefects of the Chalet School* was published posthumously in 1970), but covering 8 years in fictional time. The series ends with Jo's triplets about to leave school and embark on their university studies. Although this was clearly a suitable point at which to end the Chalet story, Brent-Dyer was unable to resist the temptation to plot the triplets' future lives beyond graduation, for one of them — Len, the eldest — is already engaged to be married and another, Margot, intends to enter the Church and work as a medical missionary.

The school, however, is set to go on forever, and so is Jo. That the series should have continued through 59 volumes is a tribute to the author's considerable ability to reposition it when necessary to maintain its credibility and the interest of her readers. This was achieved through geographical moves and adept changes in focus but also, after the first few books, by ceasing to rely on a single protagonist or small group of protagonists, as in conventional literary narratives. Instead, Brent-Dyer made community life the centre of the series. This permitted it to undergo any number of permutations, and it is interesting to speculate what might have happened to the Chalet School in the years to come.

COMING OUT AS A SCHOOL STORY FAN

One of the effects of the negative criticism levelled at school stories in the years following the Second World War has been that those of us who enjoy reading the books have often been forced to keep our mouths shut about it. To confess our preference would be to invite incredulity and ridicule. Many contributors to the fanzines have written of their relief at finding others through the fan clubs who share their preference; many use the metaphor of the closet, and speak gratefully of being able to "come out" in the company of fellow-fans. Like the lesbians and gay men from whom this metaphor is borrowed, the joy these readers' experience at meeting others like themselves is in direct proportion to the pain they suffer at having to deal, in the rest of their lives, with other people's perceptions (or misconceptions) about them and the books they love. What is abundantly clear to adult school story fans is that a liking for school stories is not simply disparaged in our society (as a liking for detective or romantic fiction might be, for example), it is generally considered bizarre, if not ridiculous.

In her contribution to this book, Sheila Ray considers the critical reception given to the Chalet School books across the 20th century.

Unsurprisingly, given the treatment of girls' school stories by literary and educational critics, they have been treated with no more respect by other cultural institutions. For example, the very title of the Bethnal Green Museum of Childhood's 1984 exhibition, *Jolly Hockey Sticks — The World of Girls' School Fiction*, implies that the books should not be taken seriously. The emphasis of the exhibition was on book covers and illustrations, rather than on distinguishing individual authors or sub-genres, nor did the exhibition offer any sustained analysis of the genre, as might have been expected.

In journalism, Arthur Marshall began a lifelong interest in parodying girls' school stories, particularly those of Angela Brazil, with a review in the *New Statesman* in 1935. He continued to publish parodies in a variety of magazines as well to to perform them on radio and later compiled *Giggling in the Shrubbery* (1985), a satirical account of the splendours and miseries of girls' public schools. Ronald Searle published candid cartoons of the awful schoolgirls of St Trinian's in magazines such as *Lilliput* and *Punch*, and collaborated with "Timothy Shy" (D. B. Wyndham Lewis) on *The Terror of St Trinian's* (1952).

His cartoons were developed into a series of comedy films by Ealing Studios, beginning with *The Belles of St Trinian's* in 1954. The Ealing series took certain elements of the girls' school story — the enclosed all-female community, a uniform which made no allowances for adolescence, girls behaving like boys and the adventure elements which crept in from the mystery and crime genres — but subjected them all to merciless parody which concentrated on the girls' physicality, with younger, pre-adolescent girls having little regard for their appearance and behaving very roughly towards their peers, while older girls and some staff members were heavily sexualised.

More recently this has been echoed on the stage in Denise Deegan's play *Daisy Pulls It Off*, which opened in the West End in 1984 and was still being produced seven years later at the 1991 Edinburgh Festival. This parody, which draws heavily on the works of Angela Brazil, features adult women playing schoolgirl roles. Significantly, whereas heterosexual sex is all but absent in the novels, it is placed at the forefront of these parodies in their representation of school life.

It has been argued that the negative treatment given to girls' school stories by both male and female critics owes much to the fact that the books were written by women and read by an almost exclusively female audience. We have seen how the growing social expectations of educational equality which played a part in the genre's demise also gave rise to a feeling that novels written exclusively for girls must be inferior to those written for boys or for both sexes. Cadogan and Craig echo this when they write that "girls' books quickly became a medium for the reinforcement of social prohibitions and expectations"[15], a comment which, like those of other critics, rests on an unstated assumption that, since girls have been and still are failing to fulfil their educational potential in the 20th century, so a medium which purports to represent girls' educational experience in that century will itself be inferior.

Further evidence to support the view that the negative critical treatment of girls' school stories might be directly related to the sex of their authors can be gleaned from the differential treatment accorded to comic book school stories for girls. Girls' comics were first created in the 1920s by male writers already writing the same sorts of stories for boys, and they continued to be written, drawn and owned by men throughout this century, with male authors often assuming female pseudonyms. Despite the hostility expressed towards comics by parents, educationists and critics from the mid-20th century onwards, and the fact that girls' school stories have not survived in comic form, critics have tended to treat them with greater respect and enthusiasm than the girls' school stories in novel form, and give much more attention to describing plots and authors. Carpenter and Prichard, for example, in their entry on "Girls' Stories", allot twice as much space to comics as to novels, while Cadogan and Craig, having scorned the work of Oxenham and Brent-Dyer, write of the comics:

> the male writers were so inventive and convincing that they managed to involve readers as well as fictional girls in the vivid situations which they created. Using a wide variety of feminine pseudonyms, they transported their audience for twopence a week through endlessly successful school themes . . . [16]

A similar preference for male authors is found in Mary Cadogan's later compilation, *Chin Up, Chest Out, Jemima* (1989), whose title alone is sufficient to indicate its approach. In the introductory chapter which gives a history of girls' school stories, "Eighty Years of the Spiffing Schoolgirl", Cadogan devotes more than half to comic stories written and published by men. Alongside girls' school stories by both male and female authors are found articles and parodies by Cadogan, Arthur Marshall, Terence Stamp and Denise Deegan. Although parts of the book, particularly the introductory chapter, are informative and historically accurate, the title and the choice of contributors suggest strongly to the reader that girls' school stories are not to be taken seriously.

Tania Modleski, writing about popular genres for adult women, has pointed out that "very few critics have taken them seriously enough to study them in any detail". She describes a double critical standard, already identified by feminists as biasing literary studies, which she claims is also operative in studies of mass culture.

> Women's criticism of popular feminine narratives has generally adopted one of three attitudes: dismissiveness; hostility . . . ; or most frequently, a flippant kind of mockery . . . It is significantly indistinguishable from the tone men often use when they mention feminine popular art . . . In assuming this attitude, we demonstrate . . . our acceptance of the critical double standard and of the masculine contempt for sentimental (feminine) "drivel".[17]

In *A World of Girls* (1992), Rosemary Auchmuty argues that this masculine contempt, which women so often share because we too have been educated to accept masculine standards of "quality", stems from men's anxiety about and fear of things which belong to women and exclude men. In a patriarchal society, women are supposed to put their energies into men. The existence of any cultural artefact or indeed, any time or space which is designed for women alone is profoundly threatening to masculine power, for it suggests the possibility that women could have other priorities — could even, in fact, put ourselves first.

The last two decades have seen considerable changes in the ways in which girls' literature has been viewed. On the one hand, feminist scholarship has provided a forum within which women's work and women's culture have come to be valued and examined from women's point of view. The pioneering study of girls' school stories, Mary Cadogan and Patricia Craig's *You're a Brick, Angela!* (1976), while very much a product of its time, nevertheless established the subject as one worthy of serious study. Since then, both Victorian and 20th-century girls' fiction have been considered in greater depth by feminist scholars in a range of fascinating studies, presenting a view which differs significantly from the earlier dismissal of the literary critics and librarians.[18]

The other impetus has come from the school-story enthusiasts themselves (which is not to say that the two groups do not overlap). There have been a number of excellent biographies and critical studies of the work of notable exponents of the genre.[19] Other very interesting work has come from the fanzines or newsletters devoted to individual writers — the *Friends of the Chalet School Newsletter*, *The Chaletian*, the *Abbey Chronicle* (Elsie J. Oxenham), *Serendipity* (Dorita Fairlie Bruce) and others — and to children's literature in general, such as *Folly* (Fans of Light Literature for the Young[20]), which is distinguished by excellent biographical and bibliographical research. Finally, an increasing number of undergraduate and postgraduate students — including the authors of three of the chapters in this book — have taken girls' school stories as the subject of their dissertations, thus continuing to add to our knowledge and ideas about the subject.

THE CHALET SCHOOL REVISITED

This centenary volume represents both these approaches. The book begins fittingly with a chapter written by Helen McClelland, whose biography of Elinor Brent-Dyer gave fans our first (and so far, only) picture of the woman *Behind the Chalet School*, and who thus inspired so many of us to take a scholarly interest in our favourite girls' school stories and their authors. Helen gives us an update on and an overview of her continuing research into the life of Elinor Brent-Dyer, "In search of Elinor".

The second chapter comes from Polly Goerres, describing the celebrations for the centenary of Elinor Brent-Dyer's birth and discussing the reasons for the Chalet School books' appeal. Polly not only wrote an undergraduate thesis on the books, she is in an almost unique position to know what fans think about them, since she is a member of the Committee of Friends of the Chalet School and also one of the hard-worked organisers of the hugely successful Brent-Dyer centenary celebrations in 1994.

Sheila Ray's *The Blyton Phenomenon* (André Deutsch, 1982) was one of the first serious considerations of the literary achievement of Enid Blyton, England's most prolific and popular children's writer, and the critical response to her work from librarians, educationists, and the reading public. Sheila examines here "The Literary Context of the Chalet School", first from the point of view of its critical reception and then in terms of the literary world on which Brent-Dyer drew, and which she presented to her readers in a wealth of allusions and references to enrich our knowledge and experience.

Juliet Gosling's chapter on the Chalet School as

an educational institution derives from research for the M.A. thesis she completed three years ago. In it she shows how the fictional world mirrored in part the real development of middle-class girls' schools in the early 20th century and in part Elinor Brent-Dyer's own educational philosophy and ideals. She reminds us, however, that these are works of fiction, and that the educational aspects of the school also function as settings for various plot devices and character development.

Rosemary Auchmuty's chapter on the Chalet School Guides and the role of girls' organisations in school stories develops the argument put forward in her book, *A World of Girls*, that the appeal of girls' school stories lies primarily in their presentation of an all-female world, and that this was also the reason why the books were critically ignored, belittled, or condemned. Here she argues that the appeal of such girls' organisations as the Guides was because they presented an all-female world, in which a range of roles and experiences were made possible outside the usual restrictions of femininity, and that for this reason, the organisations and their fictional representations were subjected to the same criticisms and pressures as stories about girls' schools.

Drawing on research undertaken for her Ph.D. on girls' fiction and her own personal interest in theological issues, Judith Humphrey analyses the presentation of religion in the work of Elinor Brent-Dyer and other school story writers. She demonstrates that the all-female world of the girls' school endowed Headmistresses with a quasi-religious power, which not only challenged patriarchal notions of authority but combined masculine headship with a feminine maternal role. Brent-Dyer's Miss Annersley ("the Abbess") is a striking example of this subversive religious imagery in the work of an otherwise orthodox Christian writer.

Co-editor of the erudite but entertaining magazine *Folly*, Sue Sims has one of the most extensive collections of children's fiction in private hands, and she is eminently qualified to discuss the appeal of the series format — and particularly the Chalet School series — for readers of all ages. Both Sue and Gill Bilski, the author of the following chapter, are collectors-turned-dealers. Gill is now one of the major dealers in girls' fiction and Guide material in Britain. One of the Friends of the Chalet School Committee, she represents the point of view of the collector and dealer in her chapter.

Finally, Clarissa Cridland, another Friends of the Chalet School Committee member and, with Polly Goerres, co-organiser of the centenary celebrations, provides a work-in-progress report on her ongoing project to survey all the dustwrappers and illustrations of Brent-Dyer's books. For many readers, the illustrations help to form our impressions of Chalet characters. Clarissa tells us about the artists and assesses their strengths and weaknesses.

In commissioning the articles for this collection, the editors have tried to draw on the knowledge and experience of a wide range of "authorities" on different aspects of Brent-Dyer's work, who approach their subject from different positions and perspectives: as fans, collectors, dealers, writers, editors, students, teachers, scholars, librarians and various combinations of these categories. We are aware that there are many others out there who are equally knowledgeable and equally competent to write about the Chalet School books, whom we could also have approached. We began, however, with the people we knew at the time; and we are aware that this collection will not be regarded as the last word on the subject. Others are making their views known through the media of the fanzines, university dissertations, articles and books published elsewhere, and we hope that *The Chalet School Revisited* will be followed by many more publications in the field.

Two things all the contributors to this book do have in common: we all love the books, and we are all writing for an audience who love them too. Without this personal engagement with the Chalet School, these chapters would probably resemble so much that has been written about girls' school stories in the past, where the books are depicted as weird specimens under a hostile microscope, or patronised and misrepresented by outsiders looking in. We are all insiders, and we hope that our enthusiasm and our love for the books shine through these pages, to meet our readers on this common ground.

NOTES

1. Friends of the Chalet School, which produces a newsletter, organises events and co-ordinates local groups, can be contacted through Gill Bilski, 4 Sheepfold Lane, Amersham Bucks HP7 9EL.
2. Antonia Forest wrote a series of books about the Marlow family, some of which are school stories and some not. Anne Digby is the author of the successful "Trebizon" series, discussed later in the Introduction. Other contemporary school story authors include Mary Hooper and Jean Ure.
3. Mary Cadogan & Patricia Craig, *You're a Brick, Angela! A New Look at Girls' Fiction 1839-1975* (Gollancz, 1976).
4. It is sometimes argued that Oxenham was not really a school story writer, since so many of her books — in particular, most of the Abbey series which were always the most freely available of her output — are not set in schools. On the other hand, all her Rocklands, Sussex Downs, Gregory's, Torment, Jinty, Deb, Camp Keema, and Wood End series, some of the Swiss and some of the Abbey books, and a number of single titles, *are* set in schools, though perhaps the focus is less school-centred (and more concerned with Guides, Camp Fire, or personal relationships) than the work of many other authors.
5. Humphrey Carpenter and Mari Prichard, *The Oxford Companion to Children's Literature* (Oxford University Press, 1984), p.208.
6. Cadogan and Craig, *ibid.*, p.9.
7. Robert Leeson, *Children's Books and Class Society* (Writers and Readers' Publishing Cooperative, 1976), pp.33-4.
8. Gill Frith, "'The Time of Your Life': The Meaning of the Girls' School story". In Carolyn Steedman, Cathy

Unwin and Valerie Walkerdine eds. *Language, Gender and Childhood* (RKP, 1985), p.115.
9. See Sheila Ray, *The Blyton Phenomenon* (André Deutsch, 1982); Barbara Stoney, *Enid Blyton* (Hodder & Stoughton, 1974), pp.164-7.
10. Elinor Brent-Dyer, *The School at the Chalet* (1925), p.15.
11. *Shocks for the Chalet School* (1952), p.22.
12. Helen McClelland, *Behind the Chalet School* (New Horizon, 1981), p.141.
13. *The Chalet School in Exile* (1940), p.60.
14. *The New Chalet School* (1938) — St Scholastika's; *Bride Leads the Chalet School* (1953) — the other Chalet School; and *The Feud in the Chalet School* (1962) — St Hilda's, though this is only a temporary merger.
15. Cadogan and Craig, *ibid.*, p.9.
16. Carpenter and Prichard, p208; Cadogan and Craig, *ibid.*, p.233.
17. Tania Modleski, *Loving with a Vengeance. Mass-Produced Fantasies for Women* (Archon Books, 1982), pp.11,14.
18. On Victorian girls' fiction see, for example, Anna Davin, "Imperialism and Motherhood", *History Workshop 5* (1978), pp.9-65; Jacky Bratton, *The Impact of Victorian Children's Fiction* (Croom Helm, 1981); Deborah Gorham, "The Ideology of Femininity and Reading for Girls, 1850-1914". In Felicity Hunt, ed. *Lessons for Life. The Schooling of Girls and Women 1850-1950* (Blackwell, 1987); Judith Rowbotham, *Good Girls Make Good Wives. Guidance for Girls in Victorian Fiction* (Blackwell, 1989); and Kimberley Reynolds, *Girls Only?* (Harvester Wheatsheaf, 1990). The appeal of 20th century girls' school stories has been discussed in Cammilla Nightingale, "Sex Roles in Children's Literature". In Sandra Allen, Lee Sanders and Jan Wallis eds. *Conditions of Illusion* (Feminist Books, 1974); Gill Frith, "'The Time of Your Life': The Meaning of the Girls' School Story". In Carolyn Steedman, Cathy Unwin and Valerie Walkerdine, eds. *Language, Gender and Childhood* (RKP, 1985); and Rosemary Auchmuty, *A World of Girls* (Women's Press,1992).

19. See, for example, Barbara Stoney, *Enid Blyton* (Hodder & Stoughton 1974); Gillian Freeman, *The Schoolgirl Ethic: The Life and Works of Angela Brazil* (Allen Lane 1976); Helen McClelland, *Behind the Chalet School* [a life of Elinor M. Brent-Dyer] (New Horizon, 1981); Eva Löfgren, *Schoolmates of the Long-Ago: Motifs and Archetypes in Dorita Fairlie Bruce's Boarding School Stories* (Symposion Graduale, 1993).
20. The *Abbey Chronicle*. Editor, Monica Godfrey. 30 Sidford High Street, Sidford, Devon WX10 9SL.
Serendipity. Editors, Stella Waring & Carolyn Denman. 3 Dudwell Cottages, Camrose, Haverfordwest, Dyfed SA62 6HJ.
Folly. Editors, Sue Sims & Belinda Copson. 9 Silver Birch Road, Erdington, Birmingham B24 0AR.

The Chalet Girls' Cook Book; Helen McClelland's *The Chalet School Companion* & *Elinor M. Brent-Dyer's Chalet School.*

IN SEARCH OF ELINOR

HELEN McCLELLAND

ELINOR BRENT-DYER . . . ? But what on earth makes you want to write about *her*? That, in the mid-1970s, was the usual reaction to my plan for a book about the author of the Chalet School series. Many of my friends appeared to think that women who wrote school stories were just a bit of a laugh. And even my husband, normally most supportive of my writing projects, failed to see why anyone wanted to devote so much time and labour to the "Shilly-Shally School" — as he called it. A gloomy pronouncement that "People who want to read well-researched, in-depth biographies, don't want to read about Elinor Brent-Dyer; and vice versa . . . " summed up his attitude. Nor was there any lack of Cassandras to join him in the chorus; the bottom line of their predictions being that the book would never find a publisher (which almost proved to be true).

Only Scottish obstinacy kept me going. Especially when it soon became clear that finding information would be difficult, for at that time very little was known about Elinor Brent-Dyer. Few of the standard works of reference, surveys and so on even mentioned her; and one that did include her name in a rather dismissive listing of school-story writers "popular between the wars", managed to misspell that name as "Eleanor".[1] The only reasonably detailed entries were those in the editions then current of *Twentieth Century Children's Writers* and *Who's Who of Children's Writers*; and both of these

— for reasons to be considered later — turned out to contain inaccuracies.

Of course some ideas about Elinor Brent-Dyer could be gleaned from her writings. A series of 59 books will inevitably reveal something of its creator; and no reader could doubt that the woman who wrote the Chalet School stories had at some time been a teacher; professional inside knowledge springs from the pages. Clearly, too, Elinor Brent-Dyer had been much interested, even though not expert, in music, history, foreign languages, legends and local customs. She had loved beautiful scenery, travel and good food. She had possessed a sense of humour. And unquestionably she had held strong religious convictions — while being unusually ecumenical in attitude for someone of her generation.

All this could be deduced from the Chalet series. And although it can be dangerous to try to guess too much about an author from his or her writings, in this case the list of preconceived ideas was to be confirmed by later discoveries.

Not so, however, the vague impression of Elinor's appearance that, quite irrationally, had grown in my mind over the years. A strong authorial presence does pervade the Chalet stories; but there was no real justification for my picturing Elinor as tall and graceful, with dark wavy hair and finely chiselled features, always elegantly attired in some flowing garment topped by a long fur stole, and generally resembling a younger slimmer version of the Queen Mother. No doubt an unconscious mingling, here, of Madge, Joey and Miss Annersley. And it came momentarily as a shock to be confronted, quite early in my researches, with a photograph — not a flattering one, either — of the real Elinor Brent-Dyer. The squarely built, rather dowdy woman portrayed, her large heavy features carefully set in a self-conscious photographic smile, was quite unlike my imagined author. Even today this particular portrait (dating from 1963)[2] does not appeal to me, although I know others would disagree. To my mind, there are many far more sympathetic and characteristic pictures of Elinor. But in any case a growing knowledge of the real person quickly dispelled the fantasy image. Besides, there were other, more dramatic surprises waiting along the road.

A LONG UPHILL JOURNEY. UNCOVERING THE EARLY YEARS

The quest for information began in earnest during November 1974, when, deaf to opposition and wise counsels, I decided to work seriously on a biography of Elinor Brent-Dyer. My own interest in the Chalet School had survived for more than 30 years, dating back to my ninth or tenth birthday when *The School at the Chalet* — a second-hand early reprint containing, happily for me, all the Nina K. Brisley illustrations — was my present from an eccentric elderly relative. She, despite her advanced years and striking intellectual gifts (a pet hobby was making verse translations of Dante) had become, and remained to the end of her life, a staunch devotee of the Chalet School. At the time I naturally didn't realise it, but she thus embodied the possibility that even intelligent adults could enjoy the Chalet books — something my parents would have found hard to believe. And to her I owe the good fortune of reading all the early Chalet stories in the correct order — always a bonus when reading a series, to my mind. With her as my guide, the world of the Chalet School became very real to me as a child, and through countless rereadings I got to know many of the books almost from memory.

That it was also possible for children of a completely different generation and upbringing to enjoy the Chalet School came home to me only when my daughters, at about ten and eight, took to the stories with huge enthusiasm. Initially I was surprised. This was the 1970s: the girls' school story was thought to be stone-cold dead and deservedly so. Publishers were becoming ever more socially conscious; and children's books, as well as having to be unisex (if not actually slanted towards boys) were expected to cover only subjects considered relevant to the 1970s. My children were happy enough to read stories in this contemporary genre (later they would nickname it "Oil Rigs and Rape"); but their enjoyment of the Chalet School books continued unabated right into their teens.

During this period, a number of immensely enjoyable holidays at Pertisau-am-Achensee — the real-life Tyrolean setting of the early Chalet stories — had fuelled our collective "Chalet-o-mania". We found Pertisau an enchanting place, and could easily see why Elinor Brent-Dyer fell in love with it when she visited the Achensee in 1924. That visit unquestionably was, and would remain, her inspiration in the Chalet series. And although the years have brought changes to the village — and many more, alas, since our first 1970s visit — nothing can alter the extraordinary beauty of the lake and mountain scenery; or change the essential atmosphere of the district, so well recaptured in the early books of the series.

Our trips to Pertisau were pure pleasure. But little did I realise how difficult the task of following Elinor's footsteps in other directions was to prove. The nearest parallel would be a treasure hunt, where not only are more than half the clues missing but most are presented in the wrong order, while false clues lie scattered everywhere. How often during the researches I would hear words to the effect: "Now, old Mrs So-and-so could have told you all about that; but of course she died last year . . . ". And quite early it became plain that Elinor herself, for reasons that didn't emerge until much later, had taken pains to cover her tracks.

My first step had of course been to contact the two publishers of the Chalet School series: W. & R. Chambers and Collins (now HarperCollins Armada). And now began a scenario that would be replayed many times, with endless irksome variations. On each occasion I would set off with high hopes and a long list of queries, only to find that — despite a friendly welcome, for people were invariably kind — I came back with little definite information. Chambers, where I talked to two editors who had known and worked with Elinor, did supply some colourful background material, but they knew almost nothing about Elinor's personal life and origins. Armada knew even less. But at least they did suggest my getting in touch with a Mrs Phyllis Matthewman in whose house, at Redhill in Surrey, Elinor had spent the last years of her life. And when Mrs Matthewman sent an amusing and friendly letter, confirming that she had known Elinor since childhood and inviting me to lunch, it seemed that at last my troubles were over. Surely, with the guidance of such an old friend, the growing list of queries would be answered.

Yet again things turned out disappointingly. Mrs Matthewman was a characterful old lady in her late 70s. Herself a writer, she could recount things with an intriguing touch of colour, and she provided a completely new slant on aspects of Elinor's personality. She had indeed known Elinor since the days, around 1905, when "She lived in South Shields with her widowed mother and her brother and untold numbers of cats".[3] But there had been a gap of more than 30 years in their acquaintance. And it was soon apparent that Mrs Matthewman's memory was far from reliable. Very few hard facts emerged, and where anything like dates was concerned she was hopelessly vague. References to "the war" turned out to mean sometimes the First World War, at others the Second. And, as transpired later, there were many things in Elinor's early life of which Phyllis Matthewman was ignorant.

The situation was particularly frustrating because all the papers Elinor had left were apparently still in the house, together with the remains of her large book collection; but this wasn't a straightforward matter. The Redhill house was both large and riotously untidy. Piles of letters and manuscripts (many of them Phyllis Matthewman's own, or belonging to her late husband) lay everywhere, spilling from dirty cardboard boxes and old suitcases. Books were scattered all around — only some of them in bookcases, and many in a state of neglect that would give a book-collector nightmares. Who knew what secrets lay buried? But plainly it would have been insensitive for me, a complete stranger, to have insisted on plunging into the chaos. Especially when the signals emanating from Mrs Matthewman suggested that she hadn't really liked Elinor very much . . .

In fact — as I gradually discovered — Mrs Matthewman's feelings towards her long-standing friend were decidedly mixed; and tinged, it must be acknowledged, with a good deal of professional jealousy. Looking back, I can see that this undoubtedly coloured the first impressions Phyllis gave me of Elinor — many of which I was later to rethink, and often to revise.

On later visits I did have the opportunity to look at some of Elinor's papers and notebooks. But it was not until after Phyllis Matthewman's death in July 1979 that I had access to them all. And, sadly, by this time some had disappeared — along with a set of our family photos taken in Pertisau that I had lent to Phyllis. However, much valuable material had survived, enabling me to add things, or occasionally change them, in the first draft of the biography.

That first, 1974, session with Mrs Matthewman did at least provide me with two new — and correct — pieces of information: Elinor had been born in South Shields, and the family name was not Brent-Dyer, but just Dyer on its own. With this knowledge and little else I set off for the National Registrar's office at St Catherine's House in London, and began to search through the four enormous volumes which record all births in England and Wales during the year 1895. Mrs Matthewman had assured me this was the right year, as had the entries in the two reference books mentioned earlier. And yet, not one single Elinor Dyer — or for that matter Eleanor, or even Mary Elinor/Eleanor — appeared to have been born in South Shields that year.

Much checking and rechecking still failed to find her. So I proceeded to search the four volumes for 1896, then for 1897 — and so on, right up to and including the 1901 volumes — that year having seemed just worth a try since I'd read in a newspaper article that Elinor Brent-Dyer was 21 when her first book was published in October 1922 (the latter date being established beyond doubt by the British Library catalogue). By this time almost a couple of hours had passed, what with lifting down and replacing those 28 massive volumes, not to mention the laborious process of checking the name: Dyer may not top the list of the most common British surnames, but there are nevertheless quite a few of them.

So now it was back to square one, with nothing for it but yet another go at 1895. This time I decided to scan every single entry under Dyer, not just the girls' names containing Elinor/Eleanor. And in the July to September volume my eye was caught by the unusual first name of Henzell. That, according to Mrs Matthewman, was the name of Elinor's brother, and sure enough this particular Henzell had been born in South Shields. But wait a minute — hadn't Henzell been Elinor's *younger* brother? Perhaps I'd been working in the wrong direction. Into reverse then, and full speed into 1894. And there at long last was recorded the birth in South Shields of a Gladys Eleanor May Dyer. Not quite the name I'd expected, but it was so near the Elinor Mary of Chalet School fame that it had to be right. I hurried to apply for a copy of the certificate and a couple of days later the date of Elinor Brent-Dyer's birth had finally been established as Friday 6 April 1894.

All that work for just one date! And the whole pattern was to be repeated over and over again. Frustration, disappointment, false trails and dead ends were everyday occurrences. However, by way of compensation there were also a few pieces of unbelievably good luck. Particularly in the matter of establishing the facts about Elinor's education. This, through almost a year of researches, had proved an exceptionally difficult area. No one appeared to recall even the place where Elinor had attended school, let alone the name of the school itself. There were plenty of vague rumours, including one that she had been for a time at the well-known Dame

Allan's Girls' School in Newcastle upon Tyne. There was also a definite statement in *The Times* obituary notice that Elinor Brent-Dyer had studied at the University of Leeds.[4] But these rumours, when checked, all turned out to be unfounded; and an enquiry to the University records office in Leeds revealed, surprisingly, that Elinor had never in fact been a student there.

Around this time the whole enterprise might well have foundered, but for a fortunate coincidence when a not too demanding professional engagement just happened to take me to the north of England. Here I found myself staying within a few miles of South Shields, and with time to spare I was able to visit the town frequently and to spend several days in the Central Public Library searching through their extensive records.

At first this process, though highly interesting in itself, did not seem very productive. True, I was learning a lot about the local and social history of South Shields during the decades round the turn of the century; and it was fascinating to find, for example, that in those days the passenger fare on the Tyne ferry between North and South Shields had cost a mere half penny, old style; while a hundredweight of best coal could be bought for about 5p. There was, too, some gentle amusement lurking in odd corners — like the census report with the ambiguously worded statement: "the increase of population in [this area] is attributed to the presence of a number of workmen temporarily employed there in building a bridge . . . ". And at least the discovery that, during Elinor's early life tuberculosis had caused several hundred deaths each year in South Shields did have some relevance to the Chalet School books, since it helped to explain why this disease plays such an important role in many of the early stories. But, where strictly essential information was concerned, the rate of my search compared poorly with glacial flow.

Then one day, quite unexpectedly, a young woman who worked in another part of the library came into ask if I was interested in meeting her former schoolteacher, who had "been at college with Elinor Brent-Dyer". That casual offer marked an important milestone. For not only was Mrs Isobel Miller, the splendidly entertaining old lady I met, able to establish that Elinor had indeed been her fellow student at the City of Leeds Training College, but, along with exact dates, she also knew the name of Elinor's school and provided a lot of information about it into the bargain as well as on a number of related matters.

Things were beginning to make progress. And only a short time later it transpired that the mother of a South Shields newspaper editor, Mrs Eva Oliver, had actually been at the same school as Elinor: it was invariably known locally as "the Misses Stewarts' School", after the two formidable women who ran it, although its proper name was St Nicholas's. Best of all, a 1908 school photograph was found, which included the 14-year-old Elinor — then called May Dyer. And when, in August 1975, that photograph appeared in the Shields Gazette, along with a request for information, the letters began to pour in (the people of South Shields being fortunately gifted with long memories, and Elinor, as one correspondent pointed out, was "Not the kind to be easily forgotten") and this brought much invaluable new information.

In the mean time the treasure hunt had slowly been going ahead in other directions. It was a complicated operation, for Elinor during her 75 years had lived at numerous different addresses, and she had used a variety of first names during her first three decades, including at one point the colourful but unlikely appellation "Patricia Maraquita". She had also, for reasons that slowly became apparent, taken pains to disguise her background. To uncover it demanded much sheer hard slog. It meant countless trips to St Catherine's House to unearth further certificates of birth, death and marriage. It involved many visits to Somerset House to scan wills; to the Office of Public Records to look at census information and other documents; to the British Library to study all manner of publications. It required much travelling around the country, visiting and talking to people who were all strangers to me at the time; that some of them would later become friends was among the unexpected bonuses offered by this particular treasure hunt. It also required a staggering number of letters and telephone calls.

Altogether a formidable undertaking. I found it exhausting and at times exasperating, but all round enormously enjoyable. In particular it was rewarding when a picture of Elinor Brent-Dyer's personality began slowly to emerge. And with this picture came at least some understanding of the reasons behind those inaccuracies in official records. For one thing it soon became clear, as I delved into the various certificates and wills, that Elinor's early life had been lived against a curious background of secrecy and evasion.

Not that there really had been anything sensational to hide, at any rate not to our late 20th century ideas. But, for example, Elinor's mother had gone to amazing lengths in concealing the complete breakdown of her marriage after barely four years, preferring to give an impression and to have it assumed that she was now a widow, whereas in fact her husband did not die until a further 14 years after the legal separation took place.

Of course it is important to remember that in those far gone days, and especially in the kind of narrow small-town world where Elinor grew up, a broken marriage was regarded as something of a social disgrace, and one moreover that often bore more heavily on the woman in the case. Society honoured widows — in theory, if not always in financial terms. But where divorce or separation was concerned there could be a tacit assumption that the wife must be at fault in having failed to "keep her man". Everything indicates that Elinor's mother, Nelly Dyer, attached prime importance to the opinions her neighbours voiced behind their lace curtains; and she would have felt the more vulnerable because, while her husband came from the faraway south of England, she herself belonged to a family that was well known and respected locally.

But it was not only her husband's continuing existence that Mrs Dyer contrived to hide by her smokescreen tactics. Already, even before Charles Dyer departed, things had not been quite as they seemed at no. 52 Winchester Street, the red-brick Victorian terraced house in a most respectable district of South Shields where the Dyers resided. Outwardly this household contained a perfectly normal three-generation family: father, mother, two small children and a resident grandmother, with the occasional uncle or cousin staying for different lengths of time. But another person might by rights have expected to live in the Winchester Street house. Charles Dyer had been a widower at the time he married Elinor's mother and by his first marriage he had had a son, named Charles Arnold Lloyd Dyer. This little boy, barely five years old when his father married again, had spent the years after his mother's death in a pathetic kind of wandering passage between lodgings up and down the country, being for the most part left in the care of landladies.

It is hard to think of any reason why poor Charles Arnold should not have come to live in South Shields with his father and stepmother once they had settled down after their marriage, for he had no other close relatives and there was ample room at 52 Winchester Street. The fact is, and this remains one of the mysteries in Elinor's background, that the child never apparently so much as visited the household. Odder still: among Elinor's surviving friends and relatives, including Mrs Matthewman and others who knew the family well in the early South Shields days, not one person to whom I talked could recall ever hearing a word of Charles Arnold's existence. Elinor herself was possibly unaware of it during her childhood. Much later on she did learn about this vanished half-brother and his son; and she even had some correspondence with the latter, although a planned meeting during the war years never took place — being prevented at the last moment, in almost Chalet School fashion, by a car accident.

So effective was the wall of secrecy built around Charles Dyer and his elder son that only the basic facts about them could be included in *Behind the Chalet School* when it was published in 1981. But in January 1983, following a broadcast in the BBC *Woman's Hour* programme, when I'd been interviewed about Elinor and Kate O'Mara had read extracts from the Chalet books, a Mr Charles Dyer rang the BBC announcing himself as Elinor's half-nephew, son of that long vanished half-brother, Charles Arnold Lloyd Dyer. And this exciting discovery led to a meeting, during which many gaps were filled. Best of all, as well as acquiring several photographs, I was at last given some impression of Elinor's father as a person.

Charles Morris Brent Dyer (no hyphen) turns out to have been quite a bohemian character, who had an unexpectedly artistic side. In particular, he played the organ and was a skilled amateur photographer. I gained the impression that he was a lively, sociable man, perhaps a trifle too fond of drink and pretty women. This seemed to fit the preconceived picture quite well and all round it was gratifying to have many of my deductions and guesses confirmed. Yes, Elinor's half-brother had undoubtedly been the innocent cause of friction between Elinor's parents. And her father had indeed formed a liaison with another woman after he and Elinor's mother separated (he'd even had another son by her — something nobody could have deduced).

It emerged, too, that Elinor's paternal grandmother had been South African Dutch; and this explained why I'd never been able to trace anything about her — records of South African births, deaths and marriages not being generally available in this country. It could possibly explain also (or is this pushing things too far?) Elinor's rather heavy physiognomy, so different from her mother's more delicate features.

Yet another thing I learnt from Elinor's half-nephew was the reason why Brent had been among her father's names. It appears that a Captain Brent (probably Morris Brent) had commanded the ship in which William Dyer (Elinor's paternal grandfather) was serving at the time of her father's birth (1856), and the captain had become godfather to the baby. Not only that: when William Dyer was drowned at sea at quite an early age, the good Captain Brent had made himself entirely responsible for his godson Charles's education. I wonder if Elinor ever knew this? If she did, it could have been a further reason for her decision in 1922 to include Brent in her surname; a choice which, or so it has always seemed to me, was a way of declaring allegiance to her dead father, and distancing herself from her mother and stepfather.

Whether Elinor and Henzell ever saw their father again after he departed from Winchester Street is unknown. In many ways it seems unlikely that they did, in view of the elaborate measures their mother had taken to make it appear he no longer existed. On the other hand, since Charles continued to live in South Shields for many years — though on the far side of the town from Winchester Street — this bizarre possibility cannot be ruled out altogether. But one thing is virtually certain: if any such meetings were arranged they must have taken place in darkest secret; and this could only have increased still further the obfuscatory atmosphere of Elinor's upbringing. Either way, it seems improbable that Mrs Dyer would have informed the children when their father eventually set up house with another woman (who was not only to provide them with a second unknown half-brother, but also to inherit almost everything of which Charles died possessed).

Nor was it only these so-to-speak discreditable matters that Mrs Dyer strove to conceal: she clearly considered that sorrow, too, even when it took the honourable form of bereavement, must at all costs be hidden. Thus when Elinor's beloved brother died suddenly and tragically from cerebrospinal meningitis, at the age of only 17, the mourning was kept strictly within the family circle. And although there is no question that Henzell was ever forgotten (to the end of her life Elinor would still note in her diary that 28 June was Henzell's birthday), it seems that after the tragedy his name was seldom mentioned, even at home. As a result people who made Elinor's acquaintance later in life were often unaware that she had ever had a brother. One friend, Hazel Bainbridge, who was a child of nine when she first met the grown-up Elinor, did learn about Henzell's sad death from her parents, but she still remembers how strongly they cautioned her never to mention the subject in front of Elinor, or more particularly her mother, for fear of upsetting them.[5] Not surprisingly Hazel assumed Elinor's brother must have died quite recently. It was only long afterwards that she learnt the actual date of his death and realised with astonishment that, by the time she heard the story, Henzell must already have been dead for almost *ten years*.

Elinor's mother unquestionably tended to deal with any form of unhappiness or unpleasantness by shutting it away and refusing to allow herself, or anyone else, to acknowledge its existence. And the lessons she gave on the vital importance of keeping up appearances, the desirability of concealing adversity behind a smooth facade and the near obligation of keeping personal sorrows hidden, were learnt early in life by Elinor, and she was to remember them always. In some respects it cannot have been easy for her. Elinor had inherited from her father an extrovert temperament, quite different from her mother's more conformist personality; by nature she was full of enthusiasm and exuberance, was considered boisterous in behaviour as a child, and throughout life had a rather loud voice, a hearty laugh and a considerable disregard for conventions in dress and manner. Friends who visited her towards the end of her time in South Shields, when Elinor was nearer her 40s than her schooldays, recall being somewhat embarrassed by the uninhibited way Elinor had talked in detail about her Alsatian bitch being on heat — "People didn't discuss such matters in those days". Nevertheless, her mother's abiding example and her early training at the Misses Stewarts' decidedly old-fashioned school, did imbue Elinor with a certain theoretical respect for the accepted pattern of ladylike behaviour and a genuine belief in the importance of good manners. The latter emerged frequently in real life — "I remember the speed with which we had to leap to our feet and open doors", comments Helen Colam, one of her former pupils — as well as throughout her books.

Elinor's restricted upbringing also fostered in her an attitude to social class that was not quite so liberal as she herself perhaps imagined. In her books Elinor had often written against snobbery, and at times with a fervour that suggests she may have known how it felt to be at the receiving end. Take, for instance, a scene in *The Exploits of the Chalet Girls* (1933), where the aristocratic Thekla von Stift is sternly rebuked for her attitude to girls who belong, as she considers, to "the trading classes".[6] Or the passage in *A Problem for the Chalet School* (1956) where Joey Maynard speaks forcibly and at some length on the subject, making plain straightaway that the Chalet School had "always been taught that what matters is the girl herself" (in other words, not her social background) and concluding: "It's a pleasant thing to know that one comes from a long line . . . [but] when you come to the root of matters, it's you — you — YOU that matters all the time — what you are!"[7]

In that discourse Joey, who "had never had the slightest use for snobs"[8], is undoubtedly stating in fiction the opinions that Elinor sincerely believed she held. Nevertheless there are signs that in real life Elinor had a rather ambivalent attitude to the whole question; tolerant in some ways but in others less than broad-minded, as shown by the occasional remarks she let slip in conversation, and still more by such revealing moments in her books as the following from *Three Go to the Chalet School* (1949), where Mary-Lou is told by one of Joey Maynard's children: "There isn't any other [school] near, 'cept the village school, and you [with the accent on you] won't go *there*".[9]

Of course it should not be forgotten how much social ideas have changed during this century. Had Elinor been a young teacher today in the 1990s, she would most likely have been proud to claim her working-class forebears. In the early 1920s things were different. At that period the most favoured boarding-school girl — in either fact or fiction — was simply not expected to come from places like South Shields, with its down-market image of shipyards and collieries; from South Uist or South Kensington by all means, from Southampton perhaps, at a pinch from South Wimbledon but not, definitely not, from South Shields. All very silly to present-day thinking; but there can be little doubt that, in Elinor's anxiety to conceal her origins — as she most successfully did — an element of snobbishness played a significant part.

One cause could well have been her reaction to other people's attitudes. Elinor's introduction to that exclusive world of the girls' boarding-school must have happened around 1920 and hence in a fairly illiberal social climate. The actual date can only be fixed approximately; but it has now been established that for a short period before September 1923, by which time she had definitely arrived at Western House School in Fareham, Hants, Elinor was teaching at St Helen's School in Northwood,

Middx. This came to light some years after publication of *Behind the Chalet School*, when an "Old Girl" of St Helen's sent me a copy of their 1969 school magazine which included Elinor's name among obituary notices of former staff.

Why Elinor should have chosen to forsake St Helen's, which was (and still is) quite a well-known school, and move to a smaller, less prestigious establishment at Fareham, remains a matter for speculation. I was never able to find many details about her teaching career between July 1917, when her teacher-training course at Leeds finished, and September 1923 when she joined the teaching staff at Fareham. Elinor is known to have taught at various schools in South Shields, including the well esteemed Boys' High School where her brother Henzell had been a pupil, but no dates are available. On the other hand a good deal, fortunately, has come to light about the time in the early 1920s when Elinor met and became friends with the Bainbridge family. And that was a specially important time, for it was the Bainbridges who provided the essential spark to ignite Elinor's career as a published author.

THE MIDDLE YEARS.
A FINISHED BOOK AT LAST

In searching for information about this crucial period I was able for the first time to contact one of the people directly concerned: Hazel Bainbridge, to whom Elinor's first book is dedicated. From her I learnt that during the early 1920s Hazel's parents, Julian and Edith Bainbridge, were running a small repertory company in South Shields; and Hazel, who was a talented child actress, used frequently to appear in their productions during her school holidays. A warm friendship grew between the Bainbridges and Elinor, who found herself at home in their world of the theatre where her frequently exaggerated manner could be casually accepted. The Bainbridges moreover were to supply exactly the stimulus and encouragement that Elinor needed in her writing. In all previous attempts she had found it impossible, despite her natural facility for getting words on to paper, to complete anything full-length. The standard children's novel was then expected to contain at least 60,000 words; and, as Elinor herself put it, "though I'd begun quite a number of stories I always got tired of them and left them unfinished".[10] Julian Bainbridge knew of Elinor's writing ambitions, and he suggested that if she were to write a play his company would produce it. This gave Elinor not only a goal but a deadline; she accepted the challenge and the play, *My Lady Caprice*, was duly staged with both Edith Bainbridge and Hazel in the cast.

In the mean time Hazel, who adored Elinor and liked nothing better than listening to "all the wonderful stories she could tell", was so keen to know what happened next to Gerry Challoner in the story Elinor read aloud to her, chapter by chapter as it was written, that for the first time Elinor was carried triumphantly to the end of a full-length book. The result, *Gerry goes to School*, was published in October 1922 by W. & R. Chambers, who at that time was among the leading publishers of girls' stories. And the copy Elinor proudly presented to Hazel included, in addition to the printed dedication, a handwritten one: "To my own darling little sister, Hazel Mary Bainbridge".

Once started, Elinor was never to look back. A year later *Gerry* had a sequel, *A Head Girl's Difficulties*; and in the autumn of 1924 this was followed by *The Maids of La Rochelle*, the first of Elinor's Guernsey stories.

Earlier in 1924 Elinor had spent that momentous holiday in Austria which was to be the mainspring of her Chalet School series. This, at 58 full-length hardbacks and one shorter paperback, must be not only the longest running series of school stories ever known, but among the top ten series of children's books to appear in the past half-century. Sales figures for the Armada paperbacks give testimony of this: for although Elinor Brent-Dyer has never been in the bestselling class of Enid Blyton, well over 100,000 copies of her Chalet School paperbacks are regularly sold each year; and this level has been maintained over a considerable period.

Undoubtedly the Chalet School series was Elinor Brent-Dyer's principal achievement; and it is the Chalet School which has carried her name all around Britain and into many far-off corners of the English-speaking world. But she did also publish more than 40 other books: they include adventure stories, family and historical novels, educational "Readers", a collection of recipes, a couple of books with "doggy" themes, and around a dozen stories of schools other than the Chalet School.

Quite a remarkable record; bearing in mind, too, that until she was past 50 Elinor had always been occupied, at least part-time, in some form of teaching. For one period of ten years she had even run, and acted as headmistress in, her own school. The whole idea of her Margaret Roper School in Hereford had intrigued me ever since I first heard of it in Phyllis Matthewman's original letter. Especially the fascinating picture it presented of a "double life". On one hand, the ideal world of the Chalet School where, despite troubles and occasionally sorrow and the many hair-raising adventures, the good end happily and things are always "all right on the night". On the other, the endless niggling problems and the inexorable daily routine of running a real-life school, where people can sometimes be unhelpful and naughty girls cannot always be quickly reformed. Nothing I'd learnt about Elinor suggested she would be good at handling routine. How had she contrived to meet the, perhaps conflicting, demands of the real and fictional establishments?

THE HEREFORD YEARS.
A REAL-LIFE CHALET SCHOOL?

This part of Elinor's life was far easier to chart than the early years. For one thing, with less time having elapsed, many of the people directly involved were still around; and although some of Elinor's closest friends had predeceased her, former pupils of the Margaret Roper School responded well to my request for information in the *Hereford Times*, as did others from Hereford and round about.

Moreover, the back numbers of the *Hereford Times* proved to contain much basic information about the Margaret Roper School[11]; and a few sessions at the British Newspaper Library in Colindale revealed that not only had the school's principal, Miss Elinor Brent-Dyer, placed regular advertisements in the paper, there were also full reports on most school activities — speech-days, pageants in the garden, school plays, sales of work, and so on.

From these accounts, and various personal interviews, it became clear that numerous parallels had existed between the Margaret Roper School and the Chalet School. The uniform, for one thing, was almost identical, with brown and flame being the official colours at both schools. And a remarkable number of Chalet School traditions were followed at the real-life school, among them the annual Christmas play — on at least one occasion the Margaret Roper girls were actually performing the same play as their Chalet School counterparts, which in the first case was "written by their headmistress Miss Elinor Brent-Dyer", and in the second, theoretically, by *their* headmistress, Miss Madge Bettany.

On a deeper level, further resemblances can be found: the Margaret Roper School, like the Chalet School, had a strong religious tradition but it, too, was undenominational (far more unusual in those days than it would be now). Elinor unquestionably aimed to foster in her school the ideals of religious tolerance and international fellowship that have become familiar in the pages of the Chalet School books. A former pupil who is Jewish was particularly struck by this.

It was on a practical everyday level that things differed greatly, and the Margaret Roper School never enjoyed the phenomenal success of its storybook rival. For one thing, Elinor's resources were limited. No chance for her, with no spare capital and endless wartime restrictions, to summon into being by one stroke of her pen a laboratory, or a domestic economy room, or even a couple of new chalets. And, as one former Margaret Roper pupil recalled with a slight shudder: "the school meals were awful!" (Shades of Marie Pfeifen — or Karen — and those mouthwatering dishes of which they alone knew the secret . . .)

Besides, Elinor was plainly unsuited to being a headmistress. She had genuine gifts as a teacher and for making happy relationships with individual children (Hazel Bainbridge and others would confirm this), but the unremitting daily grind of running a school was simply not for her. Throughout her life she had tended to embark enthusiastically on new projects but then gradually lose interest in them, and as time went by the Chalet School began to claim an ever larger part of her time and attention. Thus, although some former pupils of the Margaret Roper School remember Elinor with much affection, others are less appreciative.

However, the Margaret Roper School did at least one good turn to the Chalet School: it kept Elinor in touch with real children in a real school. The books she wrote during her much overcrowded years as headmistress include all the "Armishire" stories, as well as *The Chalet School in Exile*, and some of these deserve to be rated among Elinor's best. Whether the gradual deterioration in quality, which becomes noticeable as the long series proceeds, was connected with the author's withdrawal from active school life remains unproven. Without question many of the later books are inferior to the earlier ones; but then it would be hard to imagine any author, anywhere, who was capable of writing 59 equally good books about the same characters in the same school. Most writers wouldn't attempt it. Arthur Ransome, for instance, in his stories of the Swallows and Amazons (and others) was content with only 12 titles. Even Enid Blyton, who must have busted more records than most, never produced a series of 59 books.

But then the Chalet School, for its author, was not just fiction; and the writing of further stories wasn't simply a matter of adding yet another book to a popular series. For Elinor it was far more a matter of chronicling actual events in the lives and world of characters who had, by this time, become absolutely real in her eyes. "Make no mistake . . . " she wrote in the first *Chalet Club News Letter*.

> So far as I am concerned, the people are there, just out of sight, but otherwise alive and panting to tell their stories. I am merely the loudspeaker through whom they broadcast . . . It is they who tell the stories. I am merely the instrument.[12]

That paragraph tells much about Elinor. In particular her choice of words is revealing; for she had already used many of the same phrases and images in a book she had written more than five years earlier — only in the book Elinor was not, at least not avowedly, writing about herself.

> "Oh I suppose a day will come [Joey Maynard explains to her adopted sister Robin Humphries] when . . .I'll have to sit down at my typewriter and be a loud-speaker again."
> "That's what you always say," Robin returned thoughtfully. "Do you really and truly feel that way about it, Jo?"
> Jo nodded. "Exactly that. The people in my stories are there, alive and kicking . . .They tell their own story. I'm just the — the instrument used for broadcasting it."[13]

The two passages are substantially the same. And interestingly, since it was the book that came first, Elinor in the *News Letter* is actually taking words from the mouth of a fictional character — not the other way round. Yet Elinor frequently and vehemently denied that any close connection existed between herself and Joey; so perhaps she was genuinely unaware of the extent to which she had been absorbed into her creature. And not only into Joey: Elinor, in later years — as a very old friend described it — "began to live more and more in Chalet lands".[14] Nor is it surprising if, as her life went by, Elinor came to prefer the glamorous fictional world she had created to her real everyday surroundings. In hard cold fact there were many discrepancies between the real-life woman, born Gladys Eleanor May Dyer in the industrial town of South Shields, brought up moreover in a broken home, and the successful author Elinor Mary Brent-Dyer — a figure whose gracious presence often seems to hover behind the Chalet stories. But Elinor's perception of herself would seem increasingly to have taken on the fictionalised image — much the same amalgam of several parts Joey Bettany/Maynard to one of the younger Madge, combined with a touch of Miss Annersley, which had formed my childhood picture. So . . . what was she really like?

THE REAL ELINOR BRENT-DYER? UNRAVELLING THE TANGLED WEBS

Even her greatest admirer must acknowledge that Elinor had an oddly ambivalent attitude to the whole matter of telling the truth. From her books no one could fail to get the impression that honesty was a highly esteemed virtue. But Elinor herself was seldom honest about her real age. Possibly, like many other women, she felt this form of deception to be harmless and justified — especially as she had always, until well into middle age, looked far younger than she was. Elinor did, however, go to the more unusual lengths of entering a false date of birth on an official form (one is in my possession where she stated it to be 6 April *1901*). And her lifelong habit of romancing — which some of her friends enjoyed — did often cause her to mix fact and fiction and to make extravagant claims. To put it another way: Elinor seems to have retained throughout life the capacity, possessed by many imaginative children, first to create and assume a fictional personality and then to believe genuinely and absolutely in its independent existence. Or so it appears to me.

For with Elinor it was by no means a matter of simply concealing her background or being evasive about her age. In her case it is arguable that a quite unusual degree of self-deception existed. How else, when describing (in the article quoted above) her own approach to the writing of her books, could she have used exactly those same images and words she had written five years earlier for Joey Maynard — and this apparently without any awareness on her part? Yet more striking; how else could Elinor have authorised a journalist who interviewed her in Hereford during the 1950s to publish an account of the early life and writing career of Elinor Brent-Dyer that contained so many inaccuracies as to be almost fiction? Maybe I too am deluding myself. Perhaps I am influenced by knowing in real life a few people who, while completely reliable in a professional capacity, can often relate their personal experience in a way that could charitably be described as fanciful. At any rate I would find it harder to believe that Elinor was deliberately making things up, than to accept that by this point she herself had come to believe entirely in the romanticised version of her story.

Why had it happened? Opinions differ as to the relative importance of heredity and environment, and Elinor may well have been someone who would always have tended to take refuge in a fictional world from the harsher realities of life. But the curiously secretive atmosphere of her early years must inevitably have influenced the shaping of her character. Today it is unfortunately not possible to do more than speculate about that early period, nor is there any way of knowing about such crucial matters as Nelly Dyer's attitude to her two children. Did Mrs Dyer perhaps, like many single mothers of only sons, incline more towards the boy in the family? Certain pointers might indicate this. Henzell is reported to have been nice-looking and he may also have inherited the charm his mother undoubtedly possessed (as related by so many people). Elinor on the other hand was considered plain as a child, rather plump in build and decidedly brash in manner. Clearly, too, Mrs Dyer was almost obsessively attached to Henzell's memory; Hazel Bainbridge's childhood picture of the household (related above) confirms this. And Hazel has another memory: she recalls vividly the occasion when she was to appear in a schoolboy role at her parents' theatre and Mrs Dyer learnt that the company had no suitable clothes. A curiously macabre scene then took place, with a grey flannel suit of Henzell's being ceremoniously unwrapped from the tissue paper and mothballs where it had been preserved through at least 15 years and solemnly handed to her (Hazel being a great favourite with both Elinor and her mother).

In any case, even had Henzell not existed, it seems unlikely that Elinor would ever have been her mother's ideal daughter. Nelly Dyer was conventional in outlook; Elinor the opposite. And although in later life, when, according to Phyllis Matthewman, "she could look quite distinguished — when she took the trouble to get herself up properly", Elinor could never have been called beautiful. That mattered a great deal in her early days, and perhaps Elinor's mother shared the view of an old lady I remember overhearing in my childhood: "Don't you think any mother would rather have her daughter praised for being pretty than for being clever?" This filled me with amazed incredulity at the time (I must have been about 11) but I think now that such an attitude was not uncommon among contemporaries of Elinor's mother.

Besides — and more important — Elinor also failed to pass another test that society imposed (and to some extent still imposes) on women. She failed to get herself married. And her claim — often repeated but never authenticated — that she had been engaged to a young man who was killed in the First World War was probably her attempt to forestall criticism, spoken or otherwise, of her single state.

Marriage, in Elinor's Chalet stories, was always to be the ultimate good conduct prize for her grown-up characters; moreover, there are definite indications that she herself thought of spinsterhood as second-best. Her wholesale awarding of the matrimonial crown to all but a handful of characters certainly suggests that she conformed on this point to the social ideas of her time. And there is a personal note of regret underlying the comment made by one of her Chalet School characters after a wedding: "So the last of our old quartette is married," Frieda spoke softly, "I am so glad. Simone is too dear and sweet *to spend all her life teaching* [my italics]."[15] What lends a stab of poignancy here is that Simone in the story is only about 23; Elinor, when she wrote the lines in real life, was a spinster of 47 and had been teaching on and off for nearly thirty years.

Of course Elinor's views on marriage, as reflected in the Chalet School series, were totally unrealistic. But her attitude to men, in particular to their dominating influence within the family, is not clear. The three leading men in the series — Dick Bettany, Jem Russell (respectively Madge's brother and her husband) and Jack Maynard (who marries Joey) — all appear to be well in command at home, and major family decisions are generally left to them; even the irrepressible Jo being often held in check by her husband. On the other hand, it must be significant that Dick — not Madge's *younger* brother but her twin — is shown to acknowledge at the beginning of the series that "all their lives . . . [Madge] had been the one to plan for them both. If she had determined to start this school, nothing he could say or do could prevent her."[16] Plainly Elinor had envisaged the possibility that Madge as a truly independent young woman would not share her brother's anxieties about how she, Joey and Mademoiselle Lepattre would fare all on their own in Austria, without a man to look after them. And that Madge is able to achieve success in her independent enterprise (with only occasional advice from minor male characters such as Herr Mensch and Herr Marani) must also be considered noteworthy.

Here Elinor could be seen as following, no doubt unconsciously, the pattern of her female forebears in the north-east, where seamen's wives, who were effectively in sole charge of the family during their husbands' long absences at sea, would frequently enter themselves on census forms as "Head of the House". But the Chalet School women show no inclination to challenge another convention of the period: the moment Doctor James Russell has carried his bride off to the Sonnalpe and installed her in the pretty chalet, *Die Rosen*, it is simply taken for granted that Madge, as a married woman, is now debarred from working regularly in the school. And right through the series this same fate overtakes all the innumerable members of the Chalet School teaching staff who leave to get married — despite the fact that a high proportion of them marry doctors at the nearby Sanatorium, and hence live within easy reach of the Chalet School.

There is, however, one important exception: Joey Maynard is never allowed to sink with the matrimonial ship. Though indubitably a married woman and with the impossibly large family of 11 children, Joey not only continues to be at heart a fun-loving Chalet School girl, she is pictured by Elinor as having an extremely fulfilling career as a writer. Of course it's fair to say that writing is one of the pursuits that can, in real life as well as fiction, be successfully combined with running a home. Although whether Jo could really have produced such a "long line of gaily jacketed books", even with the unfailingly splendid household help she always enjoyed, remains less certain.

The links between Elinor and her favourite heroine were obviously strengthened by Jo's writing activities. But Elinor could not match one achievement she allowed her fictional character: Jo Bettany is barely 18 when *her* first book is accepted for publication, whereas Elinor was 28 when hers first appeared. Not that she was ever prepared to acknowledge this. Officially it was always stated that she had been 21 at the time; and Elinor seems indeed to have attached surprising importance to this myth of early success. An outside observer might well find her many genuine achievements far more interesting: in particular the remarkable progress her career had made following *Gerry*'s first appearance. Elinor, in 1922, had been just an unknown school-teacher. By the time of her death in 1969 she was considered important enough to be given obituaries in many of the national papers, including that appreciative if rather inaccurate notice in *The Times*, mentioned earlier.

Nevertheless it is true that the basic facts of Elinor's story are not particularly impressive. A correct account for an updated reference book might read:

> Elinor Mary Brent-Dyer was born on 6 April 1894 in South Shields, where she was educated in a small private school. At 18 she began a teaching career of nearly 40 years, during which she taught in both state and private schools, working with boys as well as girls, and teaching at different times English, history, Latin and class-singing, also coaching hockey and running a folk-dancing group. Finally she founded and became headmistress of the Margaret Roper School in Hereford, which she ran herself from September 1938 to July 1948.
>
> Her first book, *Gerry Goes to School*, was published in October 1922 and during the next 47 years she was to publish more than a hundred books including the famous Chalet School series. Elinor Brent-Dyer spent the last five years of her life at Redhill in Surrey, where she died on 20 September 1969.
>
> Between 1915 and 1917 she had attended the City of Leeds Training College and in the late 1920s she was for a short period a part-time student at the Newcastle Conservatoire of Music (now defunct). Elinor Brent-Dyer was brought up in the Church of England but joined the Roman Catholic Church in December 1930.

Not, on the surface, an eventful story: no lurid love affairs, no strong political involvement, no solo journey up uncharted rivers. As put by the first publisher to reject *Behind the Chalet School*: "the trouble is that Eleanor [sic] did not have a very interesting life". And I would concede that what Elinor did, apart from her writing, was less interesting than what she *was*. To me it was remarkable that anyone whose working day was necessarily spent in the classroom would then devote her spare time to creating an imaginary school-world. But in 1979 the general attitude seemed to be (just as predicted) that nobody wanted to read about a woman whose main achievement lay in writing school stories for girls — a genre that was then considered at best foolish escapism, at worst positively harmful.

Today things have changed considerably. But the different climate that slowly came about during the next decade was a long way off in the mid-1970s. At that time Armada, incredible as it may seem, was planning to let the Chalet series die, as they saw it, a natural death. Children's tastes, so they claimed, had altered; and they, along with other publishers, rejected outright any possibility that a significant number of adults were interested in the books.

However, the Chalet School simply refused to lie down and die. In spite of general disbelief, and even a measure of disapproval, the level of paperback sales practically doubled during the 1980s; the demand for second-hand copies of the long out-of-print hardbacks also increased enormously (with prices rising at an alarming rate); and various programmes broadcast by the BBC after *Behind the Chalet School* had finally struggled into print brought countless letters confirming the Chalet series to be alive — not only in Britain but in many corners of the world. Most of the adult writers expressed surprise and delight at finding they were not alone in their Chalet addiction: in the words of a correspondent from Invercargill, New Zealand "[I had] been a fan of the C.S. books for years (I am now 23) . . . [but] living at the bottom of New Zealand, and not liking to admit to sceptical friends that I still read 'children's books' . . . I had never realised how many other adults enjoy the stories."[17]

A softening in attitudes towards the school story was gradually to increase as the 1980s went past; and by 1989, when Armada decided to publish *Elinor Brent-Dyer's Chalet School*, things had changed completely. No need with this, my second venture into Chalet territory, to search *The Writer's Handbook* for a publisher: my contribution to the compendium was actually commissioned, and the book's appearance heralded by live radio interviews (I had waited for 18 months for the BBC to take any interest in *Behind the Chalet School!*). And this time the whole experience of writing the material was unbelievably different. In the 1970s it had seemed vital to write Elinor Brent-Dyer's story from a detached, even critical viewpoint; and with the expectation of socially conscious editors in mind I had deliberately highlighted for discussion the weaknesses of the books, being aware that anything enthusiastic would be instantly rejected. Not so in 1989, when I enjoyed the wonderful freedom of writing as I liked and no longer having to appear aloof.

Of course no one, however devoted a fan, would claim that the Chalet School books have no faults: it is all too easy to point out the weaknesses and the many careless inconsistencies. Moreover, some of the later stories, to my mind, have little to offer. But there is no denying that "Miss Brent-Dyer certainly captured the imagination of vast numbers of girls to an incredible degree".[18] Nor that, while other popular series, both contemporary and comparable with the Chalet School, have now virtually disappeared from general view, the Chalet books are still being regularly bought and read by both children and adults.

In striking testimony to this, a Chalet School fan club — the Friends of the Chalet School — has now been flourishing for some years. It was founded in Australia in 1989 with just a handful of enthusiasts; but FOCS has grown so rapidly that today it is run by a committee of five — four in the U.K. and one (Ann Mackie-Hunter, the original founder) in Australia; while the membership, which increases literally every week, now includes many hundreds of fans in more than a dozen countries.

Most important of all: the books are not just being read but positively enjoyed. That the Chalet School continues to attract new readers, 70 years on, must surely speak for itself about the unquenchable vitality of the stories.

Meanwhile, although the basic facts about Elinor herself have been established and have now been corrected in several reference books, the search still continues, with scraps of new information coming to light from time to time. As when, for example, I at last managed to find and talk to one of those "missing persons" from Elinor's past: Edith Le Poidevin who had been quite a close friend during the time at Western House School but had then vanished from Elinor's life. In talking to the former Miss Le Poidevin (by this point she had been Mrs Brookes for more than 50 years) I learnt the answers to a few old questions, only to find them succeeded by new ones! Who was it, for instance, who invited Elinor to Guernsey, since apparently it was *not* Edith Le Poidevin who did so? And that's just one of the queries that remain concerning

Elinor's life story.

Today it seems unlikely that these queries can all be answered. On the other hand, a letter that was read at the FOCS Centenary weekend in Hereford has helped to bring Elinor herself to life in a completely new and remarkable way. This letter — written by Mrs Chloe Rutherford, who from an early age knew and was much attached to Elinor — presents a picture that, to me, came as a revelation. For although a biographer may painstakingly uncover the facts of a life story and, by synthesising the impressions of others, may even provide a glimpse of the real person, only a friend — and a loving friend — could have created a portrait of this calibre. The full text of Mrs Rutherford's memento will be compulsive reading for all Chalet fans, and it can be found in the FOCS special centenary publication. But here, to round off this account of my "Search for Elinor", I should like to quote a few lines from Chloe's affectionate tribute.

> To a youngster, her outward physical appearance was rather daunting . . . [and] the face of unmistakable authority made her . . . an imposing and dominant presence . . . It took me quite some time to realise this was the outward mask of the working Headmistress. Behind that facade there lurked a complex, singleminded, lovable, clumsy, stubborn, forward-thinking, spiritual, dottily humorous personality of enormous charm and innate wisdom . . . [A] very kind and generous woman, a mine of information, and a fount of good common sense.

That depicts the real Elinor Brent-Dyer far better than I ever could.

NOTES

1. Alec Ellis, *History of Children's Reading and Literature* (Pergamon, 1968).
2. Portrait taken 1963, property of W. & R. Chambers. Reproduced in final *Chalet Club News Letter*, no. 20, Nov. 1969 and in *Behind the Chalet School* (New Horizon, 1981), opposite p.24.
3. Mrs Phyllis Matthewman's first letter to H. McClelland, June 1974.
4. Elinor Brent-Dyer's obituary in *The Times*, Tuesday 23 Sept. 1969.
5. The talented child actress for whom *Gerry Goes to School* (1922) was written. Mother of actresses Kate O'Mara and Belinda Carroll.
6. *The Exploits of the Chalet Girls* (1933), p.81.
7. *A Problem for the Chalet School* (1956), p.110.
8. Ibid.
9. *Three Go to the Chalet School* (1949), p.54.
10. *Chalet Club News Letter*, no. 10, Nov. 1963.
11. *Hereford Times*, numerous dates from 1938 to 1948 including: 2 Apr. 1938, 23 Apr. 1938, 3 Sept. 1938, 17 Dec. 1938 (parents' day), 9 Sept. 1939, 13 Jan. 1940, 21 Dec. 1940, 4 Jan. 1941, 6 Sept. 1941, 3 Jan. 1942, 12 Sept. 1942, 24 July 1943 (pupils' pageant), 23 December 1944 ("The Youngest Shepherd"), 8 Dec. 1945 (carol concert), 6 July 1946 (speech day), 21 Dec. 1947 (parents' day & prizegiving).
12. First *Chalet Club News Letter*, May 1959.
13. *Joey goes to the Oberland* (1954) p.40
14. Letter from Mrs Vivien Pass (née Jewell) to H. McClelland.
15. *The Chalet School Goes to It* (1941), p.247.
16. *The School at the Chalet* (1925), p.12.
17. Letter to H. McClelland.
18. Letter from Judith Humphrey to H. McClelland.

Copyright. Some of the material concerning the research for Elinor's early life was originally part of an article, "Questions about Elinor", which appeared in the magazine *Signal*, edited by Nancy Chambers, in May 1988. Certain other biographical material has also been used previously in *Behind the Chalet School* and/or *The Chalet School Companion* (Armada, 1994). In all three cases, the copyright is the property of Helen McClelland, who is the sole owner of all rights.

EXCITEMENTS FOR THE CHALET FANS — CELEBRATING THE CENTENARY OF ELINOR M. BRENT-DYER

POLLY GOERRES

"I DON'T like the look of that sky," was the frequent comment of a Chalet School mistress, poised to take a party of schoolgirls on an expedition. On just such a day of ominous grey skies, a crowd of people gathered in a Surrey cemetery to attend the dedication ceremony of a headstone. It was to be placed on the grave of a woman most of them hadn't known, a quarter of a century after her death. Even more unusual was the fact that it had been paid for by donations from dozens more people who hadn't known her. But this is the power of Elinor M. Brent-Dyer.

The idea of celebrating Elinor M. Brent-Dyer's centenary had come to me when, as a student, I read Helen McClelland's biography, *Behind the Chalet School*. Then, I had been reading the Chalet School books for ten years. Unlike several other teenage fans I had gone on reading them unashamedly during adolescence. I had preconceived notions about the author, that she was upper middle class (the naive assumption afforded by a double-barrelled name), from the Home Counties and from a large, wealthy family. These were all speedily shattered when I learned from the biography that Elinor was the product of a lower middle-class north-eastern broken home. I wandered slowly round the students' union bar, reading it avidly. I noted then that Elinor's centenary would take place in 11 years' time, and wondered what was being planned to celebrate it. Little did I think that I would be one of the instigators of a wealth of centenary celebrations.

I kept on with my Chalet reading in the years leading up to the centenary in 1994, my life being affected by several Brent-Dyer inspired events. The first happened when I established a valued correspondence and friendship with Elinor's biographer, Helen McClelland. Secondly, with Helen's encouragement and advice, I completed an undergraduate dissertation entitled *Language, Traditions and Genre of the Chalet School Series*, now held at Sheffield University's Centre for English Language and Cultural Traditions (CECTAL). Then Helen put me in touch with Ann Mackie-Hunter who had founded a Chalet fans' society and newsletter. The following year, 1990, as a result of reading the books, I spent my honeymoon in Pertisau-am-Achensee, site of the early Chalet titles. All the while I wrote to Collins (who published the books in paperback), Ann, Helen and others asking "What are you/we/they doing to celebrate Elinor's centenary in 1994?" Ann suggested I should contact Gill Bilski, who was then UK secretary for the Friends of the Chalet School.

It seems a glib thing to say, but 16 May 1992 was a day that would change my life . . . for the next few years at any rate. This was the "*Folly* Day" at the home of Belinda Copson, co-editor of *Folly* magazine. Here I met Gill Bilski and coyly asked her what Friends of the Chalet School were doing to celebrate Elinor's centenary in two years' time. Gill seemed surprised to learn that it was to be the centenary, but a lively discussion followed. The assembled Fans Of Light Literature for the Young were keen to commemorate the birth centenary of such a great popular author. One of these fans was Clarissa Cridland, to whom I chatted enthusiastically about Pertisau, the Chalet series and, to her great surprise, football!

When, in a subsequent FOCS newsletter, Gill appealed for a committee to plan and co-ordinate centenary events, I assumed that she and her book-dealing contacts had by then effected a grand stratagem. Not wishing to be left behind in this, I wrote a desperate letter to Gill offering all the help I could with the centenary plans and hoping it wasn't too late to become involved. I need not have worried, for only one other person had offered to take on the daunting challenge . . .

Clarissa and I were brim-full of bright ideas for commemorative plaques, a travelling exhibition, trips to Elinorcentric locations, Christmas cards and a calendar, all of which we discussed at length on the telephone. But we were both hampered by time, distance and full-time jobs. We decided against turning our attention abroad, and instead focused on two principal areas: Hereford, where Elinor had lived and worked for over thirty years, and South Shields, her birthplace. Letters were written to both local councils, again in the style of "What will you be doing to celebrate the centenary . . . ?" We also tentatively considered Guernsey, the site of most of Elinor's La Rochelle series and of wartime Chalet episodes.

The first major breakthrough came when my letter to Hereford City Council ended up on the desk of Jenny Houston, Promotions Officer in the Environment Department. Jenny's great-aunt had been Miss Rose Farr Smith, an old friend of Elinor's. Jenny had met Elinor, but paid her only the amount of attention that any eight year old would to the friend of a great-aunt. Miss Farr Smith had been the dedicatee of Elinor's book *Excitements at the Chalet School* (1957). For the love of her Aunt Rose and the promotion of Hereford as a tourist centre, Jenny agreed to meet the newly formed Elinor Brent-Dyer centenary committee, to discuss a weekend celebration in Hereford. With Clarissa away on business, I took a local member, Val Mackay, with me on that first Hereford reconnoitre; her local knowledge was invaluable.

Jenny put us in contact with the City Museum and Library for our exhibition, with caterers and hotels, and offered help with the provision of a commemorative plaque on the site of Elinor's former Margaret Roper School. She also had good ideas of her own, such as an illustrated talk which would involve the people of Hereford. Clarissa and I made several subsequent visits to Hereford, originally hoping that our party could stay at Belmont Abbey School or the Royal National College for the Blind, both boarding establishments. Those who had been at boarding schools would be able to relive the illicit pleasures of midnight feasts. Those, like me, who had only ever dreamed of attending a boarding-school would be able to revel in the experience.

Father Peter Fell of St Francis Xavier's Church in the centre of Hereford, where Elinor had worshipped, agreed to let us hijack his Sunday morning Mass during our weekend. The museum and library building would hold our small exhibition, and we hired the Bishop's Palace for two illustrated talks — one for the general public and one for our members. One Saturday in July 1993 we attempted to plan a coach tour around Elinor's Golden Valley, the scenery often mentioned in her Armiford Chalet books. Accompanying us was Joy Wotton, who had spent several childhood summers in the Hereford area, and we drove around winding lanes in the pouring rain, trying to put Chalet names to real-life places. But perhaps we should not have attempted this. Elinor had a vivid imagination, and used it to transplant real-life houses into different locations. Later in the day, Jenny Houston joined us to advise on the locale. However, we concluded that the tour of the Golden Valley should be a sideshow to a main feature, and not a feature of the weekend itself. We could use it as the route to Hay-on-Wye, second-hand book capital of the western world.

We wrote to people who had bought books from Gill Bilski's catalogue and written fan letters to Helen McClelland about the biography to tell them about FOCS's existence and our centenary plans. There are many hundreds of Friends of the Chalet School throughout the world who are known to us. How many hundreds more fans are there with whom we haven't made contact? When Chalet School fans find out about the society, they seem absolutely thrilled to know of its existence. We received many letters saying "I-had-no-idea-that-FOCS-existed; I-joined-immediately", many tell us that they had believed they were the only ones who still read children's books and were delighted to find so many kindred spirits.

Admitting one's "Chaletomania" to the non-converted does not always happen easily; although I have never hidden my love of the Chalet School series, I have often felt that many people do not really understand why I still read them. Others do not find it so simple. A leading book dealer who went to the Hereford weekend explained that she had not told her boyfriend where she was going, fearing what he might think! Similarly, when the centenary committee tried to gauge interest in printing Christmas cards and calendars showing illustrations from the delightful Nina K. Brisley dustwrappers, one member wrote to explain that she would not buy any because she could not possibly admit to her business colleagues, to whom she would be sending Christmas cards, that she still read children's books!

When we held our first meeting in December 1992 we had received other offers of help from would-be centenary committee members. By then, however, we had decided that we had worked well as a duo for several months, and logistically it was easier to keep it to two, although we could not possibly have achieved what we did without the constant support of Gill Bilski and Ann Mackie-Hunter and help from others on an *ad hoc* basis. The mid-April Hereford weekend was to be the focal point of celebrations, which would kick off with a plaque unveiling in South Shields the week beforehand. Guernsey was to be the venue for a La Rochelle trip, and we thought we could round off our celebrations with a memorial service, since September 1994 would see the 25th anniversary of Elinor's death.

We decided to hold a special dinner on the Saturday evening of the Hereford weekend, and had two guest speakers in mind: Helen McClelland, who is now Patron of Friends of the Chalet School, and Luella Hamilton who, as Luella Gresham, had been a pupil at Elinor's Margaret Roper School in Hereford during the last war. As I left Clarissa's house after that first committee meeting, I asked her how many people she thought would wish to come to Hereford. "I don't think we'll get more that 20 or 30," she replied. Neither of us thought that over 160 Friends of the Chalet School would make the literary pilgrimage to Hereford 16 months later.

The planning stage stepped up a gear during summer 1993. Mo Everett and Joy Wotton helped us by making preliminary investigations about a trip to Guernsey for late summer 1994. Clarissa wrote to the priest of the church of the Holy Family in Reigate, where Elinor's funeral had been held, regarding a thanksgiving service. After several letters to South Tyneside, I made contact with Tom Fennelly, a director of tourism from South Shields, about a possible plaque unveiling there.

Clarissa, meanwhile, had discovered that the exhibition area in our hoped-for venue, the Bethnal Green Museum of Childhood in London, was now a cafeteria. We weren't disheartened and got in touch with the Curator of the Edinburgh Museum of Childhood. The Edinburgh connection was an appropriate one, since Elinor's main hardback publishers, W. & R. Chambers, were based there.

One area which certainly captured members' interest was the idea of a headstone. Many people were distressed to learn that Elinor had been buried without one, and we appealed for donations which flooded in until we had raised over £1,100. We chose a stonemason near Hereford, Diana Hoare, who specialised in memorials for people in the arts world. The figure raised purchased a large slate headstone with a simple inscription: "In Memory of Elinor M. Brent-Dyer, Author of the Chalet School Series, 1894-1969", with the FOCS logo incorporated into its arched top. It also paid for erection costs and transportation to the Redstone Hill Cemetery in Redhill, Surrey.

In July 1993 we made a three-day trip to investigate Edinburgh and South Shields. Clarissa arranged to meet John Hayes, the Curator of the Edinburgh Museum of Childhood, and Diane Peacop of W. & R. Chambers. *En route* home from Scotland we planned to meet north-eastern Friend of the Chalet School, Carol Mee, who had done some preliminary reconnaissance trips around Elinor's former homes in South Shields. Tom Fennelly of South Tyneside Metropolitan Borough Council also wished to meet us. We hoped to try to persuade his council to provide a commemorative plaque for Elinor, just as Hereford City Council had done.

The Edinburgh meetings were highly successful. Diane Peacop lent us some fascinating artefacts for our exhibitions, such as contracts and manuscripts. To Chalet fans like Clarissa and me, these were revelations. We hadn't known that *The Chalet School in Exile* (1940) had had the original working title of "The Chalet School and the Nazis", nor that Elinor had been paid so little for her manuscripts. John Hayes was so amenable to our suggestion of a Brent-Dyer/Chalet exhibition that he offered to hold it for six weeks during June and July 1994. We would have many display cabinets and a children's prize quiz; we would also give an illustrated talk to the Friends of the Museum.

The following day we travelled from Edinburgh to the north-eastern coastal town of South Shields, birthplace of Elinor M. Brent-Dyer. It was a town she seldom mentioned in her work, and few who knew her in her later life would have imagined that she came from the north-east. Carol Mee, who met us there, showed us the street where Elinor had been born 99 years previously. Winchester Street was now a car park and modern houses, so would be an unsuitable location for a commemorative plaque. So, it transpired, was Belgrave Terrace, a street of large, imposing Victorian houses where Elinor had lived with her mother after the latter's marriage to Septimus Ainsley. Belgrave Terrace, though once very grand, had certainly seen better days, and since it was quite a way from the town centre we doubted that the plaque would be seen by as many people as if it were placed elsewhere. Finally we drove to Westoe Village, a beautiful tree-lined area of listed buildings not far from the town centre. No. 3 Westoe Village was at that time the site of St Clare's Hospice, and part of the route of the Catherine Cookson trail (for South Shields boasted another author!). This had been the home of St Nicholas's School, run by the Misses Stewart, which Elinor had attended during the early years of this century and where she had later returned to teach for a term or two. Over lunch, Carol expressed a desire to make her own contribution to the celebrations. Blissfully unaware of the size of the task, she very kindly offered to make a small souvenir cake for each of the participants at the weekend. At the time we told her there would probably be 50.

Tom Fennelly of South Tyneside Metropolitan Borough Council liked our suggestion for a commemorative plaque and said that the council would fund the plaque and its erection. He said that it might be unveiled by the Mayor of South Tyneside, an event to be followed by a town hall reception for Friends of the Chalet School. We were naturally delighted and returned home with a much clearer idea of how the centenary year would take shape.

One of our members, Martin Spence, bravely offered to make a sponsored swim of the Achensee to raise funds for a commemorative plaque in Pertisau. This seemed to solve many problems, since our sketchy efforts to make contacts in Pertisau had so far come to nought. Indeed, a member of the Austrian Tourist Board failed to understand our reasoning behind wishing to provide a plaque. He had written back suggesting we got in touch with the Pertisau Tourist Office ourselves. The German, he explained, would present no problems for a former pupil of the Chalet School! Martin, however, being a fluent German speaker, both swam for, and arranged the erection of, a commemorative plaque. This was put in place early in 1994, adjacent to the Catholic church and library in Pertisau.

By the autumn of 1993 it was clear that we had underestimated hugely the level of interest in the Hereford weekend. Over 160 Friends of the Chalet School (plus a handful of non-member other halves) wished to come to Hereford. The Bishop's Palace and the hall at Belmont Abbey would be packed to capacity. (There is no truth in the rumour that we drew lots to see which of us would break the news to cake-baking Carol Mee!)

With centenary year upon us, other offers of help came in. Linda Parkington from Bury, who had taken a course in calligraphy, offered to make individual name badges for weekend participants. "Prefects'" badges were to be embroidered by Lillian Smith of Dundee. Sister Julie-Anne Donnelly from the West Country designed place settings for our dinner tables; like the Chalet School dormitories, each table was to be named after an alpine flower or similar. In addition to Carol Mee's individual cakes, Helen Ware of Wells offered to make a special birthday cake for the dinner with an icing-sugar Joey Bettany figure on top. We also planned to hold a small private book sale after church on the Sunday morning; Marie Hrynczak of London was keen to organise this. There were many others, to whom I apologise if I have failed to mention them by name, keen to give assistance. Many Friends of the Chalet School offered to be prefects in the hotels, to keep the other members in order and make sure they got on the appropriate "motor-coaches" — of course in "croc"!

The intricacies of the centenary weekend needed

to be finalised by the start of 1994. We wanted to hold a Chalet School mega-quiz on the same evening as the dinner. With my fierce competitive streak I was quite disappointed that I would have to organise the quiz, rather than take part in it. Gill did not wish to take part in the quiz, but was happy to set it, so she and Clarissa took on this task. West Sussex member, Gillian Priestman, had the excellent idea of having a school group photograph taken of the Hereford participants. We commissioned Vivian's Studios of Hereford to do the honours. Thelma Holland, our photographer, had been trained by the original Vivian, and Vivian's Studios had been used frequently by Elinor and her Margaret Roper School. They were responsible for the famous photograph of Elinor wearing a hat, which appears on the rear dustwrapper of *Behind the Chalet School*. Father Peter Fell of St Francis Xavier's Church allowed us to choose the music for the Mass, and we got in touch with Adrian Officer, the authority on Elinor's favourite composer, Ernest Farrar, so that Farrar's music could be played and sung during the Mass.

With over 160 people needing to be fitted into 4 separate hotels, Clarissa and I had the difficult task of matching people who wished to share rooms. We tried, wherever possible, to pair off people who were within ten years of each other's age. We also had three members in a triple room — our own Chalet School triplets. This nightmare task took four hours on the telephone, breaking off the call every now and again to try out different permutations. Even when we had finished we had problems. In one instance we matched a profound snorer with somebody who couldn't abide snoring!

The Chalet spirit prevailed from the very first. Some members wanted lifts to Hereford, and others offered them. Many came to Hereford from great distances, such as Arbroath and Newcastle, and were glad of company on the journey. At this time we were thrilled to hear that our President and Founder, Ann Mackie-Hunter, would be making the journey to Hereford from Sydney, Australia, and staying with other Friends of the Chalet School during her three months in the UK. Three others also came to Hereford from Australia, in addition to a couple who lived in Switzerland.

Hotels, caterers, museums, councils, coach companies . . . all were written to, and plans were checked and double-checked. We rehearsed the illustrated talk that we were to give jointly in Hereford, first to the general public and then to our members. I would introduce Elinor and her life and times, and Clarissa would talk about Elinor's books and dustwrappers. Sweatshirts, posters and facsimile paperbacks of *The School at the Chalet* were provided by HarperCollins to celebrate the event. South Tyneside Metropolitan Borough Council produced a special souvenir leaflet about Elinor, quite unwittingly printing it in brown and flame, the colours of the Chalet School.

Mindful of the mayoral reception in South Shields, the Mayor of Hereford offered to give us a small cheese and wine reception to begin our Hereford weekend. We were also lucky enough to have the Deputy Mayor of Hereford, Councillor Mrs Kit Gundy, to speak to us at our dinner. She, too, had known Elinor, and was therefore an appropriate person to unveil the commemorative plaque.

On a bright, chilly April morning, exactly one hundred years after Elinor M. Brent-Dyer's birth, a crowd of about 70 Friends of the Chalet School were bound for Westoe Village; most of them had boarded a coach at the South Shields Town Hall. Those who had travelled from as far afield as London, Dublin and Dundee mingled with the press and the three women in their 80s who had personal recollections of Elinor — two of them as their teacher, the third as a local celebrity. As the commemorative plaque was unveiled on the building which had once housed Elinor's School by the Mayor of South Tyneside, her former pupil, Veronica Cheyne, made a poignant observation. "Miss Dyer would have been flattered and delighted," she later wrote, "rushing among us, thanking us for being there."

Although she never publicised the town, South Shields was ready to forgive Elinor on the centenary of her birth and gave her fans a marvellous three-course spread, worthy of Karen the cook, or Frau Mieders, mistress of "Dommy Sci". Local press and radio coverage of the day was excellent ("Now it's Wor Elinor!" was one memorable headline), thanks to a concerted campaign by the committee. Indeed, there was healthy local coverage around all Elinor's key areas — and we even made the national press (*Guardian*, *The Times*, *Observer* and *Independent*). The town library had provided a small exhibition of Brent-Dyer artefacts, including the certificate of her parents' ill-fated marriage. The council printed a map of Elinor Brent-Dyer's South Shields.

There was barely a breathing space between the South Shields plaque unveiling and our next centenary event, just nine days afterwards, the Hereford weekend. Those present as the Mayor of Hereford welcomed us to his city saw Clarissa and me, calm, unruffled and amazed at just what a large crowd over 160 Chalet fans made. The crowd had not seen the flustered beings in chaos just two hours before, as we prepared the Bishop's Palace for the evening's illustrated talk, struggling with the slide projector. Eventually we appointed a "projector monitor" to shoo people away from the rickety edifice lest it came crashing down.

Two contributory factors to the Hereford weekend's success were that everyone came determined to enjoy themselves and that the Chalet spirit (whether it be manifested in "sheepdogging" those who looked lost, or by all pitching in and "going to it"!) was in evidence throughout. For example, a condition of our being allowed to use the Bishop's Palace was that we restored it to its previous state before we locked up and departed. Chalet fans from three of the hotels went away in coaches, while those from the Castle Pool Hotel nearby rolled up their sleeves to lift chairs, vacuum carpets and collect rubbish.

Even the bookshops joined in our celebrations. The Hereford Bookshop produced a marvellous display including a schoolgirl's straw boater. The proprietor lost track of the offers made to him for his display copy of *The Chalet School in Exile* with its rare Nazi dustwrapper!

Gill Bilski recalled that she knew we had "arrived" when she saw a police cordon around Litchfield Lodge — former home of Elinor and her Margaret Roper School, now converted into flats. The Herefordshire constabulary had to be present since Litchfield Lodge is on Bodenham Road, one of the main thoroughfares into the city; traffic was directed around a milling throng, many wearing gentian-blue centenary sweatshirts. Although we had obtained permission to erect our plaque from the residents of Litchfield Lodge, and to swarm around their car park (formerly Elinor's garden) taking photographs, many Bodenham Roadees were greatly amused by our presence. In her unveiling speech, Kit Gundy asked if Luella Hamilton would help her unveil the plaque. Elinor would have admired the neatness of this arrangement, since these two had known her personally.

The city centre of Hereford was invaded for the rest of the morning by blue-sweatshirted Chalet fans. Some were anxious to take coffee at the Green Dragon Hotel, as their idol had done more than 30 years before. Others browsed in charity shops — who knows where a rare copy of *The School by the River* (1930) might be lurking? Still more viewed the cathedral, with its priceless treasure, the Mappa Mundi. For some, the attractions of Marks and Spencer's proved too much even during the centenary weekend, and hopeful midnighters gathered in the food hall. After an hour it was time for the party to enter three of what Elinor would have termed "motor-coaches", each with a large sign proclaiming "Chalet School" across the windscreen. Clarissa, Joy Wotton and I took one coach each, and narrated tour notes about the Golden Valley as we sped past Michaelchurch, Vowchurch and Peterchurch bound for Hay-on-Wye.

Chalet fans are curious beings in many ways. The vast majority of us are not exclusively Brent-Dyer collectors. Hay-on-Wye, with its 20 or so second-hand bookshops, allowed us to break our croc and have a jolly good ramble — "I *said* ramble and I *meant* ramble" (*Theodora and the Chalet School*, 1959, p.41). No shelf was left unchecked in our search. Our final afternoon destination was Judith Gardner's Children's Bookshop, just outside Hay. Judith had erected a huge marquee for our tea tent, resplendent with magnificent signs showing jolly schoolgirls taking their tea and cakes.

Saturday evening at Belmont Abbey began in a riotous way. We can all remember the military precision with which school photographs are staged. The task does not get any easier when the schoolchildren are mostly adults. Those who were young and agile climbed up to stand on chairs on top of tables at the very back of a frightening-looking edifice. Others of moderate agility sat on chairs on top of tables in front of them. Older fans and those who had difficulty standing were afforded the luxury of chairs, while the youngest and smallest of us squatted down at the front. Twenty minutes later it was "watch the birdie", and we were immortalised on Kodak paper. Then the mental torture of Clarissa and Gill's quiz, over which they presided dressed as a 1930s schoolgirl and a 1930s Girl Guide of the First Chalet School Company respectively, sent us ravenously into dinner.

One fan wrote that it was a pure joy to sit back, close her eyes, and listen to the after-dinner speakers painting wonderful word pictures. From Helen McClelland's tale of researching the elusive Elinor's life, to Luella Hamilton's memories of her Headmistress, to Gill's message to all Friends of the Chalet School and Kit Gundy's recollections of a highly effusive personality, everything was highly entertaining. The abbey's brothers and fathers seemed rather amused at the strange variety of female guests. The FOCS committee (at that time Ann Mackie-Hunter, Gill Bilski, Clarissa and me) were kindly presented with cards and gifts, including alpine flower soap, which had been bought in secret by the members present at Hereford, and organised by Sue Sims, the other editor of *Folly*. Ann, as President and Founder of FOCS, cut Helen Ware's centenary cake; the exquisite nature of the sugaring effect and the presence of our President from thousands of miles away brought a lightning dazzle of camera flashes.

There were even a few speeches left over for Sunday, for the coach drivers were not allowed to exceed their legal maximum driving hours and had to take us back early to our hotels. This was not something which had happened to the stranded coach party in *The New Chalet School* (1938). (This, however, allowed some of us the opportunity to hold midnight feasts, and even for one miscreant prefect to re-enact the "Baby Voodoo" episode from *The New House at the Chalet School,* 1935).

Sunday was not the "gentle" day that Margia Stevens described to her parents. It started by way of a moving tribute. Father Fell found his congregation at St Francis Xavier's had virtually doubled, as many of the Chalet party attended a Mass that he had allowed us to dedicate to Elinor. Members of our committee read secular and Biblical pieces, and enjoyed renderings of Ernest Farrar's "Brittany" and "The Knight of Bethlehem" from the church choir's star soloist, Clare Quinn.

Then from the sublime, to the ridiculous — the Sunday morning book sale, where Marie Hrynczak and her band of cashiers presided over a mad rush which knocked the January sales "into a cocked hat". Members had been offered the chance to bring books — not just Brent-Dyer titles either — and rich pickings were to be had, more so even than at Hay-on-Wye. One member even emerged with three bursting carrier bags full of books.

Carol Mee's individual cakes were presented as souvenirs after lunch, where Clarissa and I made brief speeches, allowing the main ones — a humorous account of the founding of FOCS by our President, Ann, and a moving tribute from Elinor's heir, Chloe Rutherford, read by Helen McClelland — more time. When the afternoon coaches rounded up the party, many tearful farewells were said — but many more new friendships had been forged and addresses been exchanged.

With South Shields and Hereford over, the Edinburgh exhibition had now to be arranged. Several members lent us their prized artefacts for display, including Chalet School tapestries, a membership card and badge from the original Chalet Club, memorabilia from the Margaret Roper School — and of course the inevitable full set of dust-wrappered Brent-Dyer books! We were privileged to have Tony Chambers of Edinburgh's famous publishing family to open the exhibition with his recollections of Elinor. He deemed it "a pleasure because it brings back to me very pleasant memories of meetings with Miss Brent-Dyer — always Miss, never Elinor".

Almost all Chalet fans would covet the set of dust-wrappered Brent-Dyers displayed in glass cabinets at the exhibition. Indeed, one member, Alison Lindsay, wrote "somebody lend me a brick!" An interesting theory on the books' timelessness is shared by several people, including Elinor's biographer, Helen McClelland, who believes that the crusade against contemporary slang terms employed by the Chalet School authorities is a reason why the books have not dated. This is in contrast to many of Elinor's contemporary authors, including Angela Brazil, whose books were riddled with fashionable slang of her time, and have not lasted the course into the last quarter of the 20th century.

In fact, to my surprise, not all modern schoolgirl readers are aware that the books were written so long ago. When I was a child I would always turn to the publication details at the start of each book to find out its year of first publication. I thought all children did this. Having discussed it with adult Chalet friends, I now know this is only true for about half of us. At our exhibition *Back to the Chalet*

School, which ran at the Edinburgh Museum of Childhood between 4 June and 16 July 1994, a member of FOCS watched a bemused Chalet School reader of about 12 gazing at the collection of first-edition Chalet School books in original dust wrappers. The girl could not understand why these old books, dating from 1925 to 1970, were there. To her, the Chalet School series was modern, and she had never questioned the fact that the girls in the books were not her contemporaries. The FOCS member, now fellow committee member, Fen Crosbie, explained about the timescale of their publication, which shocked and even disappointed the young reader, for whom the Chalet School series were just lovely new modern paperbacks!

For our "La Rochelle" weekend, a smaller party than that at Hereford — about 40 — crossed the English Channel to Guernsey. We were relieved that the conditions were rather less tempestuous than for Jo's reverse journey in *The Chalet School Goes to It* (1941). Although Clarissa and I, as the centenary committee, had sorted out the administration with excellent support from Gill, the real planning for the event had been left to Mo Everett, a resident Guernsey member. She gave over her home in true *Freudesheim* style to an evening of delicious food, a quiz and progressive games, with a beautiful La Rochelle cake on display. The rest of her family, husband Frank and daughters Katie and Ginny, joined in with a will and made sure the party had a splendid time on the island.

A proper "croc", albeit one on wheels, traversed Guernsey, taking in the sites familiar to the Temple, Willoughby, Atherton and Raphael clans and locating the site of the Chalet School at Sarres. New-found friendships were intensified by Chalet chats on hotel stairs until three a.m. and beyond.

Matey would not have approved our unhealthy hours!

On 20 September 1994, the day after we returned from Guernsey, Father Michael Sewell, a former children's book buyer, conducted a thanksgiving service for the life of Elinor M. Brent-Dyer, exactly 25 years after her death. This took place at the church of the Holy Family, Reigate, where Elinor's funeral service had been held. Members of the FOCS committee, our Patron and Elinor's biographer Helen McClelland and Chloe Rutherford, Elinor's heir, read secular tributes, including an extract from *Eustacia Goes to the Chalet School* (1930) and a *Chalet Club News Letter*, and passages from the Bible. Again, the beautiful Edwardian notes of Ernest Farrar's "Brittany", sung by Sandra Ford, moistened many an eye. Finally, Ann and Gill laid a floral tribute on Elinor's grave, newly marked with the headstone that Friends of the Chalet School had provided, and dedicated by Father Michael.

So why the great excitement? Why did so many people wish to become involved in the centenary celebrations? Could it be the timelessness of the series? Chalet School books have been in print continuously since the mid-1920s and the original schoolgirls for whom Elinor Brent-Dyer wrote will now be in their 80s or 90s. These girls grew up in a world wholly different from the modern one. Before the 1950s, when teenage culture developed in the western world, there was no middle ground between childhood and adulthood; consequently a schoolgirl of the 1920s would read school stories for most of her teenage years, whereas many Chalet fans of my 1960s' "baby boom" generation went through phases of embarrassment if they had to declare that they still read girls' school stories during their teens and young adulthood. For many adult fans of Elinor Brent-Dyer, the reading of the entire Chalet School series is a biennial or even annual treat. They may have read each book dozens of times, and be familiar with them all, but, as one fan puts it, "I know the books so well by now that rereading each one is like greeting an old friend". In reading certain titles again after a gap of several years, I always discover new and interesting themes, insights into characters and quaint turns of phrase.

For me, the attraction is also in knowing what comes next. When I reread *Gay from China at the Chalet School* (1944), I had to find a comfortable place where I could not be disturbed because I knew I would cry my eyes out when reading how Jacynth Hardy was told of her only relative's death. I am sure that the almost naive acceptance of death as "falling asleep to wake with God" has been a comfort to many readers, and has helped them come to terms with the natural process of grieving after a bereavement.

The Chalet School books are part of my life, and have been for over 20 years. I cannot imagine a time when I will not read them. They are a piece of my childhood carried forward to my adulthood; I can remember where I was when I read each one, where I acquired them and the thrill of finding each new title. The books mature with the reader. Whereas a ten year old might read them for the lively adventures of the middle school, the adult reader can look at the skilful description of interpersonal relationships and the exquisite characterisation of almost 2,000 "paper children" (the term is Elinor's). They are far from being childish, although ostensibly written for children.

I am told that I have developed a "Chalet School mentality" in daily life. For example, my horror of procrastination stems from the teachings of "Matey", the Chalet School matron. Each new girl at the Chalet School is told in exhaustive detail, often by Matron, that there is only one way to make and strip a bed, and that it is vital to keep one's dormitory cubicle tidy. As Joey's daughter, Len Maynard says to a new girl Richenda Fry in *The Chalet School and Richenda* (1958, p.49): "Matey insists on doing it this way, and it's always best to fall in with her ideas. She's a perfect poppet when she likes; but get across her and you know all about it!" In the same way, I have developed a desire for order. Other Chalet readers I know emulate the girls in different ways, including plunging into a daily cold bath, to emerge (one hopes) "glowing and fresh from the icy sting" of the water (*The Chalet School and Barbara*, 1954, p.42), visiting the locations of the books on holiday, writing in the style of Elinor (albeit unknowingly; I was often ticked off for this in the 6th form!) and repeating many of the book's sayings. One Chalet friend of mine even calls her young son "Colin-a-bobbin", borrowing the pet form used by Madge Russell to the Robin.

For some readers, the Chalet books provide an alternative reality to an unhappy childhood, and the plots are relived in their imaginations or in role-play games in the school playground. For others, Christmas is not Christmas without reading about Jo, Madge and the Robin staying in Innsbruck with the Mensches in *Jo of the Chalet School* (1926). For others still, the world of the Chalet School is a logical extension of a fantasy world. The Chalet girls' sense of honour, loyalty to the school and intellectual ability became traits to emulate, particularly the way in which each girl seemed to become almost effortlessly trilingual. As Joey explained to Zephyr Burthill in *Jo to the Rescue* (1945, p.169), having previously lapsed into French, "I am afraid we are so accustomed to speaking any one of three languages as they come handy, we tend to forget that it isn't the same with everyone."

Each generation of fans finds that on one level the books are first class adventure stories set among the day-to-day minutiae of school life, but on returning to them in adulthood they entertain on a different level. It is the characterisation and lively interplay between diverse personalities which interest the reader more at 30 or 40 than at 10. I believe Elinor's books form an adult saga written for children. One has to call it this, for, to borrow the style from a modern blockbuster, Elinor's series sweeps majestically from the Austrian Tyrol through the war-torn Channel Islands to the peace of Herefordshire and Wales and back to the Alps, this time in Switzerland, taking about 28 fictional years and 45 real ones to do so.

The series' appeal to the child reader is easily understood. When a girl first encounters the Chalet School she is often in her last years of primary school, when the thoughts of a bigger secondary school excite her; the Chalet School takes on the form of that school in her imagination. On first attending my girls' day school at its competitive entrance examination, I wanted it to be the Chalet School. To a girl of 10 or 11, the detail with which school life is described paints a picture of a fascinating world, cubicles with cabinets which have

> a place for toilet articles, all except one's spongebag. For that, there was a hook attached to one of the standards that supported the curtain-rods round the cubicle. A second standard had another hook for your dressing gown . . . (*The Chalet School and Barbara*, 1954, p.40).

She reads of cubicle curtains, bathroom lists, bedstripping, "showing-a-leg", private prayers, the silence bell, window cubicles, dormitory prefects, Leafy and Gentian dormitories, splasheries, locker tidiness, Matey hauling transgressors out of lessons, cold baths, rising bells and the proper use of the back stairs.

Elinor had a gift for describing worlds in which readers could lose themselves, whether it be the Tyrol of Joey and Madge, the Tyrol of the peasant family from whom Joey rescues the St Bernard pup, Rufus, the hostile North Queensland climate where the Venables family failed to prosper or the genteel world of the Temple sisters' Channel Islands. All human life is there, and all human life must conform — not to a stereotype, because there are many different characters at the Chalet School, but to the ideal of "a real Chalet School girl". All Chalet readers will know who these are: Jo Bettany, Mary-Lou Trelawney and Len Maynard are the archetypes, while Rosamund Lilley, Elizabeth Arnett and Juliet Carrick begin shakily but get there in the end. On the other hand, Betty Wynne-Davies, Diana Skelton and Thekla Von Stift are never true Chalet girls. They fail to conform to the system, and in turn the system has little to offer them.

Another highly appealing factor of the Chalet School series is the growth of the school. It is enjoyable to watch Madge Bettany's small venture flourishing and a family feeling is engendered. We grow up with Jo — although Jo herself resists growing up, notwithstanding her marriage at the comparatively early age of 20, she still strives to be a schoolgirl when verging on 40. She acts as the universal matriarch to her 11 offspring, adopted children and the school as a whole. In addition to being schoolgirl adventures, the Chalet School books are about a family, initially the Bettany siblings, and later their spouses and a combined total of no fewer than 24 children. The school is the extended family; despite growing in size to several hundred, it still retains the essential family qualities.

If the minutiae of school life fail to enthral the childhood fan, then the excitement and adventure of the plots will grip her. In the same way the adult reader will gain more from the descriptions of the development of a girl's character, her conformity into the ideal Chalet School mould, and the pupils' and staff's interaction in peer groups and between groups. There are many examples of the dual-level of Elinor's appeal. While a child might thrill at Cornelia Flower's sortie into the Tyrolean caves, and her capture by a madman in *The Head Girl of the Chalet School* (1928), an adult will admire the subtlety with which Cornelia is transformed from a firebrand into a Chalet girl (albeit a mischievous one!) and eventually Head Girl. Grizel Cochrane's headstrong flight up the Tiernjoch in *The School at the Chalet* (1925) shows a wilful spirit; the writing is vivid and powerful, and Grizel's sense of adventure transmits itself to the reader. But an adult will marvel at Elinor's artistry in juxtaposing the characters of the younger Joey, Grizel's rescuer, who is imaginative and impetuous, with the older Grizel, who is wild and vengeful.

However, while an adult Chalet reader may still appreciate Elinor's craft as a storyteller and adventure writer, and a perceptive child will marvel at the fine detail of Elinor's characterisation, primarily Elinor is writing an adult tale for children. One unusual feature of her writing which illustrates this well is the staffroom dialogue. Nearly all the Chalet books contain at least one instance of a staffroom discussion, showing schoolgirl problems from the point of view of the staff. Readers learn that the Chalet staff are human, and the child reader also learns that grown-ups too are human, and that they too have their problems with the Eustacias and Theklas and Joan Bakers who inhabit the world of the Chalet School. The clearest insight into the adult world, the world of a teacher which Elinor knew so well, is offered in *The New Mistress at the Chalet School* (1957), when readers live and feel the trepidation and anxiety which young Kathie Ferrars, fresh from University, experiences when she takes her first class: "Kathie drew a long breath as the door closed . . . For a moment she felt almost panic-stricken. She also felt as if the world were made up of eyes which fixed firmly on herself." (p.57). Would these have been the recollections of Elinor, whose own teaching career had spanned more than 35 years?

But despite conforming to the ideal of a "real Chalet School girl", Chalet School pupils are encouraged to express themselves individually in many ways. Tom Gay's penchant for carpentry allows her scope to encourage others at the Hobbies Club. Nina Rutherford's musical genius means that her school timetable is rearranged allowing her to specialise. For a while, in the middle Chalet titles, a Special Sixth form exists, in which 6th form girls study the subjects they wish to pursue in tertiary education.

Elinor's heroines provide positive feminine role models for her readers. Girls find that their storybook favourites do not have to identify with men to get on, albeit in the exclusively female world of the Chalet School, but that women can be encouraged to succeed for their own sakes. Examples of this include Eustacia Benson, who becomes a great classical scholar and as "E. Benson" has her academic treatise mistaken for that of a man; Tom Gay, a "missionary" after Oxford among the boys' clubs of London; and Mary-Lou Trelawney, who thirsts to make her way in the field of archaeology.

I cannot remember being moulded by Elinor Brent-Dyer's religious teachings to make a positive effort to join the community of a church, but I can say that I felt keenly aware of the part that religion played in the lives of the Chalet girls. The idea of praying to thank God for blessings received, as well as to ask for His mercy in future things, was the single force which taught me to pray regularly, not just when I was in difficulties. Other fans have been shaped by Elinor's ecumenical attitude. One fan, Winifred Crisp, now in her 70s, wrote in *Friends of the Chalet School Newsletter 23*:

> I don't think anyone, even my parents, had a greater influence on me than E.B.D. From her I learnt the value of international understanding, leading me to become a member of the International Friendship League 47 years ago . . . She taught me religious tolerance, not very usual in those days, so that when I, as an Anglican, married a Roman Catholic, there seemed nothing difficult about it, and in fact has led me to become deeply involved in ecumenicalism.

Pertisau pilgrimages are frequent among Friends of the Chalet School's members. The Obergammeau Passion Play of 1930 was instrumental in Elinor Brent-Dyer's conversion to Catholicism from Anglicanism. A Chalet fan in her early 30s wrote back from her first trip to Pertisau: "I feel very close to E.B.D. and the books here and am keeping a diary".

There is also another appeal in the books, the

appeal of the author herself. I felt I knew Elinor Brent-Dyer as a person, but not her background, before I read Helen McClelland's biography *Behind the Chalet School* (1981). Elinor does try, albeit unconsciously, to bring herself into the narrative. Having read the biography, I wondered how someone who seemed to be a great champion of realism, for example the Jew-baiting incident in *The Chalet School in Exile* (1940), sought not to mention that such a thing as divorce occurred, given the possibility it gave for interesting plot developments, and wondered too why there was an unusually high amount of deaths and families with only one living parent. Elinor liked to give away something of herself in her dedications, "To Mother and Dad" (*A Thrilling Term at Janeways,* 1927), to use the largely northern practice of referring to lunch as dinner, and to make her characters the mouthpieces of her opinions.

The Chalet School books are all about wish fulfilment, the school we would have liked to attend, the friends we'd have liked to have. But they are as much a product of Elinor Brent-Dyer's wish fulfilment as that of her readers. This is the school she had wanted to run. Joey is the child and woman she should have been. Miss Annersley is the embodiment of the headmistress Elinor had wished to become. She portrays secure families with steady, head-of-the-household father figures, as if to compensate for the lack of such a framework in her own.

So who is the typical Chalet fan? I do not think s/he exists. There are members of Friends of the Chalet School whose ages range from seven to 83. They are about 99 per cent female. Some are schoolgirls at Chalet School-style boarding schools; others attend inner city comprehensives. Some are housewives; others are university lecturers or solicitors. They inhabit all social classes, and live in more than ten countries. Some have been reading the books since the age of eight. Others come to them later in life; in several instances through their daughters' or granddaughters' influence. The majority seem to be women who are rather forceful characters, by which I do not mean bossy. Could this be an unconscious wish to be Joey Bettany? I am convinced that, though we may like or dislike her as a person, we all aspire to be Joey in some way. We'd all love to be as popular and have as many friends as Joey does (and I'm sure Elinor wished this, too!) to be as fulfilled in career and family life as Joey is, and to be as financially secure. The force of Joey's personality is one of the major factors which make the series so appealing. Perhaps other young fans, as I did as a child, identified Joey with a senior girl at school, or a popular young teacher.

Why, as we approach the 21st century, are the books still selling nearly 100,000 paperback copies a year to the rising generation, and why are they so keenly sought in the second-hand market, sometimes for hundreds of pounds? Though the language and scenarios may appear dated to some, the characterisation and plots are as fresh and immediate as when they were first written. Today's schoolgirls may experience the same rivalries, friendships and quarrels as their forebears in the 1920s. Whether it be a reflection or an ideal, of the schooldays we are now experiencing, or a nostalgia for our own far distant schooldays, there is something within the Chalet School series which grips us. To paraphrase Joey Bettany, even when we are ancient with great-great-grandchildren, fans of Elinor M. Brent-Dyer will still read the Chalet School series.Having said that, the overwhelmingly simple reason for Elinor's continuing popularity — and the reason why her centenary was so keenly commemorated — is that she was also a jolly good storyteller!

THE LITERARY CONTEXT OF THE CHALET SCHOOL

SHEILA RAY

IN the 1920s, when Elinor Brent-Dyer's books began to appear, there was very little critical interest in Britain in books written specifically for young people, although some children's books, such as A. A. Milne's Pooh stories and collections of verse, were reviewed alongside adult books. The first professionals to take children's literature seriously were librarians: in 1936 the Library Association established the Carnegie Medal, an annual award for an outstanding children's book, and the *Junior Bookshelf*, the first British specialist reviewing journal devoted to children's books, was launched by H. J. B. Woodfield, a librarian who became a bookseller. Librarians working with children in the 1930s were very much influenced by the views of American children's librarians, who believed that they had a duty to promote only the best children's books, and who, a decade earlier, had begun to put forward ideas about what constitutes a good children's book.

Criteria for judging children's books have changed little over the years. The plot should be convincing and well-constructed, with plenty of action. Good characterisation is essential; stereotyping should be avoided and the characters should be believable, with the ability to change and develop within the story. "If the setting is . . . geographic . . . [it] should present a healthy, fair picture and portrayal of other cultures and customs."[1] The style should be readable for the age group for which the book is intended, should show an imaginative use of vocabulary and avoid clichés. Themes and ideas should offer a challenge to the young reader. Formula fiction and long series tend to be dismissed without any consideration of their possible positive qualities.

In Britain, in the first 30 years of the 20th century, school stories were published in large quantities, as books and in annuals, miscellaneous collections and magazines. Although they were stocked in many libraries, they were, on the whole, poorly regarded by adults. Constance Stern, children's librarian at Croydon in the 1930s, was typical in her condemnation of girls' school stories, decrying them as a waste of "creative energy on unpractical daydreams".[2]

Adult opinion, of course, did not affect their popularity with children. Up to the outbreak of the Second World War in 1939, Angela Brazil, who published over 50 full-length and many short school stories between 1906 and 1946, and who is generally regarded as the pioneer of the girls' school story[3], was regularly reported to be the most popular and bestselling writer for girls.[4] In a survey carried out in 1947, G. A. Carter, a librarian, reported that school stories were the most popular kind of reading amongst 12- to 14-year-olds and that Angela Brazil was the second most popular writer, with 29 nominations compared to W. E. Johns's 34. Elinor Brent-Dyer received five nominations along with R. D. Blackmore; no doubt the children who nominated Elinor were being truthful while those who mentioned R. D. Blackmore had probably just been reading *Lorna Doone* at school, as I did in the early 1940s.[5]

The *School Library Review*, which began in 1936, and the *School Librarian*, which was started the following year, were, as the titles suggest, geared to libraries in schools, and to libraries in academic secondary schools in particular; they provided book reviews and articles about authors and titles that might be enjoyed by young people, and the general impression that emerges from their pages is that, as soon as possible, children were encouraged to read John Buchan, Sir Walter Scott, H. G. Wells, Robert Louis Stevenson, Rudyard Kipling and Rider Haggard, having first cut their teeth on children's classics such as *Little Women* (1868), *Alice's Adventures in Wonderland* (1865) and *The Water Babies* (1863). One headmistress, Miss M. G. Beard of Crofton Grange, addressing a meeting of the Association of Head Mistresses of Boarding Schools in 1937 or 1938, said, "I never allow school stories," and then wondered why reading was a problem for the 11 to 15 age group.[6] The *Times Literary Supplement* began to publish an occasional *Children's Books Supplement* in 1949, but it was only in the 1950s that teachers generally began to take an intelligent interest in the contemporary books being published for children and young people.

There were few critical works about children's literature, and their emphasis tended to be on its historical development; for example F. J. Harvey Darton's *Children's Books in England* (1932)[7] and Roger Lancelyn Green's *Tellers of Tales* (1946) both include mention of Talbot Baines Reed, the populariser of the boys' school story, but not of Angela Brazil. Roger Lancelyn Green brought the history of children's literature up to date in a rewritten and revised edition of *Tellers of Tales* in 1965, but although he has a chapter entitled "Rudyard Kipling and the World of School", in which he mentions the Jennings books by Anthony

Buckeridge, he gives no indication that girls' school stories ever existed.[8]

It is only in 1949, in Geoffrey Trease's *Tales Out of School*, a survey of children's literature which broke new ground by looking at what children were actually reading at the time, that we find a mention of Elinor Brent-Dyer alongside the many other writers popular with children. In the chapter, "Midnight in the Dorm", girls' school stories are considered alongside those for boys; Trease points out that, for historical reasons, the girls' school story lagged behind the school story for boys, and mentions Brent-Dyer and the Chalet books along with Angela Brazil and Elsie J. Oxenham. This was a start, although he regards the level of writing in this field as low.[9]

Marcus Crouch, in *Treasure Seekers and Borrowers*, first published in 1962, does slightly better. He includes Elinor Brent-Dyer amongst three writers, the others being Dorita Fairlie Bruce and Josephine Elder, who "explored the convention of school-life, and the minds of their heroines with greater subtlety" and suggests that the Chalet School stories show a little of "the influence not of the traditional school-story but of the 'adult' school novels of Hugh Walpole and others".[10]

Another standard work of the period is Frank Eyre's *20th Century Children's Books*, first published in 1952; in the revised and enlarged edition of 1971, he begins the section on school stories by saying: "The school story was always an artificial type and its decline towards the middle of the century was neither unexpected nor deplored." He too mentions Elinor Brent-Dyer, Dorita Fairlie Bruce and Elsie J. Oxenham, each of whom "was responsible for several series of books about the same characters or school, of which Elinor Brent-

Dyer's 'Chalet School' series was the farthest removed from reality and Dorita Fairlie Bruce's 'Dimsie' series the nearest to it".[11]

Until the early 1960s literary criticism of children's books was largely in the hands of male critics who, even if they managed to read a Chalet School book, were certainly not likely to be able to look at it from the point of view of a typical reader. Marcus Crouch and Frank Eyre were both highly regarded critics, but the former's verdict of "subtlety" sits oddly with the latter's accusation of lack of "reality".

When, as a librarian, I first started working with children and books in the late 1950s, the only critical works in the field by women which were easily available in Britain were Dorothy Neal White's *About Books for Children* (1946)[12] and Lillian Smith's *The Unreluctant Years* (1953).[13] Both authors were children's librarians, the first in New Zealand, the second in Canada, and both believed firmly in providing only the best children's books, amongst which school stories were definitely not included. Dorothy Neal White has a brief reference to the "once popular school story", while Lillian Smith ignores it completely; both were preoccupied by the idea that children had no time to waste on reading mediocre books. It is, of course, true that school stories are a peculiarly British genre, but this fact alone does not account for the scant attention they received from these critics, especially as we now know that school stories were read eagerly in New Zealand, Australia and Canada.[14]

After 1960, there was a surge of critical interest in children's books in Britain, but by this time attitudes towards girls' school stories were firmly fixed. John Rowe Townsend published the first edition of *Written for Children* in 1965. In the third revised edition of 1987 he wrote, "the traditional boarding-school story has not revived and does not look likely to do so".[15] He concentrates on the boys' school story, although Antonia Forest is described as "bravely" keeping the boarding school story alive with the occasional Marlow title.[16]

The first British woman to emerge as a serious critic was Margery Fisher, although even she was New Zealand-born, whose *Intent Upon Reading* (1961) was quickly recognised as a landmark in the criticism of children's literature. Restricting the historical element to an account of what literary criticism had already been done in the field, she concentrated on currently available children's fiction. Although school stories are the first group to be dealt with in the chapter called "Fossils and Formulas", the Chalet books are described as a "clear example of fossilization". She is critical of "ten or twelve pages of drama concerning the dire consequences of tilting your chair while working" and the "shadowy and uninteresting characters", and describes the new generation of schoolgirls as being "untouched, apparently, by the passage of time".[17] At this point she clearly did not anticipate the survival of the Chalet books into the 1990s!

However, in her *Who's Who in Children's Books* (1975), there is an entry for Joey Bettany in which she says, "Though the episodes and the idiom of the stories now seem laboured and out of date, the character of Jo can still claim attention".[18] Her last review of Chalet books appeared in *Growing Point* in 1985, when she reviewed the paperback editions of *A Leader in the Chalet School* and *The Chalet School Wins the Trick*. Here she takes an even kinder view:

Elinor Brent-Dyer has developed a most entertaining series of episodes as individuals vary from one book to another . . . Jack, determined to make her mark on the school quickly, disrupts discipline with practical jokes and ill-conceived experiments, while Len . . . restores the balance through a strength of purpose that has no self-esteem in it.

Both stories are described as extending "the saga of a school which, however old-fashioned it may seem now in social terms, still faces the same dissensions and definitions of personality which are the basis of fiction in general and of school stories in particular".[19] Since the quality of the Chalet books, in my opinion, declined rather than improved as time went on, to what can one ascribe this change of attitude? The mellowing of age? Or the realisation that the Chalet books were obviously surviving despite the odds?

By 1985, the girls' school story had received rather more attention. The first edition of *You're a Brick, Angela!* by Mary Cadogan and Patricia Craig had appeared in 1976. In looking at the whole range of books and magazines published for girls between 1839 and 1975, the authors performed an invaluable service but, in covering so much ground, some of their comments were bound to be superficial and they undoubtedly trod on many people's dreams[20], when they criticised Brent-Dyer for her "religious sentimentality" and the fact that she felt that her characters' adulthood could "best be expressed by supernatural fecundity.[21] They looked at the books with an adult knowingness, and were unable to avoid poking fun at the stories in a way that is not very far removed from the mockery of Arthur Marshall.

When Marshall reviewed *Excitements at the*

Chalet School in 1957 he began:

> Excitements at the Chalet School vary. There is an avalanche ("A whacker to judge by the sound of it"), a past headmistress (Miss Bubb), a landslide. Miss Annersley in her crimson twin set, and Margot Maynard (forget-me-not eyes), who "fell into Lucerne last March".[22]

Arthur Marshall made a name for himself as a humorist on the subject of girls' schools and girls' school stories, both in writing and on the radio. The editor of the *New Statesman* would know, when inviting Arthur Marshall to review a Chalet book, exactly the sort of review he would get — certainly not one to be taken seriously. It is significant that a quotation from Marshall ("Such brilliance, energy and expertise. It's all super!"), appears on the cover of the paperback edition of *You're a Brick, Angela!*.

Two books which focus on the English school story, Isabel Quigly's *The Heirs of Tom Brown* (1982) and *Happiest Days* (1988) by Jeffrey Richards, devote, respectively, one chapter and no space at all to the school story for girls. Isabel Quigly says, "Elinor M. Brent-Dyer set the enormous Chalet School series in the Austrian Tyrol, and went back there after the Second World War",[23] which piece of misinformation is typical of attitudes towards girls' school stories prevailing into the 1980s, and probably lingering on into the 1990s: the sternest critics do not see any need to get their facts right. Jeffrey Richards contents himself with saying that "girls' fiction is a universe of its own" and refers readers to the "perceptive analysis" of *You're a Brick, Angela!*.[24]

In 1981, Helen McClelland's *Behind the Chalet School* filled a large gap, although it did not come from a mainstream publisher.[25] It was only when feminist criticism turned its attention to girls' stories that the girls' school story was taken seriously by critics. Judith Rowbotham's *Good Girls Make Good Wives* (1989)[26] and *Girls Only* (1990) by Kimberley Reynolds[27] pointed in the right direction, but both were concerned with fiction published before the First World War. Rosemary Auchmuty's *A World of Girls*, published in 1992, which dealt with the novels of Elsie J. Oxenham, Dorita Fairlie Bruce and Elinor Brent-Dyer, therefore marked an important step forward.[28]

I believe that girls who enjoyed school stories from 1910 onwards recognised, if only subconsciously, the fact that the world of an all-girls' school provided a satisfying environment for their fantasies. It was a world in which the female viewpoint was important, in which females took positive decisions and could be seen as leaders, and in which they succeeded and achieved, or could do so, both physically and intellectually. And, at least, they were never required to do the washing up or undertake other mundane domestic chores, except, possibly, for fun or in an emergency.

THE CHALET BOOKS CONSIDERED

It has already been said that, in the criticism of children's books and in establishing whether a book is a good children's book, consideration is generally given to plot, to characterisation and to style and themes. Children and young people demand a good story, an author who can tell one holds their attention and keeps them turning the pages. However, by the time girls reach the stage of reading the Chalet books, they are likely to be fluent readers and do not need the enticement of a good plot. The Chalet books are not plotted in the accepted sense of the word; they are held together by a central character or characters and by a specific time-scale, usually a school term. Where there is a unifying and recognisable plot such as the rivalry of the two schools in *The Rivals of the Chalet School* (1929) or the kidnapping of Elisaveta in *The Princess of the Chalet School* (1927), this is not an exclusive or dominant feature. Life goes on as usual, independently of the central theme, and there are many incidents which do not contribute to the unfolding of the plot.

One of the attractions of the books must be the minutiae of school life and organisation, which are seen from all points of view. During the course of a book, the viewpoint can shift from that of the older girls to that of the youngest, and the reader is also told what the staff and Head do, think and feel in certain situations. It may have been this feature of the books that Marcus Crouch had in mind when he saw in the Chalet books the influence of the writers of adult school novels.

Many of the books, particularly in the case of the later titles, are concerned with the fortunes of one particular character and the way in which she settles down at the Chalet School. In the earlier books Elisaveta, Eustacia, and Joyce Linton, for example, are all such central characters, but the books do not deal entirely with their concerns and the viewpoint from which events are seen shifts frequently. In the typical school story in which a new girl arrives at the school, meets problems but is gradually accepted and settles down, everything is usually seen from her angle, but Brent-Dyer presents a more rounded picture of school life and this may be one reason for her continuing appeal. Perhaps, to the young reader, the books seem more realistic because of it, despite their comparatively exotic settings. Young adolescent girls usually seek in their reading some guidance about what it is like to grow up and about what lies in the future. The Chalet books give 11- and 12-year-olds a foretaste of the responsibilities and challenges that lie ahead.

The characters are clearly defined but there is little real characterisation. Brent-Dyer has the advantage of being able to differentiate between her characters through nationality — English Jo, French Simone, American Cornelia — and goes even further by making a distinction between the two Austrian girls, Frieda, the North Tyrolean, and Marie, the pretty Viennese. The girls, however, develop very little through their experiences. Some settle down, some become truly reformed characters as the result of some incident, such as Eustacia through her accident or Joyce Linton because of her unfortunate involvement with Thekla, but, on the whole, the characters remain very much as they are when we first meet them — Simone is a rare exception.

Each emerges on to the Chalet scene with her physical appearance, nationality and main characteristics already established. Sometimes these are reinforced in more detail; for example, a distinction is frequently made between Grizel's good but mechanical playing of the piano and the way in which Margia Stevens plays with real feeling and expression. Characters can be relied upon to behave or react in a certain way; their characteristics are often used to develop the plot. In *The New House at the Chalet School* (1935), the campaign against the new matron is carried a stage further when Margia is "longing to get" at her new Brahms and meets a disbelieving Matron (p.183). Later in the same book, Jo's fear of the dentist, when she finally succumbs to the pain and confesses to Matron, leads to a major expedition to the dentist in Innsbruck and the subsequent meeting with Jem's long lost sister, Margot Venables.[29]

There is a large cast of characters, but 50 years after reading the earlier titles I find it easy to recall even some of the minor characters and their distinguishing features. However, I was fortunate in that the first Chalet book I read (in about 1940) was *The New House at the Chalet School*; I then caught up on all the earlier titles, and read the later ones up to and including *Lavender Laughs in the Chalet School* (1943), while I was a schoolgirl. I read them many times, partly because there was a shortage of books during the Second World War, so the characters and incidents of these early titles are engraved on my memory. It is possible that girls coming first to one of the much later titles might be confused by the many characters and lose interest quite quickly. However, I have recently come to the conclusion that one of the reasons why the Chalet books were, and have remained, so popular with succeeding generations of schoolgirls is that it is comparatively easy to find out what other titles exist and in which order they should be read, since the complete list of them is usually included in each book.

In style, the Chalet books are very much part of popular literature. There is no fine writing, phrases are repeated, much of the story is told in dialogue and there is little in the way of demanding vocabulary, even allowing for the use of foreign words and phrases. Nevertheless, Brent-Dyer had a gift for description. Most readers of the early books set in the North Tyrol must feel that the Tiernsee really exists, and cannot be surprised when they discover that it is in reality the Achensee, and that the lake steamer and the rack-and-pinion railway are there for the viewing. As a schoolgirl in the 1940s, I pored over an atlas trying to identify the Tiernsee, without success. I learnt of its existence in the early 1950s while on a train between Bolzano and Munich and finally went there in the early 1960s. I found not only the reality but that the light fell on Briesau (Pertisau) in exactly the way I had always imagined from Brent-Dyer's descriptions.

It is, however, the themes and the way in which they are treated that offer the most scope for constructive discussion of the Chalet books. Elinor Brent-Dyer drew heavily on the contemporary conventions of the girls' school story. She even appears to have copied ideas from her contemporaries, in particular from Elsie J. Oxenham and Dorothea Moore. The concept of a music school in her Ruritanian, non-Chalet story, *The School by the River* (1930), seems to be modelled on Dorothea Moore's *Guide Gilly* (1922). Even more obviously, the idea of an English school linked to a sanatorium in healthy mountain air had already been used by Elsie J. Oxenham in *The Two Form Captains* (1921), some years before *Jo of the Chalet School* was published in 1926. In *The Princess of the Chalet School* she uses the conventions of the typical Ruritanian school story: the Ruritanian princess sent to an English school incognito from which she is kidnapped by men plotting against the crown. The set-piece in which the brave English girl, who has rescued the princess, rides through the Ruritanian capital is a popular one, and Brent-Dyer makes the most of it.

However, although she describes activities portrayed in the typical school story, such as folk-dancing, Guides, drama and games, Brent-Dyer builds on these and treats many of them in a new and enriching way. She describes small events and makes them interesting, as can be seen in *The Chalet Girls in Camp* (1932), where there is no need to introduce spies or criminals to keep the action going; she relies on a succession of quite plausible happenings to make an enjoyable story.

Most notable are Brent-Dyer's internationalism and her emphasis on the importance of international understanding; she does not display the British chauvinism so typical of many of her contemporaries. There is never any suggestion that British girls are more honest or more brave than girls of other nationalities. Non-British teachers are not mocked or teased; the first Deputy Head, later to become Head, of the Chalet School is a French woman, and the various French Mademoiselles are never the figures of fun that they are in most girls' school stories. The Chalet girls do not make fun of accents or misunderstandings of languages. A rare example of this is Grizel's mix-up of *heiliges* and *heisses* in *The School at the Chalet* (1925), when she, Madge and Jo have just arrived in Austria and Madge take the two girls to a hairdresser's shop in Innsbruck; even then Jo realises that she is being unfair in drawing attention to the mistake later. Elinor Brent-Dyer's attitudes are very different from Elsie J. Oxenham's attitudes in her stories about St John's and St Mary's Schools in Switzerland (1921-7)[30] and from Angela Brazil's in *The School in the South* (1922). In these, there seems to be little attempt to show pupils being encouraged to take advantage of opportunities to learn the local language, to study the local culture or even to meet any nationals.

Elinor Brent-Dyer's internationalism culminates in the formation of the Chalet School Peace League in *The Chalet School in Exile* (1940) and its continuance through the subsequent books set during the

Second World War. *The Chalet School in Exile* was a very informative book for many British schoolgirls reading it in the early years of the war, just after its publication in 1940. At the time, although there were some school stories which included refugee schoolgirls who had escaped from Nazi Germany to England,[31] Brent-Dyer's book was unique in the way in which it described what was happening in German-occupied countries. The treatment meted out to Jews was brought to life for me when, at the age of 11 or 12, I read about Jo and Robin trying to protect Herr Goldmann, the jeweller. Sitting in a Gasthaus in Spartz, enjoying coffee and cakes, they see him being chased by a crowd of youths throwing stones and rotten fruit, and rush out, Robin to put her arms around Herr Goldmann and Jo to harangue the pursuers (pp.119-20).

In her portrayal of the staff and girls, and their relationships, Brent-Dyer is both moderate and generous. New girls are treated well and they continue to be accepted; there is no petty bullying or quarrelling. If there is a difference of opinion, it is soon sorted out. The behaviour of the Chalet girls, when they cause the St Scholastika girls, whom they regard as rivals, to go home with wet feet after the two schools meet on a narrow path, is quickly condemned. There is little of the snobbishness which was the much criticised hallmark of many girls school stories, and the domestic staff are real people. One of the events of *The Head Girl of the Chalet School* (1927) is the wedding of Madge's maid Marie; this is described in far more detail than any of the weddings of the main characters, most of which take place off stage.

There are good relationships between girls of different ages; despite the heavy sighs on the part of the prefects about the behaviour of the middles, or of a particular form or of individual trouble-makers, the older girls are practical and caring and take a healthy interest in the concerns of the younger girls. This may have happened at first because of the smallness of the school, so that girls of all ages are thrown together, but it continues. For example, in *The Exploits of the Chalet Girls* (1933) there is a major expedition, packed with incident, to the Barenbad Alps, designed to show just how awkward and unaccommodating the new girl, Thekla, really is. Marie does her best with her young and unpleasant cousin, making conversation to the best of her ability; she is supported by her peers, including Frieda Mensch and Sophie Hamel, to whom Thekla is positively insulting. Frieda later has to take the younger Cornelia, shaky after falling into a hole, back to school. As they grow tired, the younger girls are given an "older guardian" to look after them. Throughout the sixth and seventh chapters which describe this outing, the older girls face up to the task of looking after the younger ones, trying to make sure they have a good time and don't come to grief. This tradition of caring continues through the series. In *Tom Tackles the Chalet School* (1955), when a match against Monkton Priory has to be cancelled because of bad weather, the older girls rally round to arrange alternative attractions, including an impromptu gym tournament, and find suitable prizes from amongst their belongings (p.59).

Concern for the less fortunate is frequently shown, in caring about what is happening to the local people and in raising money for good causes through the Christmas play or the annual sale of work. Brent-Dyer cannot be faulted in providing role models for girls which might encourage them to grow into caring, well-adjusted and responsible members of the community.

How does she fare when looked at from a feminist point of view? One of the great advantages of the girls' school story is that it provides a microcosm in which females are seen in positive roles and girl readers are shown that they too can achieve academically, socially, politically and so on. Brent-Dyer does not make a great song and dance about the alternatives (as they were then) of taking up a career or getting married. She very much reflects the climate of opinion at the time when she was writing, and which continued to be the general view until well into the 1960s. She does not offer much choice in the matter of careers, but here again she is reflecting reality. Those girls who do not have a special gift which will lead to a career in, say, music or, in Jo's case, writing, become teachers, doctors (at least not always nurses) or school secretaries, and marriage is seen as the normal goal for most of them. Of the early central characters, Marie becomes engaged while she is still at school; Jo, in the tradition of many popular heroines, has always despised the idea of marriage so it takes her somewhat by surprise, but at a fairly early age; Frieda goes into it in the natural course of events, but Simone, like Juliet and various other Old Girls, goes to university and embarks on a teaching career because she must earn a living, although she too eventually marries.

LITERARY REFERENCES IN THE CHALET SCHOOL BOOKS

In the 1920s and 1930s writers for girls were generally middle-class women who had read widely even if they lacked formal educational qualifications. They were beneficiaries of the changes which had taken place in society in the latter part of the 19th century. Urbanisation had brought about the growth of schools, libraries, concert halls and art galleries. The Education Act of 1870 had merely officially confirmed progress towards universal literacy. Although many families lived in poverty, the changes affected not only the growing middle classes but many working-class families. Philanthropists such as Andrew Carnegie were replacing the landed entry in providing opportunities for poorer people; Sunday schools and Settlements run by the universities and religious bodies supplemented the work of weekday schools in poorer areas. Even those children who left school early learnt to read and write and continued to use these skills. Both my grandmothers, born in the late 1870s, had left school by the age of 12, but were great readers to the end of their lives.

Magazines provided accessible reading material at a reasonable price. Dickens's novels were published in weekly penny parts in the 1840s and as time went on 19th-century classics were published in cheap editions. They were also abridged to make them accessible to young people and excerpts, perhaps simply retold, appeared in school readers along with stories from history and about life in other countries. In this way a wide range of children acquired a working knowledge of the plot and characters of many literary classics as well as a knowledge of history and geography through learning to read. In an age when there was no radio or television, and when the cinema was in its infancy, reading was one of the few forms of escapist activity. My mother, born in 1901 and not particularly academic, used to tell how, at the age of 14 or 15, during the First World War, she was reading Charles Reade's *The Cloister and the Hearth* (1861), crouched in front of a dying fire, when a policeman knocked on the door because a light was showing. Most young teenagers faced with Reade's book, a minor classic, today would regard it as an impossible challenge.[32]

What Gillian Freeman says of Angela Brazil — "widening the horizons of her readers in so many spheres, literary, geographical, historical, archeological and botanical, as well as creating awareness of music and the visual arts"[33] — is also true of Elinor Brent-Dyer. Historical and geographical information, languages, music and literature are all topics which are introduced naturally into her books. From the early Chalet books the reader must also absorb a great deal of background information about Austria, its history, geography, social conditions, customs and folklore.

To give some idea of the richness which is imparted to the Chalet books by these elements, I am going to consider in some detail the literary references which can be found in the first 17 books of the series; these are the titles which I read as a schoolgirl, and which I can therefore relate to my own experience. In fact, after the 17th book, *Lavender Laughs in the Chalet School*, Brent-Dyer seems to have made less reference to literary works, and relied much more on invented titles, including the books supposed to have been written by Jo, such as *Gipsy Jocelyn* which is one of the prizes in the gym tournament in *Tom Tackles the Chalet School* (p.60). (In the same book, however, there is a nice piece of publicity for Chambers Dictionary, which is of course published by the publishers of the Chalet books in hardback — pp.193-5). One can only speculate about the reasons for this change. Did Brent-Dyer realise that her knowledge of what most girls read was out of date? Did her publishers persuade her to drop specific references to make her books more readable for girls differently educated? Having invented so many books by Jo, and the Lavender Laughs series, and with so many past events to which reference could be made, were the literary references just crowded out?

Reading is an important activity for the girls of the Chalet School and literature lessons are always an important part of the curriculum. After she marries and goes to live at the Sonnalpe, Madge frequently comes down to the school to give her special lessons in English literature, at least during the time-span covered by *The Head Girl of the Chalet School* (p.16). Later in the same book the girls "rejoiced loudly" at the news that she had come on a few days' visit, and requested a Shakespeare lesson (p.115).

Jo is an omnivorous reader. I have always assumed that she was named for L. M. Alcott's Josephine March in *Little Women*; did Brent-Dyer plan right from the start to make her a writer too? Jo's gift for writing is established in the second book of the series, *Jo of the Chalet School*, when she wins a prize in a writing competition. It is significant that, in *The Princess of the Chalet School*, another nail is hammered into the new matron's coffin when Madge discovers that Matron has stopped the girls reading in bed on Sunday mornings; this has always been allowed on condition that they sit up, have a good light and wear bed-jackets.

The nature of the books and stories to which reference is made ranges widely. In *Jo of the Chalet School*, Jo begins her literary career with a simple folk tale about a poor forester, which was published in the first issue of *The Chaletian*, and then secretly submitted for a competition by Jem. Brent-Dyer, like many of her contemporaries, was well acquainted with the traditional tales of Europe, and references to them are scattered through the books. The girls are described as imitating Kay and Gerda in Hans Andersen's *The Snow Queen* (first English translation, 1846) by warming pennies and using them to make small round holes in the frost on the window panes (*Jo of the Chalet School*, p.136). This is an experience unknown to most late 20th-century schoolgirls living in centrally heated homes, no doubt, but a practice familiar to me when I read the book in the early 1940s. Traditional tales also provide points of reference; in *The Head Girl of the Chalet School* (p.69), Bernhilda is likened to "one of the princesses in Grimms' Tales" (first English translation, 1823-6), while in *Eustacia Goes to the Chalet School* (1930, p.113), Jo compares a house out of which she always expects an old witch to appear to the one in *Hansel and Gretel* (another tale of the brothers' Grimm).

Elinor Brent-Dyer also demonstrates an interest in local folk tales. On the expedition to the Zillerthal in *The New House at the Chalet School*, Frieda tells a Tyrolean legend about the building of a church (pp.236-7). Elsewhere in the same book there are references to Biddy O'Ryan's Irish folk tales (pp.189 & 198), and in the later *The Highland Twins at the Chalet School* (1942), Fiona McDonald's tales of Highland kelpies, seal women and black hares are mentioned (p.152).

There are also references to well-known children's classics. In *The Head Girl of the Chalet School*, George MacDonald's *At the Back of the North Wind* is being read to the youngest girls (p.116) and in *The Rivals of the Chalet School*, Mary Burnett, the Head Girl, goes off to read *Peter Pan* to the Robin (p.272). In *The Princess of the Chalet School* Jo is reading *Little Women* (p.264) and in *The Chalet Girls in*

Camp, when Jack Maynard tells her that she'll have to grow up some day, Jo replies, "Not a day before I have to! I'll be like Jo March in Little Women, and 'wear my hair in two tails until I'm twenty'!" (p.165). In *The Chalet School Goes to It* (1941), Gwensi explains how salmon are poached to Daisy and Beth: "They have flares and hold them low under the water, you know, and the salmon come to the light — it's all in *The Water Babies*." (p.181). Fiona and Flora, safely installed as *The Highland Twins at the Chalet School*, are "provided with story-books from the Junior library, and Fiona revelled in *The Secret Garden* . . . while Flora was lost in *Five Children and It*" (p.84).

Charles Kingsley's *The Water Babies* (1863), Louisa Alcott's *Little Women* (1868) and George MacDonald's *At the Back of the North Wind* (1871) are likely to have been known to Elinor as a child as they have seldom, if ever, been out of print. She would have been ten when J. M. Barrie's *Peter Pan* was first performed in 1904; although it did not appear as a book with a text by Barrie himself until 1911, there were several "books of the play" before that and, as Barrie was a leading literary figure of the day, *Peter Pan* quickly took its place amongst children's classics. E. Nesbit's *Five Children and It* (1902) and Frances Hodgson Burnett's *The Secret Garden* (1911) are also by writers who were well-known literary figures in the first decade of the 20th century. By 1942, when *The Highland Twins at the Chalet School* was published, both books had been reprinted many times, were regarded as children's classics and were likely to be known to most girls reading Brent-Dyer's books.

Alongside the references to children's classics and folk tales are those to contemporary girls' school stories. There is an oblique reference to Dorothea

Moore's *Guide Gilly* in *The School at the Chalet* when Gisela is talking about a book she has read and Wanda says, "It was a Girl Guide . . . Her name was the same as yours, Gisela, but they called her 'Gilly'" (p.235). In *Lavender Laughs in the Chalet School*, Lavender's library book is *The Two Form Captains* (p.138), presumably the book by Elsie J. Oxenham. Thus Brent-Dyer acknowledges the two books from which she used basic ideas, the music school in a Ruritanian country, and the link between an English school and a sanatorium. When the school moves to Howells village in *The Chalet School Goes to It*, Jo looks at Gwensi's bookshelves and comments, "Here's a whole shelf of Elsie Oxenham, and another of Dorita Fairlie Bruce and Winifred Darch. If the kid's a fan of anything, it's of school stories."(p.75).

However, like many of her fellow writers, Brent-Dyer was well aware of the low regard in which school stories were held by adults in the 1920s and 1930s. Teachers and librarians believed that they misled readers, portraying boarding-school life in a more romantic and glamorous light than it deserved. This belief, which has continued to the present day[34], is reflected in the Chalet books. When, in *The School at the Chalet*, some girls put forward the idea of having a school magazine, and suggest organising a party to celebrate the Head's birthday, both undertakings having been gleaned from the purely imaginary *Denise of the Fourth* by "Muriel Bernadine Browne", Jo tells them that some school stories "are awful tosh" (p.129).

Another invented book, *Pat the Pride of the School*, inspires Polly Heriot to ring the alarm bell in *Jo Returns to the Chalet School* (1936). "It seemed to Polly that if she could ring that bell . . . they would be so thrilled by the daring of the act that she would become a real live school heroine" (p.130). The real consequences are very different: the alarm bell rouses the whole valley, making Mademoiselle Lepattre and the school look foolish, several of the girls are badly upset and everyone, of course, is, as Jo says, "hauled . . . out of bed on a freezing night for no good reason" (p.156). Jo, embarked on her career as a writer of school stories, has already discarded *Malvina Wins Through* on Matron's advice, burnt the manuscript and started afresh with *Cecily Holds the Fort*. Now, vowing that this will contain "nothing that might not have happened at the best regulated of schools" (p.71), she resolves to remove descriptions of "any pranks . . . that might . . . incite brainless Juniors to imitation thereof" (p.158).

If school stories were held in low regard by many adults, what were young people expected to read? As was said earlier, articles and reviews in the *School Library Review* and the *School Librarian* in the 1930s show that, once at secondary school, young people were encouraged to read adult novels. Sir Walter Scott, Charles Dickens, Robert Louis Stevenson, H. G. Wells and John Buchan were all regarded as authors who tell a good story and might therefore be enjoyed by readers from the age of 11 or 12 onwards. Up to the 1950s they were looked upon as standard reading fare for the young and, sometimes in abridged editions, were used as class readers. My younger sister, who started at a Yorkshire grammar school in 1946, not only had Scott's *Rob Roy* (1817) as a class reader in the first year but also had his *Red Gauntlet* (1824) as a set text at A-Level.

Nineteenth-century novels were readily available to many girls, and omnivorous readers like Jo were quite happy to tackle them. In *The School at the Chalet* (p.18), when we first meet her, she is reading

Scott's *Quentin Durward* (1823); later (p.126) she's reading *John Halifax, Gentleman* (1857) by Mrs Craik (Diana Maria Mulock) and she's also described (p.191) as having read George Borrow's *Romany Rye* (1857) and *Lavengro* (1851), while Grizel, confined to her room in disgrace (p.275), seeks refuge in Thackeray's *Henry Esmond* (1852). Brent-Dyer's characters also link books to places. Paris reminds Jo of Baroness Orczy's *The Scarlet Pimpernel* (1905) and Dickens's *A Tale of Two Cities* (1859), when they go there on their way to Austria in *The School at the Chalet* (p.36), while *The First Violin*, very much a book of its time and scarcely known today[35], inspires Grizel's mad journey to the Falls of Rhine in *The Head Girl of the Chalet School*, an adventure which raises the whole question of whether she is really fit to be Head Girl.

Even if they were not as well read as the Chalet girls, most of her readers would at least have heard of these books in the 1920s. Perhaps one of the appeals for girl readers was the fact that reading is always seen as a commendable activity. Nobody ever seems to be told to take their nose out of a book and go out and get some fresh air and exercise or help with some domestic chore, which must in reality have been the experience of many readers.

Nor are references confined to English literature. It is interesting that when, in *The Rivals of the Chalet School*, Jo says that she's going to be a writer and not get married, Simone quotes the examples of Madame Le Brun and Madame de Stael, "two of our greatest writers", who were both married, as was the English writer, Mrs Gaskell (p.32). In *The Exploits of the Chalet Girls*, Jo mentions that she's read Josef Egger's *Geschichte Tirols* and learnt from it that there might be an earthquake in the Tyrol (p.169). Hilary sits down to do a little work with *Les*

Pensées de Pascal in *The New Chalet School* (1938) (p.200), while in *The Chalet School Goes to It*, Simone is teaching with the aid of "La Dernière Classe"(1873), a short story by Alphonse Dudet which had a particular poignancy in the early 1940s (p.223). It describes the last class taught in the French language in a school in Alsace-Lorraine, an area about to be transferred from France to Germany as a result of the 1870 Franco-Prussian war. The work of a distinguished French author and about children (the story is told by one of the boys), "La Dernière Classe" turned up frequently in French text books used in British schools up to the 1940s.[36]

A writer who seems to have been particularly important to Brent-Dyer is Rudyard Kipling. Grizel, leaving home in *The School at the Chalet*, receives a new Kipling as a farewell present from the Rector and his sister (p.30). When, in *The Highland Twins at the Chalet School*, Fiona goes to ask if she can use her gift of second sight to try to "see" Jack, reported drowned, Jo's eyes fall "on the row of red, leather-bound Kiplings which she had collected through the years. That sort of thing had happened to the unpleasant youth in *Captains Courageous*" (p.249).

Twice, at least, Brent-Dyer uses the phrase, "that, as Mr Kipling says, is another story", once in *The School at the Chalet* (p.335) and again in *The Chalet School and the Lintons* (1934) (p.269). When, in *Jo Returns to the Chalet School*, Polly Heriot's alarm bell prank goes seriously wrong, Jo sends her to the school library to ask the junior librarian for *Stalky and Co*, and tells her to digest what "The Three have to say about Old Prout", and we learn that, as a result of this, "the Immortal Trio's views on the subject of 'Popularity Prout'" complete Polly's demoralisation and provide a successful antidote to reading too many school stories (p.157).

In her enthusiasm for Kipling, Brent-Dyer was like many other people in the early part of the 20th century. From about 1890 to 1930 he was the most popular writer in English, in both verse and prose, throughout the English-speaking world. Widely regarded as the greatest living poet and story-teller, he received the Nobel Prize for Literature in 1907, and his books were popular far beyond academic and literary circles.[37] His work continued to be widely read after 1930 and his stories and some of the more memorable lines of his poetry became common property. I clearly recall being read one of his short stories "Rikki-Tikki-Tavi", about a mongoose, at the age of about five, and a prefect reading some of the *Just-So Stories* (1902) to us when I was in the first year at secondary school, when she had to take the class for an absent teacher. My adult relations used to recite and quote bits of Kipling's verse, and I was somewhat surprised, when I arrived at university in 1948, to find that Kipling was so highly regarded by academics that my English professor wrote books and articles about him. The wide availability of *The Jungle Book* (1894) on video in the weeks leading up to Christmas 1993 is an indication of the powerful hold Kipling has had on the Anglo-Saxon imagination for over a century.

Even Robert Louis Stevenson, whose books are referred to more than once — for example, the donkey in the Christmas pageant which takes place during *The Exploits of the Chalet Girls* is named Modestine after the donkey in *Travels with a Donkey* (1879, pp. 296-7), while, in *The Chalet School Goes to It*, Daisy is reading *An Inland Voyage* (1878) aloud (p.57) — is upstaged by Rudyard Kipling. "Read us something exciting ... Something like *Treasure Island* would be nice. I love pirates!" requests Jo, but when Miss Maynard returns with *Stalky and Co*, Jo utters a squeal of delight (*The Head Girl of the Chalet School*, 1928, p.167). This incident puzzled me for years after I first read it at the age of 11 or 12. I must have known both books well enough to think that if Jo had expressed an interest in *Treasure Island* (1882) and pirates, *Stalky and Co* (1899), a school story, even though it might have been my own first choice, would be a poor substitute! Only on rereading the book quite recently did it seem to make sense; Brent-Dyer, with her fondness for Kipling, would see the substitution as more than acceptable.

One author who features frequently in the early Chalet books, who is a more surprising choice, is Martha Finley, although she is never actually mentioned by name. All Chalet book readers, however, will be aware of the Elsie books, even if they have never seen one. In *Jo of the Chalet School*, when Jo is convalescing, Dr Jem brings her six Elsie books, of which Jo has heard but never read, "Aren't they about an awfully good little girl . . . ?" (p.249). Martha Finley (1828-1909) was a prolific and popular American writer for girls, whose books outsold every other children's book except *Little Women* for three generations. *Elsie Dinsmore* was published in the USA in 1867, a year before *Little Women*, and in London in 1873, but Martha Finley was never as well-known or as popular in Britain as she was in her native country, although she seems to have made a great impression on Brent-Dyer. The fact that the books inspire Jo to want to know more about American history may have something to do with their less than successful voyage across the Atlantic, most girl readers being put off by their historical background rather than wanting, like Jo, to know more.

There were 28 Elsie books altogether, but by 1926 Brent-Dyer may have come across only the first six which have some structural unity revolving around the relationship between Elsie and her father, and which have something of the charm of a soap opera — they are "good bad books".[38] Jo is so inspired by them that she writes her own Elsie book and we are told that she has "caught the style of writing exactly" (p.255). In *The Rivals of the Chalet School* American Evadne suggests that her friends call themselves the Ku-Klux-Klan to "fight for their rights" and, when everyone is doubtful about what the Ku-Klux-Klan did, they refer to Jo's Elsie books and are "thrilled" by the account of the Klan's doings (pp.51-52).

In *Exploits of the Chalet Girls* Jo says, "I've been talking like an Elsie book all this term — the fruits of being head-girl! (p.119) while, in *The Chalet School and the Lintons*, Frieda suggests that for their entertainment on staff evening, the staff are going to perform some of the Ku-Klux-Klan scenes out of "those Elsie books of Jo's" (p.117). As late as *The Chalet School Goes to It*, Betty Wynne-Davies declares that Elizabeth Arnett is going "all goody-good and pi and must have been reading the Elsie books" (p.210). Were they still reading Jo's original six, one wonders?

Brent-Dyer's preoccupation with the Elsie books is surprising for two reasons. First they were not nearly as accessible as *Little Women* and other American girls' books, such as the Katy books by Susan Coolidge; although copies can now be picked up on the second-hand market I didn't see any until the early 1970s, when an American student lent me one. Secondly, and even more surprising, is the apparent sympathy for the Ku-Klux-Klan, a secret society whose members dressed weirdly in white robes, masks and pointed hoods, which grew up in the southern states of the USA after the Civil War to oppose the right of black people to vote, and which still exists. Brent-Dyer, otherwise very liberal, tolerant and progressive in her views about nationality, religion and race, never seems to have questioned the morality of the Ku-Klux-Klan organisation and their methods. In this she was reflecting the general British view of the time; it was not until the 1960s that white Americans and white British people began to rethink their long-established attitudes to race and colour, and we know that it is a long and painful process to change these.

Some books inspired Chalet School entertainments. In *The Chalet School and the Lintons*, far from re-enacting Ku-Klux-Klan scenes, as suggested by Frieda, the staff choose to present Mrs Jarley's Waxworks. Marie realises this as soon as the curtains go back to reveal Miss Wilson clad in an "ample" black skirt, Paisley shawl and coal-scuttle bonnet, and made up with heavy black eyebrows and to look as if some of her teeth are missing, while her colleagues take the part of waxworks. Mrs Jarley, proprietor of a Waxworks Show, is one of the notable characters whom Little Nell and her grandfather meet during the course of their travels in *The Old Curiosity Shop* (1840), a lady "stout and comfortable to look upon who wore a large bonnet trembling with bows".[39] Like Mrs Jarley, Miss Wilson has a wand with which she indicates a character while she comments on their known weaknesses and points morals, referring to incidents such as Miss Norman's shrieks when "a mouse had been introduced into prep" (p.120) or Matron's belief in the efficacy of castor-oil, at which Joyce, Thekla and Mary, who have received doses after their recent midnight feast, all go scarlet (p.121). No mention is made either of Dickens or the title of the book in which Mrs Jarley appears; perhaps Brent-Dyer assumed that her readers were as well read as the Chalet girls although it scarcely matters as the entertainment is enjoyable in its own right.

Later in the same book, however, there is a quite detailed discussion of Charlotte Yonge's work when the St Scholastika's girls borrow one of her ideas for the Magic Cave which is their contribution to the annual Sale of Work. Charlotte Yonge's Magic Cave was created in a conservatory and Brent-Dyer seems to have added one to the Chalet buildings at this point for the same purpose as it's not mentioned elsewhere. The Chalet girls are curious about what St Scholastika's are planning and Hilary Burn hints that it is something to do with Charlotte Yonge's *The Three Brides* (1876); Jo says they haven't got that particular title in the school library although they have several others (p.288). Brent-Dyer's version of the Peri's Cave follows that described in *The Three Brides* quite closely, with "unseen musicians", Hilary Burn as the Peri, the use of two of the original rhymes, the blindfolding of the "victim" and the present which the victim finally receives.[40]

When some of the girls, including Jo, have to spend the half-term holiday at school in *Jo Returns to the Chalet School* and are invited by the staff to "a Grand Sheets-and-Pillowcase Party" (p.223), they are puzzled. Jo explains that they have to manufacture a fancy-dress costume from two sheets and a pillowcase, which may be pinned or lightly stitched but on no account cut, and that there will be prizes for the prettiest, the funniest and the most outstanding. Brent-Dyer may not have remembered the source of this idea, but it seems possible that she was subconsciously recalling a similar event described by Mrs George de Horne Vaizey in *Pixie O'Shaughnessy* (1903), where Bridgie issues the young people with a pair of sheets and a pillowcase to keep them happily occupied one afternoon in making themselves costumes for a party in the evening. In that book the party is a key event because the beautiful Esmeralda is wearing her costume when she is first seen by her future husband. The three Pixie books were all serialised in the *Girl's Own Paper* in the early years of this century before being published as books, and they continued to be popular with girls up to the outbreak of the Second World War; it is quite likely that Brent-Dyer read them as a young girl.[41] Of course, sheets and pillowcase parties may have been a fairly common event in days when people had to make their own entertainment, especially when there were domestic staff to wash and iron them afterwards.

Religious books are also included amongst the reading of the Chalet girls. Madge, faced with providing a service for a multi-denominational assembly in *The School at the Chalet*, chooses a short reading from Thomas-à-Kempis (p.58) and offers the same book, albeit under its title, *The Imitation of Christ*, to the girls to read quietly when they cannot get to church because of bad weather in *The Exploits of the Chalet Girls* (p.213). In *The School at the Chalet*, she is reading *The Little Flowers of St Francis* to the girls (p.187), and in a later book this is described as "a favourite book at the Chalet" (*The Chalet School and Jo*, p.171). The religious books no doubt reflect another of Brent-Dyer's own reading preferences, particularly in the period leading up to her conversion to Catholicism in 1930.

One of the few books mentioned by Brent-Dyer not long after publication is H.V.Morton's *In the Steps of St Paul*, a book with a strong religious interest. This was published in 1936; in *The Chalet School Goes to It* (1941), it is being read by Robin (p.35). H.V. Morton wrote a series of *In Search of . . .* books, which covered England, Scotland and Wales (these may even have inspired the idea of the Lavender Laughs books) and which were very popular during the 1930s and 1940s. Even in the early 1950s, when I was working in public libraries, there were waiting lists for Morton's books.

References to Shakespeare, all kinds of fiction, poetry, history, the classics, religious books, biography and to books in languages other than English are found throughout most of the first 17 Chalet books. The significance of some of these might have been lost on most readers; for example, there is an animated discussion in *Jo Returns to the Chalet School* about whether Cyrano de Bergerac would have had a handkerchief (p.241), without any mention of his prominent nose. Nevertheless such references enrich the text.

However, reading does have its dangers. Not every book is approved, although the first forbidden book to be mentioned is being read by a St Scholastika's girl, Vera Smithers. Miss Browne finds what is described as a light novel which "had no business there or in the building at all" in Vera's desk in *The Rivals of the Chalet School* (p.261); she tells Vera, "You know you are all forbidden to read any of this author's works while you are still at school . . . we want you to retain your purity of mind for as long as possible" (p. 267). Possession of the forbidden book, combined with writing anonymous letters to the King of Belsornia and Crown Princess

Elisaveta, leads to Vera's expulsion. There is no indication of the author of this "light" novel, nor do we learn the nature of the book which Eustacia Benson borrows from the staff shelves in the library without permission in *Eustacia Goes to the Chalet School* (p.85), an act which results in her being banned from the library until half-term.

In a much later book, *The Wrong Chalet School*, the American novel *Gone With the Wind* is specifically named as "not exactly the type of book any schoolgirl is permitted to read in school — certainly not any schoolgirl of fourteen or fifteen" (p.162). Jennifer Penrose is in dire disgrace for smuggling it into school and passing it around her friends in the traditional brown-paper cover. To readers 30 years later, Miss Annersley's reactions must seem a shade over the top; even in 1952, the year when *The Wrong Chalet School* was published, many teachers would probably have been pleased to find 14- and 15-year olds reading Margaret Mitchell's classic. Certainly both my sister and I had read it by that age in the 1940s, and did so quite openly. According to a comment in a *Friends of the Chalet School Newsletter*, *Gone With the Wind* was changed to *Forever Amber* in the first paperback edition and later changed again, although the third title had been forgotten by the correspondent, Marilyn Gowland.[42] Kathleen Windsor's *Forever Amber* was regarded as much more sensational and would have been about right for a "banned" book in 1952, but perhaps Brent-Dyer would have been wiser to follow her earlier practice of not giving any details and leaving those to the imagination of the reader.

By the 1970s the Chalet books themselves had achieved mentionable status in other children's books. Eleven-year-old Jane Reid, the heroine of Catherine Sefton's *In a Blue Velvet Dress* (1972), who always has her head in a book, takes a large suitcase full of them when she goes to stay with the Hildreths while her parents go to Scotland. When she opens her suitcase, she is horrified to find in it her father's clothes and rock samples; Mr Reid, meanwhile, is "staring aghast at a suitcase full of Chalet School stories, Roald Dahl books, and lots of others".[43]

CONCLUSION

As can be seen from the discussion and comment in the pages of the *Friends of the Chalet School Newsletters* and *The Chaletian*[44], Brent-Dyer's literary references offer a challenge to adult readers. Many of them, however, would have been recognised by her schoolgirl readers up to about 1950. When I was enjoying the books in the 1940s, I was not unduly concerned if I came across a reference to an author or title which I did not know; sometimes, later on, I found a book which she had mentioned, and then welcomed it as a long lost friend, although I don't ever recall going out to look for one specifically.

The references reflect Brent-Dyer's own reading tastes and preferences. It seems unlikely that she was indirectly recommending books which she thought girls should read; if this had been her intention, she would surely have given more details, not just the author or title, as is often the case. In the *Chalet Club News Letters*, which began to appear in 1959, Brent-Dyer did suggest authors and titles to her readers; these lists also cover a wide range of books and sometimes the detail is not precise. For example, "study the books of Winston Churchill" in *Chalet Club News Letter 5*; as Churchill's multi-volumed history of the Second

World War was a best-seller throughout most of the 1950s, and there were always long waiting-lists in the library as each new volume was published (although I don't recall it being read by teenage girls) these *News Letter* recommendations too, to some extent, probably reflect Elinor's own reading both past and present.

Kipling is missing from the lists of recommended authors and titles at which I looked in issues 5, 8, 12 and 15, but certain authors who are, rather surprisingly, not mentioned in the early Chalet books at least do appear; Jane Austen and the Brontës. Of the books to which Brent-Dyer refers in the first 17 Chalet titles, relatively few can be described as being specifically for girls and young women: the school stories, *Little Women*, the Elsie books and the works of Mrs George de Horne Vaizey and Charlotte Yonge. Although they did not write only for women, the great 19th-century women novelists are conspicuously absent. Mrs Gaskell is mentioned by name, as an example of a married woman novelist. The fact that Charlotte Brontë's *Jane Eyre* (1847) is never mentioned is particularly surprising as this book appeared in abridged editions for young people, as did George Eliot's *The Mill on the Floss* (1860), and many of Brent-Dyer's early readers would have been quite familiar with Jane's adventures at school. Perhaps the omission of these authors is accidental, or perhaps Brent-Dyer felt that a proper appreciation of their novels depended upon girls having an emotional maturity, which she thought her own readers might not have acquired.

By the late 1960s, when Brent-Dyer was writing her last books, British authors had not yet taken on board the need to challenge long-standing ideas about gender, race and class. There had already been some stirrings of unease about the undesirability of promoting Helen Bannerman's *Little Black Sambo*, recommended for the "younger folk" in *Chalet Club News Letter 15*, but the organised movement which expressed concern about racism, sexism and the middle-class bias of children's books was not launched until the early 1970s, when Rosemary Stones, one of the most influential campaigners, mounted an exhibition at the Exeter Children's Literature Conference in 1974.

As far as sexism is concerned, Brent-Dyer, in writing school stories for girls, was making some contribution to providing readers with positive role models; although the earliest Chalet girls, such as Gisela Marani and Bernhilda Mensch, are expected to live at home until they marry, by the time of the books written in the 1940s, college and careers are common expectations for most of the girls.

With respect to class, Brent-Dyer's books are firmly middle-class. Although she appears to have been ahead of her time in condemning extreme snobbery, she still reflects the generally held, pre-war, middle-class views about state schools; for example, in *Three Go to the Chalet School* (1949), Gran tells Mary-Lou, "there isn't a decent school near enough for you to go to" (p.12). Brent-Dyer's attitude is slightly more relaxed in *The Chalet School and the Island* (1950), when Jo tells Jack that Stephen can "go to the village school for a year or two, which won't hurt him' (p.22), although Jack says, warningly, that he may "pick up all sort of language" (p.23).

Apart from her apparent endorsement of the Ku-Klux-Klan, there is no overt racism in Brent-Dyer's books; unlike many of her contemporaries, she doesn't use words such as "nigger", which came to be regarded as totally unacceptable. Her attitudes towards Jews and her portrayal of the Kashmiri girl, Lilamani, who appears in *Lavender Laughs in the Chalet School*, suggest that she would have readily accepted the new attitudes about the role of people from minority groups in books for the young.

However, Brent-Dyer's books must be examined in the context of the period at which they were written; tinkering with details, as has apparently been done in some of the later paperback editions, cannot change underlying attitudes. Above all, it must be recognised that Elinor Brent-Dyer has provided hours of enjoyment for several generations of girls. Her literary references enrich her early Chalet books in a way for which she has never been given full credit.

NOTES

1. Ann Parker, "Materials selection in Hertfordshire: a policy in action". In Vivien Griffiths ed. *Buying Books* (Library Association Youth, Libraries Group, 1983), p.15.
2. Constance Stern, *Library Association Record 38/6* (1936), p.245.
3. Gillian Freeman, "Angela Brazil". In Tracy Chevalier ed. *Twentieth Century Children's Writers* (St James Press, 3rd edition, 1989), pp.124-5.
4. T. Joseph McAleer, *Popular Reading and Publishing in Britain 1914-1950* (Clarendon Press, 1992), Chap. 5.
5. G. A. Carter, "Some childish likes and dislikes". *Library Association Record 49/9* (1947), pp.217-221.
6. *The School Library Review 1* (1936-1938), pp.218-220. *The School Library Review* and the *School Librarian* were the journals of the School Libraries Section of the Library Association and the School Library Association respectively. In the 1940s the two organisations merged as the School Library Association and the journal continued as the *School Librarian*, in which form it is still published today.
7. F. J. Harvey Darton, *Children's Books in England: Five Centuries of Social Life* (Cambridge University Press, 2nd edition, 1958). First published 1932.
8. Roger Lancelyn Green, *Tellers of Tales* (Edmund Ward, revised edition, (1965). First published, as a book for young people, 1946.
9. Geoffrey Trease, *Tales Out of School* (Heinemann, 2nd edition, 1964). First published 1949.
10. Marcus Crouch, *Treasure Seekers and Borrowers* (Library Association, 1962), p.41. Crouch presumably had in mind not only Walpole's *Jeremy at Crale* (1927), but books such as Rudyard Kipling's *Stalky and Co* (1899) and Horace Annesley Vachell's *The Hill* (1905); I feel the influence is minimal.

11. Frank Eyre, *British Children's Books in the Twentieth Century* (Longman, revised and enlarged edition, 1971), pp.82-5. First published as *20th Century Children's Books*, 1952.
12. Dorothy Neal White, *About Books for Children* (Oxford University Press, 1946).
13. Lillian H. Smith, *The Unreluctant Years* (American Library Association, 1953).
14. Evidence is provided by the existence of societies and magazines for Brent-Dyer enthusiasts in Australia and elsewhere, some of which (such as the Australian Friends of the Chalet School) pre-dated similar British organisations.
15. John Rowe Townsend, *Written for Children* (Penguin, 3rd edition, 1987), p.265. First published 1965.
16. Ibid., p.265.
17. Margery Fisher, *Intent Upon Reading* (Brockhampton, 1961), p.179-180.
18. Margery Fisher, *Who's Who in Children's Books* (Weidenfeld and Nicolson, 1975), p.159.
19. Margery Fisher, "Review". *Growing Point 24/2* (1985), p.4461-2.
20. For use of this phrase, taken from W. B. Yeats' poem, "He Wishes For the Cloths of Heaven", I am indebted to Peter Hunt, who used it in his title for a paper on Arthur Ransome delivered to the Arthur Ransome Society in November 1991.
21. Mary Cadogan and Patricia Craig, *You're a Brick, Angela!* (Gollancz, 1986). For example, see p.154, pp.201-4. First published 1976.
22. Reprinted in Arthur Marshall, *Girls Will Be Girls* (Hamish Hamilton, 1974), p.139. It is not clear exactly where this review originally appeared, but probably in the *New Statesman*.
23. Isabel Quigly, *The Heirs of Tom Brown* (Chatto and Windus, 1982), p.220. The title comes from Thomas Hughes's pioneering boys' school story, *Tom Brown's School-days* (1857).
24. Jeffrey Richards, *Happiest Days: The Public Schools in English Fiction* (Manchester University Press, 1988), Acknowledgements, page not numbered.

25. Helen McClelland, *Behind the Chalet School* (New Horizon, 1981).
26. Judith Rowbotham, *Good Girls Make Good Wives* (Basil Blackwell, 1989).
27. Kimberley Reynolds, *Girls Only* (Harvester Wheatsheaf, 1990).
28. Rosemary Auchmuty, *A World of Girls* (Women's Press, 1992).
29. The incidents and quotations in and from the Chalet books are identified in the text. References are taken from the hardcover Chambers editions.
30. These are *The Two Form Captains* (1921), *The Captain of the Fifth* (1922), *The Troubles of Tazy* (1926) and *Patience and her Problems* (1927), all published by Chambers.
31. For example, Mary K. Harris, *Gretel of St Bride's* (1941) and Josephine Elder, *Strangers at the Farm School* (1940).
32. For more background to the social, economic and educational factors which shaped Brent-Dyer and her early readers, see Richard D. Altick, *The English Common Reader: A Social History of the Mass Reading Public, 1800 — 1900* (University of Chicago Press, 1957) and Joseph McAleer, *Popular Reading and Publishing in Britain 1914-1950* (Clarendon Press, 1992).
33. Gillian Freeman, *The Schoolgirl Ethic: The Life and Work of Angela Brazil* (Allen Lane, 1976), p.20.
34. In December 1993, a newspaper report about a girl's suicide began, "A girl who chose to go to boarding school after reading stories about midnight dormitory feasts killed herself because she feared she would be expelled for smoking. Alice Clover, 13, who loved reading Enid Blyton's tales of adventure at Malory Towers hanged herself in the showers at Cawston College, Norfolk, an inquest was told." *The Times*, 16 Dec. 1993, p.8.
35. Miss Jessie Fothergill, The First Violin (Guildford, 1877). See "UK Corner", *Friends of the Chalet School Newsletter 20* (May 1993), p.13 (actually unnumbered), and the follow-up comment by Cynthia Castellan, *Friends of the Chalet School Newsletter 21* (Aug. 1993), p.12.

36. Looking for a copy of the text in connection with this essay, I found one in *Short Stories from Modern French Authors*, edited by a group of professors under the direction of Jules Bue (Librairie Hachette, 1928). My daughter-in-law found a slightly adapted version in another French reader of the same period in her school, while my husband recalled reading the story in an English translation in the 1920s, probably in one of the "gift books" published to raise funds during the First World War. All this suggests that it was widely available in the early part of the 20th century and would be familiar to Brent-Dyer's readers. The story originally appeared in Alphonse Daudet, *Contes du Lundi* (1873).
37. Andrew Rutherford, "General Preface", Rudyard Kipling, *Puck of Pook's Hill* and *Rewards and Fairies*, World's Classics (Oxford University Press, 1993), p.vii.
38. M. Sarah Smedman, "Martha Finley". In Glenn E. Estes ed. *Dictionary of Literary Biography, Vol. 42: American Writers for Children before 1900* (Gale, 1985), p.182.
39. Mrs Jarley first appears in Chapter 26 of *The Old Curiosity Shop*, from which this quotation is taken. In the following chapters Little Nell (a happy coincidence of forename?) is shown how to talk about the waxworks to customers.
40. For a detailed discussion of the parallels, see Stella Waring, "The Peri's Cave", *The Chaletian 5* (1993), pp.19-21. In the Macmillan edition of *The Three Brides* which I used, the account of the Peri's Cave appears on pp.135-8.
41. Mrs George de Horne Vaizey's novel *Pixie O'Shaughnessy* was first published in book form in 1903. I used the serial version which appeared in the *Girl's Own Paper Vol. 3*, Nos. 1136 (1901) to 1165 (1902). The sheets and pillowcase party takes place in Chap.s 18-20.
42. *See Friends of the Chalet School Newsletter 21* (1993), p.3
43. Catherine Sefton, *In a Blue Velvet Dress* (Faber & Faber, 1972; Walker Books, 1991), p.10.
44. *The Chaletian* (1990-1994); the *Friends of the Chalet School Newsletter* 1989-.

"SCHOOL WITH BELLS ON!"
THE SCHOOL AT THE CHALET AND AFTERWARDS

JULIET GOSLING

AS every fan will know, Elinor M. Brent-Dyer was inspired to write the first book in the Chalet School series, *The School at the Chalet* (1925), after spending the summer of 1924 in the Tyrolean village of Pertisau beside the Achensee. Having begun her career as a teacher at the age of 18 in 1912[1], by this time she must have accepted the possibility that, rather than marry, she would spend the rest of her life working in education.

It is clear from the detailed descriptions of the Tyrol, which was the school's setting up to the Second World War, that the area had made a striking impression on her during her visit. It is equally clear that she felt a great deal of emotional involvement with both the scenery and the Tyrolean people, and it is not unreasonable to suppose that in an ideal world Elinor Brent-Dyer would have liked to have spent the rest of her life in Pertisau. But she had to work to support herself and, even if an "English school" had been founded there along the same lines as the Chalet School, her responsiblity to her mother — with whom she lived for most of her life — would probably have prevented her from taking up a position.

But while Brent-Dyer was unable to move to the Tyrol and teach in reality, there was nothing to prevent her from doing so in her imagination. Given the detailed descriptions of the area in *The School at the Chalet*, it is reasonable to assume that she conceived the idea for the book while still on holiday, and took the opportunity to research locations and to begin to develop characters and plots. Her first two books had been school stories — *Gerry Goes to School* (1922) and *A Head Girl's Difficulties* (1923) — and the third, *The Maids of La Rochelle* (1924), made good use of local colour (in this case, Guernsey). Her fourth book was to combine both elements.

Although we know from Helen McClelland that Brent-Dyer later came to identify strongly with Joey[2], at the time she created *The School at the Chalet* she may well have had a greater empathy for Madge, the young teacher who, unlike her creator, was able to follow her dream and set up her school on the shores of the Achensee. There are many grounds for supposing that, in Madge, the 30-year-old Elinor created the character and life which she wished for herself.

While Elinor and Madge both had to earn their own living, Madge was six years younger and extremely good-looking, and therefore faced a future in which marriage was much more likely. While Elinor had grown up in a modest terraced house in the northern industrial town of South Shields, without a garden or inside sanitation[3], Madge came from a higher social class, and her Cornish home was in a more gentrified part of the country. And while Elinor was forced to hide the fact that her father had abandoned her family when she was still a toddler, Madge's parentage was above question or scandal.

But also unlike Elinor, Madge's parents were dead — no mother or stepfather existed to deny her independence or to thwart her ambitions. And while Elinor still grieved over the loss of her adored brother Henzell, who had died of cerebro-spinal fever (a type of meningitis) in 1912 aged 17[4], Madge's brother Dick remained alive — although living sufficiently far away to allow Madge to be totally independent of him. Madge was also fortunate enough to have the company and custody of her little sister Joey, and it is interesting to speculate on the part she played in Brent-Dyer's original fantasy, given life in *The School at the Chalet*.

In 1921 Brent-Dyer had become deeply attached to the child actress Hazel Bainbridge, whom she liked to pretend was a little sister and for whom she had written *Gerry Goes to School*.[5] Hazel's life cannot have been easy, and the demands of touring would have meant that her childhood experiences were far from the innocent, stable childhood which was later portrayed in so many of Brent-Dyer's books. But although Brent-Dyer might have wished she was Hazel's sister, in reality she had no such status or influence.

In the early books, then, before Brent-Dyer came to identify herself with Joey, Joey's character appears to fulfil her wishes for both her "little sister" Hazel and her dead brother Henzell. Madge had care of Joey from infancy, and Joey had a stable home and retained her childhood throughout her teenage years — in fact until about two hours before she became engaged (in *The Chalet School in Exile*, 1940). Although her health was very delicate, she was always saved by a combination of her sister Madge (assisted by her husband, Dr Jem Russell) and the health-giving air of the Tyrol. And while Brent-Dyer never married or had children of her own, Madge, of course, had not only "Dr Jem" but, eventually, a large family of six.

There are grounds, too, for assuming that Brent-

Dyer's school at the Chalet represented her ideal as an educational institution, and that Madge's life — at least initially — was the life she herself would have liked to have led. And yet Brent-Dyer's teaching career ensured that her descriptions of school life were written from experience, and it is this combination of idealism and authenticity which helps to account for the fact that over the years a number of readers have written to the publishers to ask for a prospectus, hoping if not wholly believing that the school is real.[6]

Madge's school began in the mid-1920s as a small, privately owned establishment of nine pupils, an "English school" set in the Austrian Tyrol. By the time the last Chalet book was published, 45 years later, it had become a large boarding-school of over 400 pupils, with its own finishing branch and public examination centre which, together with an "English" branch in Wales, was owned by a public company still headed by its founder. In this the school mirrored the development of actual educational establishments for middle-class girls, for whom boarding-schools were a common experience in the late l9th and the first half of the 20th century, and this probably helped to maintain the series' credibility.

The first girls' public school, St Leonard's (in St Andrew's in Scotland), had opened its doors in 1877, less than 50 years before the publication of the first Chalet School book. Others, such as St Felix, Southwold, followed in the first quarter of this century. Alongside these well-known and highly academic schools existed hundreds of much smaller, less academic establishments, many dating from the early l9th century. Boarding-schools flourished between the wars, and in the 1920s and 1930s many new schools were opened; for example, Benenden in

Kent in 1923. But after the Second World War the implementation of the 1944 Education Act brought free education to middle-class girls and regulated school standards, leading to the gradual disappearance of many boarding-schools. Those schools that remained were larger, catered for a more exclusive group of girls, and had more uniform academic standards.[7]

It is important to remember that Brent-Dyer herself was not a product of the type of school she was writing about. Instead she was educated at a small private day school, established in the 19th century and run by a pair of sisters who were almost certainly, like Madge, without teaching qualifications.[8] Nor do the books reflect Brent-Dyer's teaching experience: the quality of her own early education meant that her most prestigious post was at the Boys' High School in South Shields during 1917, and she spent much of her teaching career at local authority schools. Later, she did teach at girls' schools, but the most notable, Western House in Hampshire, was a day school rather than a boarding-school. And while she was competent as a teacher, the evidence suggests that she lacked the management and leadership skills needed to become as successful as her fictional headmistresses when running her own school, the Margaret Roper School in Hereford, during the ten years between 1938 and 1948.[9]

In fact, as with the vast majority of school stories, the educational aspects of the Chalet School play a secondary role in the plots of individual book. Lessons are used primarily as settings for tricks or amusing incidents; for example, the cookery lesson described in Chapter 9 of *The Chalet School and the Lintons* (1934) provides a background for Cornelia Flower to flavour apple pies with garlic cloves by mistake. Instead, the boarding-school setting essentially provides a realistic *raison d'être* for the autonomous all-female community that is the true subject of the series.

THE CHALET SCHOOL CURRICULUM

Nevertheless, academic achievement and the curriculum in general do play a significant role in the series, and are given greater prominence than in most other girls' school stories. The school initially begins with a curriculum consisting of "English subjects", French, German, sewing and music. However, this soon broadens out as the school grows and more staff are appointed, and for most of the series the standard curriculum includes Latin, science, mathematics, art, domestic science, religious studies, English, history and geography, as well as sewing, music and foreign languages; and senior girls are entered for public examinations. The curriculum of the school, in other words, is similar to that found in many real middle-class girls' schools of the period.

Penny Summerfield's study of middle-class girls' schools in the first half of this century, "Cultural Reproduction in the Education of Girls; a Study of Girls' Secondary Schooling in Two Lancashire Towns, 1900-50", shows that there was a great deal of emphasis placed on academic achievement, although interestingly given that the Chalet School was inter-denominational, this was less pronounced in Catholic schools.[10] However, while in reality the academic performance of girls has always been found to decline as they reach adolescence[11], this does not appear to happen in the Chalet School. While this can be partially explained by the fact that the Chalet School is a girls' school — even today, evidence shows that girls achieve better academic results when taught separately — the fact that descriptions of adolescence are generally absent from the series must also be relevant.

Mary Evans, writing about her girls' grammar school in the 1950s, recalls that:

> Academic achievement was never allowed to be everything (hence the universal dislike of the swot and the equally universal award of the school prize to the good "all rounder").[12]

This was duplicated in the Chalet School, where swot and sneak Eustacia Benson is at first universally disliked. Later in the series, the adult Joey presents a prize for "the girl who . . . has done most to help other people".[13] Prize-winners include Mary-Lou Trelawney, one of the role model characters in the series, who is told that the prize "is given to the girl who most fulfils the ideal the pupils of the Chalet School always have held before them".[14] That ideal is service to others rather than academic success. Evans also recalls that:

> To be assured of high academic honour within the school, the subjects to excel at were English Literature and History. Being good at science and mathematics had no great cachet or appeal.[15]

This is not quite true of the Chalet School, where girls go on to study science subjects in higher education, but it is true that Joey's own subjects are history and English literature, while her "ideas of maths are wild and woolly in the extreme"[16]. Mary-Lou's chosen career is archaeology, a specialism with strong links with both subjects.

Out-of-school activities include the Hobbies Club,

the school magazine (*The Chaletian*), Brownies and Guides, and an annual sale. These will have been familiar to many readers, and to a lesser extent remain so today. Valerie Walkerdine, who has written extensively about girlhood, stresses their importance:

> Proto-fascist organisations are embarrassing to those who stand outside the familiarity of one of the mainstays of suburban life. Yet, it was the church, the school, the Brownies, the Guides and the fêtes and competitions which helped to provide the building blocks of my formation.[17]

Sewing, first mentioned as a subject when the school begins, is still on the syllabus in *A Problem for the Chalet School*, published in 1956. Evans points out that sewing was a skill still much in demand in the 1950s:

> mass availability and mass consumption had not yet given the physical object the kind of fleeting importance that it was later to acquire . . . Perfectly respectable and comfortably-off women still mended their stockings in those very recent days.[18]

That sewing is seen as useful and valid rather than as an accomplishment is also shown by Brent-Dyer's serious treatment of Sybil Russell, Madge's eldest daughter, who wishes to study embroidery at "the South Kensington School" (the Royal School of Needlework), and then earn her living sewing "church embroideries, like altar frontals and stoles and copes".[19]

Other domestic subjects were introduced in the Chalet School in 1934, when the then Headmistress tells the school: "While we wish you to become cultured women, we also desire that you shall be home-makers".[20] However it is doubtful that Brent-Dyer was sincere in her commitment to this, as these lessons in particular were used as settings for tricks or amusing incidents like the one described above. In this the Chalet School appeared to reflect the mixed message which real middle-class schoolgirls continued to receive over the first half of the century. Penny Summerfield has noted that:

> the schools themselves relegated them [domestic subjects] to a secondary positon. In so doing they conveyed a message to girls about the relatively unimportant place which preparation for domesticity occupied in the schools' agenda.[21]

Evans recalls a different message by the 1950s, but points out that:

> The responsibilities of the housewife and the mother were given full credit by the staff and "making a home" was an ideal which was accorded full status by a staff that was largely unmarried.[22]

It is probable that both the fictional and non-fictional dichotomies arose because both fictional and non-fictional Headmistresses were forced to reflect the dominant educational emphasis on domestic subjects for girls, while not necessarily agreeing with it. Deirdre Beddoe points out that educationists have differentiated between the purpose of education for boys and girls for much of this century, in reference to official education reports.[23] Two years before the publication of the first Chalet book the Hadow Committee, reporting on *The Differentiation of the Curriculum for Boys and Girls Respectively in Secondary Schools* (1923), stated that "We do not think it desirable to attempt to divorce a girl's education from her home duties and responsibilities" (p.125). Hunt quotes the *Journal of Education* which, in August 1932, claimed that girls who did not become mothers were failures as women, and which commented that women teachers and office workers really needed "marriage, a home and a family".[24] By 1943, when the 17th book in the series was published, the Norwood Report of that year still saw girls being educated as future wives and mothers.

This view of girls' education continued after the war and for the rest of the time that Brent-Dyer was writing. Summerfield refers to John Newsom's book *The Education of Girls* (1948), in which he concluded that: "the vital educational objectives for women are to enable them to become accomplished homemakers, informed citizens and to use their leisure intelligently".[25] The Crowther Report of 1959 claimed that the incentive for girls to equip themselves for marriage and home-making was genetic, while the Newsom Report of 1963 stated that the main social function of girls was to make a suitable home for their husbands and children and to be mothers.

ASPIRATIONS AND CAREERS

However, the lack of commitment with which many middle-class girls' schools pursued domestic science subjects did not mean that they were offered an equivalent education to boys. Deirdre Beddoe has pointed out that:

It is worth noting that the education offered in girls' "public day schools" (i.e. private secondary schools) was far more academic and less sex differentiated than that offered in State schools. Domestic subjects were looked down upon but, on the other hand, science and mathematics were not given the provision which they had in boys' schools in the same sector. Consequently, when many middle-class girls went to university, they had already opted for arts subjects.[26]

This was not strictly true of the Chalet School. As early as 1927, Brent-Dyer writes that Juliet Carrick, Madge's ward, is leaving the school to study mathematics at London University.[27] By the 15th book, *The Chalet School Goes to It* (1941), fifth formers' ambitions include being a surgeon, and later in the series one of Joey's triplet daughters, Margot, wishes to go to medical school (*The Chalet School Triplets*, 1963). Daisy Venables, Jem's niece, also becomes a doctor (*Tom Tackles the Chalet School*, 1955), although she marries soon after qualifying and then abandons her career. Throughout the series many of the girls aim for higher education and professional careers, including teaching, nursing, gardening, librarianship, farming, law, museum curatorship and interior design. Summerfield has noted that in actual middle-class girls' schools:

> Not surprisingly from the earliest point girls developed a strong impression that academic success and entry to higher education, especially university, but also teacher training college, were what these schools required of their pupils, and that any other objectives they might have were of little interest to the heads and their staffs.[28]

She adds that this is despite the fact that the actual numbers going to university each year were small. In another study she states that only 0.5 per cent of 18-year-old girls entered higher education during the 1920s.[29] In fact Oxford Universty did not open its degrees to women until 1920 and Cambridge until 1948, although women studied there and took the exams from 1879 and 1869 respectively.

Annie Nightingale, one of BBC Radio One's first women disc jockeys, writes of her girls' public day school in the early 1960s:

> I was not considered particularly academic and I think they rather disapproved of me. When I left and said that I wanted to be a journalist, it was not considered the right thing to do. If you weren't going to university you were supposed to go to secretarial college.[30]

Evans agrees, and notes that this emphasis on academic achievement did not reflect what was considered to be important in the outside world.

> We lived in a semi-fictional world in which education, and educational success, mattered more than anything else. If we chose to believe in this fiction then we could be assured of adult success, and we could also be assured of the approval and support of the school.[31]

Evans believes that the main reason that academic success was emphasised for middle-class girls was to reinforce class structures in English society.

> Our security depended on our parents' (particularly our fathers') ability to earn a living and to earn a living that would support the detached

house and car. To do the same we would have to pass exams and learn skills that might command considerable financial rewards.[32]

She adds that:

> In one sense, of course, we were being encouraged in a lie. As middle-class girls it was highly unlikely that we would spend our adult lives in employment . . . Such an attitude on the part of teaching staff is nowadays sometimes interpreted as a fervent feminism, a determination to ensure that girls can gain access to higher education. That determination was undoubtedly there, but so too was the determination . . . that middle-class girls should remain in a middle-class world. The surest way to do this was . . . to go to university or training college or medical school or some other enclave of middle-class expectations and aspirations.[33]

However, four years before the Chalet School series began, the census of 1921 showed that nearly one in three women had to be self-supporting[34], while about 18 per cent of women aged 20 to 45 never married during the interwar period.[35] Tinkler quotes research carried out by Edith Mercer in 1940, which found that all the girls interviewed from a girls' secondary school wanted a profession, while the majority also wanted to marry.[36] And in 1951 more than one in five married women and half of all unmarried women were in employment.[37]

While many of the women employed at the time the books were published may have been working class, there is nothing to suggest that Brent-Dyer's readers reflected the social class and educational background of the Chalet School pupils, and the need to work would probably have seemed quite natural to many of them. Brent-Dyer herself needed to work throughout her life, suggesting that her portrayal of a career as a serious option for most middle-class girls was quite sincere.

ROLE MODELS

Brent-Dyer offers both the Chalet School pupils and her readers a wide range of role models. These consist of older girls, teachers and former pupils whom Brent-Dyer continues to reintroduce as adult characters throughout the Chalet School series. Pupils (and perhaps readers) are expected eventually to make the transition to role model status, beginning when they become seniors. For example, in *The Chalet School and Jo* (1931), Jo initially resists accepting the position of Head Girl because she does not want to take on the responsibility. Gisela, the school's first head girl and now a wife and mother, tells her that it would be "cowardly" to evade responsibility and to refuse to grow up.

Jo subsequently agrees to accept the post, and later admits that (p.284) : "In one way, you know I'm fearfully proud of being head girl; and — I suppose all that about being fed-up with it isn't really true. I — I *do* like it, now I'm accustomed to it." By the time that Jo has left school and returned temporarily to teach, the then Headmistress comments: "I only wish we might keep her here always. Her influence is excellent."[38] Of course, Jo does remain with the school for "always", and continues to be the school's most important role model throughout the series. In a later book, *Tom Tackles the Chalet School*, Brent-Dyer is more explicit about the function of older girls as role models when she has Matron explain to Tom:

It's a good thing for younger girls to look up to the Seniors; good for them and good for the Seniors. If an elder girl finds that younger ones are influenced by what she says and does, if she has any decency in her, it makes her careful. As we all need some sort of ideal as soon as we can think for ourselves, it's right that girls should be able to find that ideal among themselves.[39]

Brent-Dyer illustrates this with the example of Daisy Venables as an ideal role model for Tom.

Daisy, with her fresh, pink and white face, well-groomed fair hair in its thick pigtail, and jolly grin, was just the kind of girl to appeal to any Junior's imagination. She had showed herself uniformly kind to all the new girls. Above all, there was about her an air of straight dealing and uprightness that Tom was quick to sense and appreciate.[40]

Detta O'Cathain, who attended a middle-class girls' school in the early 1950s, recalls that she too regarded older girls as role models. She writes: "I remember when I was a youngster looking up to all these fifteen- or sixteen-year-olds and thinking they were gods — or goddesses. They were role models."[41]

Members of the Chalet School staff, who are often former pupils, are also role models for the girls. Because many of them, like Joey, are first described as teenagers, the distinction between staff and prefects is deliberately blurred. The very first role model is Madge Bettany, and the first to treat her as such is Juliet Carrick, who becomes Madge's ward when her parents abandon her in *The School at the Chalet*.

> Juliet had not suddenly become an angel as a result of her present Head's treatment of her. She was a very human girl; but she was deeply grateful, and since she was thorough in whatever she did, she was making valiant efforts to become the same sporting type of girl as that to which her headmistress belonged.[42]

Later in the series Juliet tells Grizel that Madge is "the sort of person people *do* come to. She's a dear, and I adore her".[43] By the time that Juliet returns to the Chalet School to teach, however, it is she who has become the role model — "when she came among them like one of themselves they all became her instant slaves".[44]

In reality, pupils at middle-class girls' schools seem to have had a mixed response to the staff, or perhaps to have had different experiences depending on which school they attended. Evans, for example, recollects that by the 1950s "The very women who had battled for entry into this [patriarchal] world had made themselves unacceptable to us as role models because they seemed to have rejected men".[45] However, Julia Pascal recalls that her school was "weighed down in petty details of school uniform and model behavour, but a place where I saw that women could hold positions of power and authority".[46] And Sheila Rowbotham remembers that:

> Our teachers were the nearest guides because they had travelled these routes before us (though of course we wouldn't *teach*). Their attitudes to literature, art, fashion and politics were seized upon, devoured, turned over, re-sited.[47]

Perhaps the most interesting way in which teachers function as role models in the Chalet School series is in Brent-Dyer's portrayal of their work and leisure time. Here teachers are seen as happy and leading a full life, with no sense of lack because they are not married. For example, in *Carola Storms the Chalet School* (1951), "the Staff, having seen all but the prefects safely to bed, were relaxing in the Staffroom, drinking coffee, eating chocolate biscuits, smoking, and otherwise refreshing themselves".[48] Their working environment is also shown to be attractive; for example, on one occasion Miss Annersley is pictured "gazing absently out of the open window at the flower garden, where roses still bloomed magnificently and the borders were aglow with tall spikes of gladioli and great clumps of cactus dahlias".[49]

Staff are often, though by no means always, portrayed as physically attractive. They are not teaching because they cannot attract a partner, but as an alternative or as a prelude to a relationship. For example:

> Hilary Burn, ex-pupil and former head-girl of the school when it was in Tirol, was a great favourite with everyone, perhaps because she so frequently forgot that she was grown-up. She was a very pretty person, with a "Bubbles" crop of golden-brown curls, wide blue eyes, and a rose-petal skin.[50]

Hilary later becomes Hilary Graves, one of the many former pupils who marries a sanatorium doctor. She thus continues to be associated with the school after marriage; Brent-Dyer's way of getting around the contemporary dictum that married women did not teach.

Perhaps not surprisingly, Brent-Dyer also positions married women with children as role models alongside single women. Many women did not want to have to choose between marriage and a career, although they commonly wanted to stay at home when their children were young. Elizabeth Wilson, writing about the post-war period to 1968 when Brent-Dyer was producing the final Chalet School books, quotes a letter from Margaret Stacey which said that "women older than me chose *either* a career or marriage . . . *we* said, I and my friends, we would be mothers *and* women in our own right".[51]

In reality, Stacey's generation, Brent-Dyer's readers, had far more opportunity to do this than Brent-Dyer — who "chose" a career — and the first Chalet School pupils, who inevitably gave up their chosen career on marriage. Beddoe writes that:

> In the inter-war years only one desirable image was held up to women by all the mainstream media agencies — that of the housewife and mother. This single role model was presented to women to follow and all other alternative roles were presented as wholly undesirable. Realising this central fact is the key to understanding every other aspect of women's lives in Britain in the 1920s and 1930s.[52]

This image enjoyed a resurgence after the war, continuing the pressure on Brent-Dyer to produce images of contented domesticity alongside positive images of independence. Wilson also points out that part-time work was seen as the ideal solution for married women in the 1950s as there was, as there is today, an underlying assumption that young children needed the constant presence of their mother.[53]

It is obviously significant that Joey, who embodies all the most desirable qualities of a Chalet School girl, has a successful career as well as eleven children, including one set of triplets and two sets of twins (although her ability to cope is dependent on the employment of servants and is thus not a realistic option for contemporary readers). No one could accuse Jo of curbing her fertility for "selfish" reasons, as the 1950s media did to women with small families — in reality it is likely that she would have been accused of irresponsibility for having so many children — nor could she be accused of neglecting her family as she worked from home.

Jo is thus able to have it all — a large family, a husband and a career — without any contentious constructs of femininity, so it is perhaps not surprising that she remains so popular with readers today. Given that Brent-Dyer came to identify closely with Joey, it is possible that Joey's domestic situation also represented Brent-Dyer's ideal.

INTERNATIONALISM, RELIGIOUS TOLERANCE AND HEALTH IN EDUCATION

Throughout the series, there are three characteristics of the Chalet School which distinguish it from other schools, both fictional and non-fictional. These are its commitment to internationalism; the fact that it takes both Catholic and Protestant pupils in roughly equal proportions; and its avowed function to protect the health and well-being of its pupils.

Madge Bettany founds the Chalet School on "English lines"[54], but of the first pupils at the school, only one-third are English or American and the rest are French, German and Austrian.[55] With the exception of the years during and immediately following the war (when the school was situated in Britain), the school continues to take pupils of differing nationalities, the bulk of the pupils being European with others coming from America or the Commonwealth.[56] While most pupils are white, one Asian pupil is mentioned, in *Lavender Laughs in the Chalet School* (1943). Although it was not uncommon for real English schools to be based in the Alps, anecdotal evidence suggests that this mix of nationalities would be highly unusual in reality, with the majority of pupils normally drawn from the UK.

When the series begins, lessons in all subjects except languages are given in English. But within a fictional four-and-a-half years Brent-Dyer is writing that the girls "naturally had to be tri-lingual, learning French, German and English".[57] By the 13th book, *The New Chalet School* (1938), the school speaks and writes a different language each day, alternating between French, German and English (something which, in practice, it is difficult to imagine could work). This policy is abandoned during the war years, perhaps because Brent-Dyer felt that it might cause offence at a time when Germany was the enemy and France was occupied, but is reintroduced in the first of the post-war books (*Three Go to the Chalet School*, 1949).

The school's trilingualism is often highlighted in the books by the horrified reaction of new girls, who are reassured that "when you hear nothing but French round you for two days every week and nothing but German on two others, you'll soon pick up words and phrases and begin to use them naturally".[58] Quite how they were supposed to produce written work in the mean time was never explained. These new girls were likely to be in the same position as Mary Evans and her school friends in the UK in the 1950s: "Confronted by real-life French or Germans or Spanish we were collectively confounded by the ability of these people to speak in tongues that we had only read about".[59] While most of the reported conversation in the series is nevertheless in English, French and German phrases are not uncommon. McClelland has noted that the trilingual policy of the Chalet School encouraged readers to emulate the pupils, although in fact Brent-Dyer's own knowledge of languages was limited, leading her to make "glaring errors" of grammar in the texts.[60]

The school also adopts some of the customs of its host countries (Austria, then Switzerland) when abroad, most notably with regard to meals and telling the time. The dining-room is the *Speisesaal*, breakfast (*Frühstück*) — consists of "coffee, hot rolls, butter and jam", tea is replaced by *Kaffee und Kuchen* (coffee and cakes), supper is *Abendessen*. Time is told in central-European style (e.g."Lessons begin in the afternoon at fourteen-fifteen, and finish at sixteen-fifteen") for, as Headmistress Miss Annersley explains to pupils, "we are in Central Europe and naturally we must use Central Europe times".[61]

Perhaps this would not have appeared so "natural" to real English schools based abroad. Evans has written that the pupils attending her middle-class girls' school in the UK in the 1950s were "children of a culture which had already inculcated belief in the superiority of the British and the benefits of British influence".[62] However, Evans goes on explain that:

> Access to "abroad" was a mark of real status: anything French had the immediate effect of sending us into the kind of haze of veneration that

some of our parents obviously shared . . . our definition of what was worth travelling to (France, Italy, Spain and India) corresponded exactly to the limits of the eighteenth- and nineteenth-century Grand Tour and the most obviously civilised of the ex-colonies.[63]

It is probable that readers interpreted the inclusion of such details as references to "abroad", increasing the appeal of the series for them, rather than believing that a real English school would adopt "foreign" customs.

However, Brent-Dyer's genuine commitment to internationalism is demonstrated in the books written during the war years. Before the German and Austrian pupils are forced to leave the school by the Nazis in 1938, the girls "had solemnly formed a peace league among themselves, and vowed themselves to a union of nations, whether they should ever meet again or not".[64] The founding document, signed by "every girl there", pledges:

We swear faithfully to do all we can to promote peace between all our countries . . . we will try to get others to work for peace as we do . . . we will always remember that though we belong to different lands, we are members of the Chalet School League of Peace.[65]

The founding of this league is one of the causes of Joey and Robin's subsequent flight from the Nazis. Later in the book, when the school is in Guernsey, Miss Annersley tells the girls:

If war should come, remember that to many of those whom we must call the enemy it is as hateful as it is to us. In our League there are girls of German and Austrian nationality, as well as those of British, French, and Polish birth. They are our members, and we must never forget them.[66]

The Peace League plays a small but significant part in the series until the war is ended. For example, a member helps the husbands of two Austrian girls to escape from a concentration camp[67], and the German brother of two other former pupils drops a message of support for the Peace League from his aircraft and later deliberately crashes to avoid taking any further part in the war.[68] Later Joey, Robin and Simone explain to new girls that one of the aims of the League is "to remember that whatever our nationality may be, we are all Chalet School Girls"[69] — the implication being that the membership of this all-female community is more fundamental than nationality. Brent-Dyer is also careful to distinguish between Germans and Nazis: "'It isn't the Germans who are doing it,' said Robin. 'It's the Nazis.'"[70]

Given the school's commitment to internationalism, it is probably not surprising that from the beginning pupils and teachers from both main Christian denominations are seen to be members. In addition, when the school changes to having two Headmistresses following an accident to Miss Annersley, one is a Catholic, Miss Wilson, showing that the author really did treat the two denominations as being of equal status. This would be unusual in real English schools for middle-class girls; Evans claims of the 1950s that "what did constitute social deviance and marginality in those far-off days was largely constituted by two factors — having a mother with a job, and belonging to a religion other than Church of England".[71]

In the Chalet School, Catholicism is seen as quite natural, and in the Austrian books Catholic girls outnumber Protestants. Religious services are taken separately, but on some occasions Protestant girls attend Catholic services. In an early book Eustacia Benson, shown by her actions and authorial comment to be an undesirable character when she first arrives at the school, questions this and is told by Joey, the series' ultimate role model:

> it's only *one* of the roads to God. If you think that way, then it's best for you. If you think another way, then *that's* best. But they all go to the same end.[72]

Jo later grows up to marry a Catholic, Jack Maynard (although in one of Brent-Dyer's characteristic errors he has been referred to as a member of the Church of England in an earlier book), and her children are brought up in the Catholic Church. Although there is no reference to Joey's conversion in any published manuscript, she is described as attending Mass in *Jo to the Rescue* (1945), so presumably she is by then a Catholic.

Brent-Dyer was herself formally received into the Roman Catholic Church in December 1930, having previously been a practising member of the Church of England.[73] Thus it is probable that she had already taken her decision in principle at the time of writing Jo's speech to Eustacia. Nevertheless, Brent-Dyer continues to promote the idea that both denominations are equal, and while the school is set in Herefordshire stresses that the school's two chaplains "were great friends".[74]

Perhaps it is understandable, given Evans' recollections, that Brent-Dyer never extended the school's concept of religious tolerance to include

Jewish girls, although girls from other Christian groups such as Quakers are occasionally mentioned (see *The Chalet School and Richenda*, 1958). However, Brent-Dyer does make plain her opposition to anti-Semitism. The incident which precipitates Joey's flight from the Nazis is her defence of an old Jewish jeweller who is being tormented by a mob (he is later murdered). Later Joey deplores a state where there are "such horrors as concentration camps and protective detention, and beating up of helpless people just because they are Jews".[75]

The third distinguishing characteristic of the Chalet School is its avowed aim to protect the health of its pupils. One of Madge Bettany's main reasons for starting the Chalet School is Joey's poor health, which makes it desirable that she moves to a drier climate, and one of Madge's first pupils, Amy Stevens, is sent there for the same reason. Later, when the sanatorium is founded nearby and Madge marries its head, Dr Jem Russell, the school's function to protect its pupils' health becomes more explicit, with particular concentration on combating TB.

> So many of the girls had one or both parents at the sanatorium undergoing treatment, and the doctors were all of the opinion that prevention was infinitely better than cure. "Catch the children early, give them a good foundation and we may save them," Dr Jem had said on one occasion.
> So plenty of milk, sleep, fresh air, and exercise were enforced at the school, and the girls throve on the treatment.[76]

This continues when the school moves to England:

"ever since the establishment of the two [school and sanatorium], great stress had been laid on the care of the girls' health . . . The school was planned with an eye to this, and the Staff knew it".[77]

In reality, there were English schools in the Alps where the children of sanatoria patients studied, and these had previously been fictionalised in Elsie Oxenham's Swiss school stories. By the 1950s, when the school and a branch of the sanatorium had moved to Switzerland, antibiotics were well-developed and the continued stress on TB patients was becoming anachronistic. However, the sanatorium also functioned as a place where former pupils found husbands, thus ensuring that they remained close to the school, and this made it too important to the series to alter.

Health was also a consideration for some real parents when deciding to send their daughters to boarding-school. Sheila Rowbotham has written that "at eleven off I went . . . to a Methodist boarding school in East Yorkshire, close to the sea. 'Healthy air,' my father said. 'Good for the chest, bracing.'"[78] It is equally important to remember that the supposed fragility of girls' health had been of concern to educationists during the late 19th and the first quarter of the 20th century, with fears that giving girls an equivalent education to boys' would affect their general health and particularly their fertility.[79] Hunt points out that one of the main ways in which headmistresses combated these concerns and preserved a full academic curriculum for girls was by concentrating "heavily on health and medical care and this included rules about dress, holding medical inspections and encouraging gymnastics and games".[80]

It is possible, then, to interpret the stress that Brent-Dyer places on the school's function to protect its pupils' health as a means of extending the choices available to the girls rather than limiting them, and it is probable that she genuinely believed that girls' health in particular needed protecting. It is also likely that the death of her brother Henzell had left her with lifelong insecurities about illness, which the emphasis on the fragility of health reflects. In retrospect, the constant references to smoking, the high levels of dairy products and caffeine which staff and pupils alike consumed and the insistence that girls kept their coats on when climbing may seem to mitigate against good health rather than promote it. But having regard to the period in which Brent-Dyer was writing, her sincerity is unquestionable.

ELINOR BRENT-DYER'S EDUCATIONAL PHILOSOPHY

Brent-Dyer's dual professional status — as a teacher and an author — is evident at a few points when she uses the series to air what were almost certainly her own beliefs about educational theory and practice. As a teacher it is probable that she would have been aware of educational developments, both in state and in private education, during the time she was writing the Chalet School series, and would be able to compare and contrast them with her own experience. And despite Brent-Dyer's own shortcomings as a headmistress, McClelland points out that at least one lesson described in the books — Joey teaching history to new girl Polly Heriot (*Jo Returns to the Chalet School*, 1936) — has been validated by an experienced teacher as "a model in miniature of how it should be done".[81]

McClelland suggests that Brent-Dyer was dissatisfied with her own educational background, and that this is reflected in the series when old-fashioned teaching methods are criticised. For example, in *Jo Returns to the Chalet School*, new girl Polly Heriot's work is decribed by the staff as being "at least fifty years behind the times!". The staff go on to explain in detail exactly why this is the case: "she doesn't even know how to do arithmetic. Her science is conspicuous by its absence; botany, mid-Victorian; geography, the limit . . ."[82]

Perhaps it is not surprising, given that Brent-Dyer was educated and trained at the beginning of the century, that modern teaching methods also come in for criticism in the series. In the first Swiss book, *The Chalet School in the Oberland* (1952), staff are concerned about a girl who has come from a school where:

> Two new governors were appointed and they both have the idea that emulation is all wrong for children and there should be neither prizes nor marks nor form positions in school . . . The girls raged about it and a good many of them either did no work at all or else worked so badly that they might just as well have left it alone.

One of the other staff members comments:

> what a pity it is when cranks get the upper hand anywhere — especially where youngsters are concerned. I do feel that elder girls ought to manage without any incentive, though, human nature being what it is, I know the majority of them do work much better if they're going to gain something tangible in the end. Where younger girls come in, I agree with prizes every time![83]

Another device that Brent-Dyer uses to illustrate her opinions about modern teaching methods is the invention of another Chalet School, run on very different lines. It makes its first appearance in *The Wrong Chalet School* (1952), when a pupil tells a new girl:

> last year they had a new Head and she has the maddest ideas. She believes in you learning *what* you like and *when* you like. It sounds very nice, but I think it must be an awfully untidy way of doing things. I'd a lot rather do as we do and have time-tables.[84]

In a later book, *Bride Leads the Chalet School* (1953), the two schools merge and the results of these teaching methods are demonstrated for the readers:

> it was found that, with very few exceptions, the girls from the Tanswick school were a good year behind their contemporaries on the Island. Free discipline does not make for hard work unless the pupils are born students and the general tone of the Tanswick school had not made for that.[85]

Given her attacks on both old-fashioned and modern teaching methods, it is likely that Brent-Dyer agreed with headmistress Miss Annersley when Miss Wilson claims that "There's quite a lot to be said for some of the old-fashioned methods of teaching, you know." Miss Annersley replies: "I believe in mingling the old *and* the new — making the best of both, in fact."[86]

Whether or not this was the secret of the Chalet School's success educationally, there is no doubt that readers found the school both believable and attractive. Writing about the series' popularity, Helen MoClelland points out that:

> Just as important for the readers was their belief in the Chalet School itself, as an abiding institution whose customs gradually evolve but whose traditions remain constant throughout the series. Maybe it was only a few fans who actually wrote and asked the publishers to send prospectuses of the school. But most readers could recite from memory the Chalet School's history, rules and constitution, could explain the time-table and take on the "sheepdog" duties of guiding a new girl around the school.[87]

With the Chalet School, then, Elinor Brent-Dyer succeeded in creating a school which was as much an ideal for her readers and fictional pupils as it was for herself. Jenny Price is typical of many readers when she says that: "My introduction to the Chalet series was *Barbara*, borrowed from the school library and I was hooked (so much so that I told all and sundry that I wanted to go to this school in Switzerland)."[88] Likewise new girl Barbara Chester, on arriving at the Görnetz Platz to start school, "gave a cry of rapture. 'Oh, isn't it marvellous! Oh, I'm so glad I've come! This will be school wth bells on!'"[89]

NOTES

1. Helen McClelland, *Behind the Chalet School* (New Horizon, 1981), p.43.
2. Ibid., pp.155-6.
3. Ibid., pp.1-2.
4. Ibid., pp.41-2.
5. Ibid., pp.63-72.
6. Ibid., pp.166
7. See Gillian Avery, *The Best Type of Girl* (André Deutsch, 1991).
8. McClelland, ibid., p.33.
9. Ibid., pp.145-149.
10. Felicity Hunt, ed., *Lessons for Life: The Schooling of Girls and Women 1850-1950* (Blackwell, 1987), pp.152-69.
11. Sue Sharpe, *"Just Like a Girl". How Girls Learn to be Women* (Penguin, 1976), pp.134-5.
12. Mary Evans, *A Good School: Life at a Girls' Grammar School in the 1950s* (Women's Press, 1991), p.22.
13. *Gay from China at the Chalet School* (1944), p.234.
14. *The Coming of Age of the Chalet School* (1958), p.222.
15. Evans, ibid., p.13.
16. *Jo Returns to the Chalet School* (1936), p.85.
17. Liz Heron, ed., *Truth, Dare or Promise. Girls Growing Up in the Fifties* (Virago, 1985), p.65.
18. Evans, ibid., p.86.
19. *Carola Storms the Chalet School* (1951), pp.111-2.
20. *The Chalet School and the Lintons* (1934), p.64.
21. Hunt, ibid., p.157.
22. Evans, ibid., p.29.
23. Deirdre Beddoe, *Discovering Women's History. A Practical Manual* (Pandora, 1983), pp.59-62.
24. Hunt, ibid., p.3.
25. Ibid., p.131.

26. Beddoe, ibid., p.59.
27. *The Princess of the Chalet School*, (1927) p.119.
28. Hunt, ibid., p.158.
29. Gail Braybon and Penny Summerfield, *Out of the Cage: Women's Experiences of Two World Wars* (Pandora, 1987), p.138.
30. Jackie Bennett and Rosemary Forgan, eds., *There's Something About a Convent Girl* (Virago, 1991), p.132.
31. Evans, ibid., pp.39-40.
32. Ibid., p.37.
33. Ibid., p.38.
34. Hunt, ibid., p.18.
35. Deirdre Beddoe, *Back to Home and Duty: Women between the wars 1918-1939* (Pandora, 1989), p.148.
36. Hunt, ibid., p.67.
37. Rosemary Deem, ed., *Schooling for Women's Work* (Routledge & Kegan Paul, 1980), p.114.
38. *Jo Returns to the Chalet School*, p.204.
39. *Tom Tackles the Chalet School* (1955), p.56.
40. Ibid., p.46.
41. Bennett and Forgan, ibid., p.138.
42. *The School at the Chalet* (1925), p.279.
43. *Jo of the Chalet School* (1926), p.30.
44. *The Chalet School and Jo* (1931), p.152
45. Evans, ibid., p.60.
46. Heron, ibid., p.41.
47. Ibid., p.208.
48. *Carola Storms the Chalet School*, p.169.
49. *Shocks for the Chalet School* (1952), p.13.
50. *Tom Tackles the Chalet School*, p.141.
51. Elizabeth Wilson, *Only Halfway to Paradise. Women in Post-war Britain 1945-1968* (Tavistock, 1980), p.47.
52. Beddoe, *Back to Home and Duty*, p.8.
53. Wilson, ibid., pp.22, 59.
54. *The Exploits of the Chalet Girls* (1933), p.23.
55. *The School at the Chalet*, pp.65-6.
56. For example, *A Chalet Girl From Kenya* (1955).
57. *The Exploits of the Chalet Girls*, p.23.
58. *The Chalet School and Barbara* (1954), p.114.
59. Evans, ibid., p.17.
60. McClelland, ibid., p.177.

61. *The Chalet School and Barbara*, p.66.
62. Evans, ibid., p.15.
63. Ibid., p.33.
64. *The Chalet School in Exile* (1940), p.55.
65. Ibid., p.57.
66. Ibid., p.202.
67. Ibid., p. 332.
68. *The Chalet School Goes to It* (1941), p.215.
69. *The Highland Twins at the Chalet School* (1942), p.95.
70. *The Chalet School in Exile*, p.228.
71. Evans, ibid., p.28.
72. *Eustacia Goes to the Chalet School* (1930), p.191.
73. McClelland, ibid., p.117.
74. *Tom Tackles the Chalet School*, p.73.
75. *The Chalet School in Exile*, p.162.
76. *The Chalet School and Jo*, p.66.
77. *Gay from China at the Chalet School*, p.62.
78. Heron, ibid., p.197.
79. See Hunt, ibid., pp.9-11.
80. Ibid., p.9.
81. McClelland, ibid., p.132.
82. *Jo Returns to the Chalet School*, pp.82-3.
83. *The Chalet School in the Oberland* (1952), pp.78-9.
84. *The Wrong Chalet School* (1952), p.19.
85. *Bride Leads the Chalet School* (1953), p.94.
86. *Three Go to the Chalet School* (1949), p.156.
87. *Friends of the Chalet School Newsletter 6*, Aug. 1990.
88. *Friends of the Chalet School Newsletter 17*, October 1992.
89. *The Chalet School and Barbara*, p.28.

The original dust wrappers of the first six books, published by Chambers and illustrated by Nina K. Brisley.

THE CHALET SCHOOL GUIDES — GIRLS' ORGANISATIONS AND GIRLS' SCHOOL STORIES

ROSEMARY AUCHMUTY

JOEY *Goes to the Oberland* (1954) is, in every sense, a transitional book. Published as no. 29, it appeared roughly halfway through the Chalet School series. It marks the end of the school's British record; from now on, readers will only be concerned with the Swiss branch. In its pages, certain popular characters are settled — Daisy gets married, Robin enters a convent — while others, absent for a period after the war, make a welcome reappearance. "You know, Jo, I have a feeling that from now on we're going to pick up a lot of threads we've had to drop," Primula confides.[1] On the journey to the Oberland, Jo makes contact with Evadne, Simone and Frieda; and in the books that follow, many of the girls who had been at school with Joey before the war return to play a new role in the series.

Jo is following the Chalet School back to the Continent — not to its first home in the Austrian Tyrol, which remained under Russian occupation until 1955, but to the Bernese Oberland. Though a traditional site for English boarding-schools and sanatoriums, Switzerland represents a fresh start for the Chalet School. Having decided to locate the finishing branch there (*The Chalet School in the Oberland*, 1952), Brent-Dyer quickly realised the attraction of transferring the main school as well; the passing of 25 years and a major war since the visit to Achensee which inspired the series had destroyed the Tyrol of Brent-Dyer's memories, and the setting needed an update.

Jo's role was to provide the thread of continuity. Ostensibly she is moving to Switzerland because her husband has been appointed head of the new Sanatorium on the Görnetz Platz. From an artistic point of view, however, she has to go with the school because she has become indivisible from it; in Brent-Dyer's presentation, she is as much a part of the school as the staff and pupils, symbolising (we are told) its very spirit.

But in leaving Britain, there are losses, too — for Jo, for the school, and for the series itself. This is not simply because the British books are among the best of Elinor Brent-Dyer's writing (particularly those set in "Armishire"); by 1954, she was simply not writing so well, and the Swiss books — with the occasional exception — are among the least inventive and most repetitive of the series. It is also because, while former connections are revived and new ones forged in the Swiss books, others are broken. This new life will lack many of the features of the old.

One thing that is left behind is the Girl Guides. In *The Chalet School and Barbara* (1954), the girls express the hope that Guides will be resumed in the new school. Though their Captain, Miss Edwards, has remained behind in England, there are other experienced Guiders on the staff, and Miss Wilson, their former Captain and District Commissioner, is nearby at the finishing branch. Miss Annersley, the Headmistress, is also keen to continue with Guides. But the removal to Switzerland has meant a great many changes, and the Head decides that "until they were in full running order, outside things like Guides must wait, although she fully intended that they should begin presently".[2]

In fact, as readers know, they never do. Chalet fans and critics naturally wonder why. In Tyrol, in Armiford and on the island, Chalet Girls were the most enthusiastic of Guides. Practically everyone in the school belonged. Readers of all the books from *The Princess of the Chalet School* (1927) to *Changes for the Chalet School* (1953) must be familiar with the Saturday morning meetings, the hikes and weekend camps, the skills acquired and badges earned. In the first half of the Chalet School series, Elinor Brent-Dyer proved herself one of the most fervent of the large band of literary advocates of the movement. In the second half, she ignored them. This chapter will examine the significance of girls' organisations in girls' school stories; and in so doing, will attempt to find an answer to the conundrum of the strange disappearance of the Guides in the Chalet School books published after 1953.

GUIDES IN THE EARLY CHALET SCHOOL BOOKS

Elinor Brent-Dyer's interest in Guides probably dates from around the time that the first Chalet School book was published, in 1925. None of her books published before this date features Guides; they first rate a mention in *The School at the Chalet*, where Gisela has been reading an English girls' school story about a Guide, "but I did not quite understand it. It is not the kind of guide we know here."

> "Girl Guides, was it?" asked Joey with interest. "I always wanted to be one, but my sister would never let me, because in England I caught cold over everything."[3]

Thus the seeds of interest are sown. In *Jo of the Chalet School* (1926), Grizel returns to school "full of the Girl Guide movement".[4] A company has been formed in the High School where she and Jo were once pupils, and her father has given her several books on the subject. She hands these around the seniors and middles, and their enthusiasm results in a deputation to the Headmistress to ask her to form a company in the Chalet School.

Miss Bettany asks the girls why they want to be Guides. Grizel replies: "It bucks you up and makes you smart!" Gisela likes "the idea of learning to do many useful things". Juliet says that "it will make for oneness".[5] Miss Bettany thinks so too. She tells them of her plan to attend an instruction course for Guiders in the Easter vacation in England. Helen McClelland suggests that Brent-Dyer herself may have attended such a course at that time, held at the Girl Guide training centre at Foxlease in Lyndhurst in the New Forest, not far from her Fareham home. Foxlease had been opened only four years before, in 1922.[6] Helen found no evidence that Brent-Dyer was ever involved in actual Guiding: the books, she points out, "tell nothing about Guides that Elinor could not have learnt second-hand".[7]

Evidence may in fact be found in the pages of the *Chalet Club News Letter*, run by Brent-Dyer's publishers, W. & R. Chambers, in the last decade of her life. In no. 4 (Oct. 1960) the author quoted a letter she had received from Miss Helen Crampton which said: "I don't know whether you will remember me, but I used to be a member of the 1st Herefordshire Lone Ranger Company when you were Captain." Brent-Dyer did remember Helen "and what a keen Ranger she was". The Lone Branch was set up in 1919, with the first company being formed in 1921, for girls who lived in isolated areas and could not get to regular meetings. Lone Guides received a monthly training letter through the post, which took the place of a company meeting.[8] Whether Brent-Dyer was ever involved with an ordinary Guide company is unclear. In *News Letter 17* (Dec. 1967) she wrote, "I loved my own Guiding days". Recently Gill Bilski expressed the view that Brent-Dyer's descriptions of Guides have the ring of experience about them.

> As a Guider, it struck me on reading *Chalet Girls in Camp* that Elinor must have been to a Guide camp . . . It is possible to get most of the information from books, but she captures the feel of a Guide camp; the endless search for wood (and the girls who always seem to find green wood); the near panic when it rains in the night and how it's always the few who have to get up to loosen the guys . . .[9]

At any rate, Guides feature significantly in most of the Tyrolean books and in other non-Chalet books of the period, such as *Judy the Guide* (1928). In *The Princess of the Chalet School* (1927), a chapter is devoted to Elisaveta's enrolment, and we learn that her father, the Crown Prince of Belsornia, plans to establish a branch in his own country: "it seems to me that it is just what is needed for our young girls". Not even the men of his own regiment, we are told, could show greater smartness than the Chalet Guides. The activities of the Guides and Brownies are described in great detail: ambulance work, signalling and Morse. The Brownies show the prince "a remarkable version of the life of Florence Nightingale in the Crimea".[10] Tests dominate the girls' thoughts, and their benefits are revealed when Jo is able to track and rescue the princess when she is captured by her father's mad cousin. "How thankful she felt that she had given up a whole Saturday afternoon once to teach the woodcraft signs to Elisaveta!"[11]

Guides are an important feature of *The Rivals of the Chalet School* (1929), in which one whole chapter is devoted to "The Chalet Guides". One fine Saturday, abandoning the Christmas tree they are decorating for the local children, the Chalet Guides have a march-out round the lake to Seehof. This takes them past the windows of the rival school on the Tiernsee, St Scholastika's, situated at Buchau. The Chalet girls' singing attracts the attention of the "Saints". Their Head Girl, Elaine Gilling, longs to be a Guide, but the headmistress, Miss Browne, objects to the movement, saying it is "unnecessary" for her pupils.[12] Elaine nurses a grievance against the Chalet School which, fed by this additional envy, leads indirectly to an outbreak of disobedience and the near tragedy in which Jo Bettany almost dies after rescuing one of the errant "Saints", Maureen O'Donovan, from the frozen lake.

When Miss Browne laments over the behaviour of her pupils, her colleague Miss Anderson suggests that "our girls wanted more than we have given them". Miss Browne cannot understand this. "They have a good library, games, a debating society. What more can they want?" The answer is Guides. "I am not a Guide myself," Miss Anderson says, "but I know what tremendous good they have done wherever they have been started".[13] St Scholastika's duly starts its own Guide company, tactfully assisted by the experienced Chaletians; and by the time of *The Chalet School and Jo* (1931) the two schools are going on weekend camps together.[14]

The Chalet School and Jo introduces Biddy O'Ryan, an orphaned runaway found wandering around the Tiernsee by a group of Chalet School middles. Rather than allow her to be sent to the Cecilia Home for Orphans, the Guide companies of the two schools undertake to pay for her education and support.[15] This must have been a major responsibility, even allowing for the fact that she is evidently housed free of charge by the Chalet School in term time and by Madge Russell and, later, Jo Maynard in the holidays. At first Biddy is sent to the local school at the head of the lake, and a future as a lady's maid is planned for her. But she soon proves, as Brent-Dyer quaintly puts it, to need better schooling than the village can provide and is transferred to the Chalet where she makes good. This takes her to Oxford and a job in Australia before, repaying her debt to the school, she returns as its history mistress in *Carola Storms the Chalet School* (1951). One of the most popular characters in the series, Biddy O'Ryan is permitted by the author to join that select band of Chalet girls who, like Joey, marry doctors at the Sanatorium and settle on the Görnetz Platz, thus retaining their connection with the school to the end of the series.

Much emphasis is laid in these early books on Guide values. Forced to take the long way home over the mountain in *The Rivals of the Chalet School*, when the path breaks away on a winter's walk, the girls of St Scholastika's sulk and complain; the Chaletians, on the other hand, "as became people who had been in the country for some time, and who were Guides, said nothing, but set their teeth and went at it".[16] The Chalet Guides do not complain in adversity[17]; they are neat and tidy[18]; they "laugh and sing on all occasions".[19] In *The Exploits of the Chalet Girls* (1933), Thekla, who initially refuses to join the Guides "since it was an English institution" and she despises all things

English, changes her mind when the prompt action of the Chalet Guides saves her from injury when her petticoat catches fire.[20] "Guides always help, don't they?" observes little Daisy Venables, justifying her action in stopping Jo and Frieda in an Innsbruck street.[21]

By the time of *The New Chalet School* (1938), the last fully Tyrolean book, the Chalet School boasts three large Guide companies, a Ranger and a Cadet company, and all the Juniors are Brownies. That year the annual garden party at the end of the summer term was to be a "Guide affair".

> The Rangers would see to Kaffee und Kuchen, and the Cadets were to have a couple of stalls in aid of the free beds at the Sonnalpe which the school had maintained ever since the opening of the Sanatorium. The Brownies were to give a display, and it had been decided that they should present the story of Grace Darling . . . The Guides were more ambitious. They were to represent hospital work in war-time . . . [22]

Thus presciently prepared, the Chalet School Guides pass into war-time and exile. The girls' training comes in handy during their escape from Nazi-occupied Austria: "How thankful they were that, as Guides, they had all had plenty of tracking practice!"[23]

Re-opening in Guernsey, the school includes first-aid classes in its curriculum as part of their war effort; "and as all were Guides, they had taken to the lessons like ducks to water"; indeed, "most of this work was revision for the Seniors, who had done it in their Guide tests".[24] Jo, now an established author, makes use of her own experiences in the two Guide stories which are among her earliest published novels for girls: *Patrol-Leader Nancy* and *Nancy Meets a Nazi*.[25] Later, *The Robins Make Good* joins the list.[26]

GUIDES IN THE BRITISH BOOKS

That Guides were an important feature of Chalet School life in Britain is not so surprising. Many girls' schools had their own Guide companies at this period; indeed, Helen McClelland tells us that there were Guides at the school Elinor Brent-Dyer herself ran between 1938 and 1948.[27] A clear picture of the range of Guide activities is given in *The Highland Twins at the Chalet School* (1942). When the school secretary is hurt in an accident, the Cadets and Rangers taking their clerk's badge share out her work between them.[28] A poignant note is struck when Elisaveta, now a refugee from her Nazi-occupied homeland, declares her intention of earning her living after the war by taking in washing: "I've got my laundress badge, Joey, as you may remember."[29]

Guides become a symbol of right thinking in the Armishire books. Betty Wynne-Davies, who resigned from her company after falling out with her friend Elizabeth Arnett, goes on to betray war secrets to the Nazis, and is expelled. Her friend Florence Williams, while less culpable, is "too lazy" to be a Guide.[30] Lavender Leigh's babyish helplessness is depicted as the result of an over-indulged upbringing by an aunt who "doesn't approve of the Guides". But when her schoolmates ostracise her for anti-social behaviour, they are taken to task by one of the prefects: "If any of you had been the good Guides you ought to be," Biddy O'Ryan declares, "you'd have given her a helping hand . . . "[31]

The opposition of Miss Bubb, locum headmistress when Miss Annersley and Miss Wilson are hospitalised after a bus crash, is represented as an integral part of a package of anti-Chalet values. It is taken for granted that her dislike of Guides, as of all activities outside schoolwork, is wrong.[32] But Tom Gay, raised as a boy, is simply misguided when she declines an invitation to join ("No blinking fear! They had 'em in the parish all right, but I never had any use for 'em").[33] As soon as she is assimilated into girls' school values, she becomes a keen Guide; and by the time of *The Wrong Chalet School* (1952) she is an even keener Patrol Leader.[34]

Weekend camps become an attractive possibility again when the school moves to an island, and a whole chapter of *The Wrong Chalet School* is devoted to one such camp. Here we meet many old friends. Miss Wilson is now District Commissioner for Carnbach Guides ("very trig in her uniform"); Miss Burn, former Head Girl of the Chalet School, is Captain of the First Chalet Company, with Miss O'Ryan as one of her Lieutenants. Unlike the Chalet girls of Tyrol days, the Guides now pitch their own tents; but like their predecessors, they enjoy the swim that follows — until they run into a shoal of jellyfish![35] In the last British book, *Changes for the Chalet School* (1953), these weekend camps are still being talked about.[36] And then — silence.

THE MYSTERY OF THE MISSING GUIDES

Why did Elinor Brent-Dyer drop Guides, which had been a central feature of her Chalet School books for almost thirty years? "Elinor seems characteristically to have lost interest in the subject," writes Helen McClelland[37]; and if her assessment of the author's character is correct, this may be the simple answer.

In 1954 Brent-Dyer was sixty years old; she had given up her school six years before, and was now writing full-time. In 1953 she published no fewer than five full-length books, and in 1954, six. Interested or not, she might not have had the time and energy to keep up with Guides in any personal capacity.

Elinor Brent-Dyer's own explanation for the absence of the Guides in the Swiss books was that *the girls themselves* would have had no time for them. In the *Chalet Club News Letter 15* (Sept. 1966) she writes: "The Chalet School Guide Company has not carried on in Switzerland because there is little or no time for it. The English branch has, however, a flourishing Company." There is a sense of *post hoc* justification about this, as in quite a lot of Brent-Dyer's answers to readers' queries, and it really doesn't stand up to close examination. What is it that fills the Swiss Chaletians' time that the English girls do not also do? Rambles, perhaps? But when they were all in England, they went for long walks, and they also played a great many matches against other schools, which they don't do in Switzerland. In *Challenge for the Chalet School* (1966), the Saturday schedule is given as "Games on Saturday morning and a ramble in the afternoon, weather permitting. Dancing and games in the evening".[38] Even with the addition of mending, there is surely room for a Guide meeting here.

Another explanation is that Guides were too closely associated in Brent-Dyer's mind with a particular kind of English boarding-school culture, which she was anxious to get away from. There were two aspects to this apparent attempt to distance the school from its earlier Guide-centredness: geographical and temporal. Paradoxically, although the Girl Guide movement was internationalist in intent and had spread to countries all over the world by the outbreak of the Second World War, it was nevertheless often portrayed in children's literature as a strongly patriotic, imperialist organisation, focused on England and English virtues.[39] This tendency was of course exacerbated in wartime, when patriotism was paramount. For Brent-Dyer, the sisterhood of Guides was always cross-national, and she was exceptional in distinguishing between the Nazis, who were England's enemies, and Germans generally, who were not.

This was emphasised in the scene in *The Highland Twins in the Chalet School* (1943) where Emmie and Joanna Linders, former Chalet School pupils and Guides, don Guide uniform to tell the story of their escape from their native Germany during the war to the assembled Guides in the school.[40] A comparison with Dorita Fairlie Bruce's presentation of the Girls' Guildry, a parallel girls' organisation, in *Dimsie Intervenes* (1938) — where Dimsie has her famous confrontation with Miss Carver over the parish hall piano — clearly illustrates how unusual was Brent-Dyer's approach in the Chalet School books.[41]

Nonetheless, in Brent-Dyer's novels — even those set in the Austrian Tyrol — the values promoted by the Guides remain utterly English. "Guide honour" is a refrain which accompanies many a schoolgirl assurance. When Madge Bettany praises the Guide movement in *Jo of the Chalet School* (1926), she says that "it gives you a big outlook, and strengthens one's ideas of playing the game and being straight".[42] And therein lies the other distance: that of time. It is clear from the Swiss Chalet School books that Brent-Dyer wanted to present her fictional school as completely up to date. Not only its educational methods but its uniform, its attitude to make-up for the girls, Jo Maynard's egalitarian relationship with her daughters, are all presented as thoroughly "modern". Brent-Dyer may have felt that the image of the Guide movement (still promoting the old ideals of honour, straightness and playing the game in the 1950s and 1960s, as women who were Guides at the time assure me) was a little old-fashioned for her new model Swiss Chalet School.[43]

Doubly paradoxical, however, is the fact that although Brent-Dyer professed to be internationalist and up to date in the Swiss Chalet School books, in reality her focus remained stubbornly English and traditional. She seems to have had no desire to turn her Chalet girls into *Swiss* Guides; she wanted them to retain their English identity, even though Guides had existed in Switzerland since 1913; indeed, "Our Chalet", the Guides' World Centre from 1932, was located in Adelboden in the Bernese Oberland![44] A Swiss contingent attended the Scout and Guide International Folk Dance Festival in London's Hyde Park in 1947, and ten years later Switzerland provided the site for one of four gigantic World Camps to celebrate the centenary of Baden-Powell's birth.[45]

No such dilemma had presented itself when she introduced Guides into the Chalet School in the Tyrol, since (as she claims in *The Rivals of the Chalet School*) Guides were unknown there at that time.[46] In fact, Gill Bilski tells me, the first Austrian Guide company was formed in 1914. But owing to the First World War and its aftermath, Guides ceased in 1918; were resumed in 1924; dwindled, and were officially restarted in 1935 — to cease again soon after because of the Second World War. Gill suggests that they may only have existed in the cities, so Brent-Dyer's claim may well be correct; the

Achensee ("Tiernsee") being fairly off the beaten track.

In Switzerland the Chalet School takes pupils from many countries but it remains an English school. Though the number of "foreign" girls increases book by book (and to do her justice, she does point out that the English girls are the foreigners in Switzerland, though significantly some English girls have trouble grasping this fact)[47], not one becomes Head Girl; it seems that British girls alone have the requisite qualities for the work.

As for the much-vaunted "modernity" of the school (or of Jo Maynard for that matter) in their approach to the upbringing of young women in the 1950s, this seems to be more honoured in assertion than example. Discipline, for instance, is much stricter in these later books: compare those regimented files from dormitory to dining-room with the freedom of Jo and her friends to run downstairs as soon as they were ready!

Yet of course Miss Bettany's sentiments would have been absolutely modern and radical when she expressed them, in the mid-1920s. The principles underlying Guides fitted so comfortably into the healthy, organised, educational regime of the early Chalet School that we tend to forget how new was women's access to such ideas. Education for girls based on an intellectual training, games, devolved leadership and a code of moral values dates only from the late 19th century; organised leisure in the form of girls' associations like the Girl Guides from the early years of the 20th.

A BRIEF HISTORY OF THE GUIDES

The Girl Guides began in 1909, three years after their brother organisation, the Boy Scouts. Though not the first organisation for girls, they were to prove far and away the most popular. Lord Baden-Powell took the credit for both Guides and Scouts, but in reality the Guides were more or less thrust upon him, and somewhat against his will. He had not at first envisaged scouting activities as suitable for girls. But within two years of the establishment of the Boy Scouts, at least 6,000 girls had set up their own troops in imitation. To rid the Scouts of these hangers-on — some of whom even gate-crashed Boy Scout events — the General (as he was then) drew up a schedule of aims and regulations for a proposed parallel association for girls.

Their zeal for activities exactly like the Scouts' was, however, quickly diverted into more feminine channels once the Baden-Powells (the General, his sister and his wife) took control. The Schedule of 1909 set the tone:

> If we want the future manhood of the country to be men of character — which is the only guarantee for [sic] safety for the nation — it is essential in the first place that the mothers, and the future wives (the guides of those men), should also be women of character.[48]

By 1909 British feminists had fought for and won a wide range of new rights and opportunities for women in education, work, the law and politics, and had been vigorously campaigning for votes for women for over half a century. The suffragettes were making their presence felt by the use of militant tactics which challenged every Victorian tenet about women's nature. But General Baden-Powell's document was not framed in terms of the rights or even needs of girls *per se* — only as future wives and mothers of men.

> Decadence is going on in the nation, both moral and physical; proofs are only too plentiful . . . Much of this decadence is due to ignorance or supineness of mothers, who have never been taught themselves.

How was this to be achieved?

> As things are, one sees the streets crowded after business hours, and the watering-places crammed with girls over-dressed and idling, learning to lead aimless, profitless lives; whereas, if an attractive way were shown, their enthusiasm would at once lead them to take up useful work with zeal.[49]

What Baden-Powell meant by "useful work" was, of course, the traditional servicing role of women: nursing, cooking, sewing. What the girls who had set up informal Girl Scout troops in imitation of the boys had wanted were all the interesting parts of Scout work like tracking, signalling and camping. Not surprisingly, many were reluctant to give up their Scouting for the new feminine offering.

Knowing this, the compilers of the first Handbook of the Girl Guides (1912, titled *How Girls Can Help to Build Up the Empire*) contrived to incorporate all the popular skills and training from the Boy Scouts' handbook which they were adapting, disguising them where necessary by the insertion of a "Womanly Purpose".

> For instance, the section devoted to stalking, tracking, signalling, camping, and all the out-door pursuits the girls had seized upon with such avidity, was cleverly camouflaged with the heading "Finding the Injured" . . .[50]

By 1935 there were 600,000 Guides in Britain and another 400,000 around the world (though they were banned in Nazi Germany).[51] As well as separate organisations for younger (Brownies) and older girls (Rangers), there were Cadets who were training for Guiding work, Lone Guides in isolated places, Sea Rangers, and an Extension branch of troops of girls with disabilities. Badges were awarded for achievement in activities ranging from "Home Craft" to all the outdoor skills.

> "Basket-worker for me," proclaimed Joey that morning, as she was putting on her stockings. "Also, I rather want a shot at Pioneer."
> "I will do Basket-worker too," agreed Frieda. "And I should like to take Boatswain, if I may. I have done the Turk's Head, and I know all the knots, and can swim."[52]

As for camping, the word became synonymous with the Girl Guides. The first recorded girls' camp was held in a private garden in 1910. It represented something of a radical departure for girls, and was at first strenuously opposed. An article in the *Glasgow Herald* in 1909 protested:

> It can hardly be desirable that this new movement among girls should be taken seriously when it is remembered how much independence, fatigue, and exposure to all weathers are the unavoidable experiences of the Boy Scout. That the healthy young boy suffers no harm from these necessities of the work, all interested in the question appear to agree. But few will, I think, allow that it is wise to allow girls of the same tender age equal freedom and equal opportunities of "roughing it".[53]

Very soon camping became the high point of every Guide's experience, as both the ideal testing ground for so many of the more interesting skills and the first opportunity for most girls to get away from home with others of their kind. *The Chalet Girls in Camp* (1932) is an English version of a genre much more common in American girls' fiction[54]: the novel which is wholly devoted to the story of a summer camp in the school holidays. Here the Chalet Guides camp on the shores of a particularly lovely lake in the Austrian Tyrol, experiencing the joys of self-sufficiency in the outdoors. The message that women can rough it too, unprotected by men, is somewhat muted by the greater emphasis on the acquisition of useful domestic skills by these pampered middle-class girls, accustomed to having everything done for them by mothers or, more probably, maids. An amusing incident revolving around the Middles' attempt to launder their own clothes provides an opportunity for Miss Wilson to announce that the school is planning to introduce Domestic Science lessons into the curriculum the following term.[55]

GIRLS' GUILDRY

Two comparable organisations much featured in girls' school stories were Girls' Guildry, beloved of Dorita Fairlie Bruce, and Camp Fire, most closely associated with Elsie Oxenham. The Girls' Guildry was started in Glasgow in 1900 by Dr W. F. Somerville. He had observed the work of the Boys' Brigade and, regretting that there was nothing similar for girls, planned the Girls' Guildry to fill the leisure hours of listless young women with organised Christian activity.

At the time, the idea of such a movement was

relatively new. The Church of England had its Girls' Friendly Society, founded in 1877, but this was English and generally confined to girls from working-class districts. Somerville's concern was for those young women of the middle class who were too old for children's play but not yet admitted to adult society — a need much more apparent at the close of the 19th century than it had been when life for women was more domestic and confined.

The Girls' Guildry had a religious though nonsectarian base. Initially each company was attached to a church. There were several ranks of membership, Maid, Maid of Merit, Maid of Honour, Maid in Waiting, each dependent on awards won; every Company was headed by a Guardian who might have one or more assistants. The distinctive uniform of blue skirt, white blouse and red sash was deliberately both patriotic and para-military. It was also simple and had the effect of submerging class differences among members, an important objective at a time when dress was so clear a class indicator. The organisation prided itself on the fact that well-to-do girls who joined Guildry were sartorially indistinguishable from the working-class Guildswomen whom the officials increasingly tried to recruit.

With the uniform the girls wore a white panama (later, a blue felt) together with a badge in the form of a lamp, the symbol of service. Herein lay the clue to the movement's aims. In 1903 the President stated that its object was:

> to induce girls to become Christian women in the truest sense, and to develop those qualities of womanly helpfulness by which they might become potent factors in brightening and improving the world.[56]

The activities arranged for members were designed to further this aim — learning First Aid, for example. Some were of less obvious benefit, such as the practice of drill. Drill seems to have been immensely popular with girls at the beginning of the 20th century, doubtless because more strenuous forms of physical activity were denied them.[57] It gave healthy exercise, at the same time inculcating the virtues of team-work, grace and style. Its military potential may have been a reflection of the times (the Boer War was in progress at the date of the Guildry's foundation) as well as a recognition of the lack of other models for young people's clubs.

Other Guildry activities included sewing; nursing; dancing (allowed from 1910, when country dancing superseded the more frivolous type); "domestic economy"; camping; and — from the 1930s — zealous social and mission work among Depression-torn poorer districts and a new emphasis on "citizenship", particularly appropriate following the extension of the vote to all women over 21. The movement quickly spread to England, Ireland and Wales and later to Canada, Livingstonia (in Africa) and Jamaica; but remained most popular in Scotland.

Dorita Fairlie Bruce was closely associated with the Girls' Guildry for well over 30 years. In December 1916 the *Girls' Guildry Gazette* reported that the No. 1 Ealing Company had performed a pageant entitled *The Daughters of Britain*, "specially written for the girls by one of the Assistant Guardians, Miss D. Bruce". In 1920 she took on a company set up to train Guardians in Ealing, and by 1926 she was one of the Vice-Presidents of the London Centre. When Guildry in the capital became large enough to support three centres, Bruce was elevated to "Centre President" of the West London Centre.[58] By this time her name was one of those most frequently found in the *Gazette*'s successor organ, the *Lamp of the Girls' Guildry*. Her novels were reviewed therein, and she contributed articles on various Guildry events and activities.

That Bruce should have espoused the Girls' Guildry rather than Guides or Camp Fire is not surprising given that she herself came from the west coast of Scotland. She was a fervent advocate, arguing that even in areas where Girl Guides were strong, there was a place for the Girls' Guildry; "the Guides themselves say that the Guildry can reach and help girls to whom Guiding makes no appeal".[59] But she does not tell us who these girls were and why Guildry succeeded where the Guides failed.

The movement features most importantly in the Maudsley books.[60] But although Nancy and her friends are keen Guildry Maids, Bruce makes it clear that the role of middle-class girls within the organisation was largely missionary. A distinction is drawn between the leaders (and those destined to be leaders, like Nancy) and the led — the rank and file. In a movement which aimed to reduce class differences, Bruce really only identified with her bourgeois heroines. In one of her articles in the *Lamp*, Bruce's plea for more women to come forward as Guardians included the remark, "there is actually one perfectly good slum Company, complete in every particular except an officer".[61] In her fiction, the point is most forcibly exemplified in *Dimsie Intervenes* (1937). Here Erica Innes, former Head Girl of the Jane Willard Foundation, sets up a Guildry company for the local girls, gets the rector's daughter to run it and asks her girlfriends to "take a kindly interest" in it. She observes that:

If I'm to be a politician some day, as I hope and intend, I've got to learn something about social work, and naturally I'm interested in girls. They learn order and discipline and self-control in the Guildry, and to go to church on Sundays . . .[62]

CAMP FIRE

Many writers for girls wrote about Camp Fire, but in Britain it was dearest to the heart of Elsie J. Oxenham. *A School Camp Fire*, her first novel on the subject, was published in 1917. Dedicated "To the girls who sit with me around the Camp Fire . . . with love and all best wishes from their Guardian", it was to be followed over the next 20 years by 13 more stories in which Camp Fire was central to the plot, as well as several in which it played a subsidiary role.

Oxenham set her fictional Camp Fires in Sussex, Oxfordshire, Wales and even Switzerland; yet for all her allegiance to things English and folk, this favourite movement was an American idea, whose lineage went back no further than 1912. Camp Fire set out to provide girls of 12 to 18 with "romance, beauty and adventure in everyday life, and to make the homely task contribute to the joy of everyday living".[63] What this meant was that girls worked towards honours in specified useful subjects, as in Guildry and Guides; and that among the seven categories of "Craft", the first was labelled "Home". (The others were Health, Camp, Hand, Nature, Business and Patriotism, later retitled Citizenship.) The honours were not badges, as in Guides, but beads of different colours, which were strung on leather thongs around the wearer's neck. The beads went with the Camp Fire "uniform", which was based on the dress of the native American, partly as a concession to the national heritage of the movement. The fact that it had no real basis in native American culture made it no more irrelevant when transplanted to Britain.

The founders of Camp Fire, Dr Luther H. Gulick and his wife, expressed the firm belief that men and women were inherently different and that society benefited most when those differences were recognised and catered to, not diminished. For this reason alone, "to copy the Boy Scout movement would be utterly and fundamentally evil". Girls should be encouraged to be "womanly", and for the Gulicks that meant domestic.

> The bearing and rearing of children has always been the first duty of most women, and that must always continue to be. This involves service, constant service, self-forgetfulness and always service.[64]

When they expounded their ideal of service, however, it was not confined (as was Lord Baden-Powell's, for example) to service of husband and children.

> Teach her the possibility of leading other girls — one of the greatest services that she can render ... Try to teach the girls how to do for other girls what has been done for them ... The factory girls, for instance, the city girls, the country girls.[65]

In Oxenham's novels the Abbey girls also exemplify this ideal of leading girls less fortunate than themselves; and though only Maidlin (the dreamy, sensitive one) joins Camp Fire, she does it for this very reason — as a service to the village girls.[66]

Alongside service, another womanly ideal which

Camp Fire fostered was "beauty". Gulick argued that throughout history, "beauty has been in the custody of women", and that it likewise deserved a place in public life. But its espousal had a pragmatic purpose too:

> Teach the old folk lore, the old folk dances, the old customs, sometimes dancing and singing by night about a fire — have that combined effect upon the senses, and you can make people over in the process and do it pretty quickly.[67]

This stunningly cynical observation makes it clear that Gulick envisaged Camp Fire as a form of social engineering — admittedly, not such a dirty word then as it is now — by seducing its victims with ritual and romance.

The Gulicks articulated a feminine version of a theme familiar in the closing years of the preceding century, that industrialisation had created an alienated workforce, deprived of beauty, variety and the opportunity to make meaningful human relationships. "So monotonous is the daily work in the shop, school, or home, that some inner vision is needed to show the real beauty that is back of daily work." The increased employment of women and girls, they felt, was taking women away from the secure home environment with its ready-made social circle, and nothing had replaced it.

> The net result is loneliness. It is not enough to provide things to do. Somehow or other the opportunity which we now lack for affection, friendship, comradeship, must be given; it is as basic as hunger . . . It is necessary to have games, and to camp out, and to build up better celebrations and a thousand different things, good in themselves,

but the main significance of which is the human relations that are established in the process of doing things that we like, and having common experiences which we share.[68]

With these words, Dr Gulick got closer to the true meaning of these organisations for girls than any of the pious exponents of women's role. In the end, it did not matter what you did in Guildry, Guides or Camp Fire, although naturally there was pride in doing something you believed was worthwhile. What really mattered was that you were doing it with other girls and women who became your friends.

Where Camp Fire differed from Guildry and Guides was in its avoidance of the quasi-military aspects of the other organisations. There was no drill in Camp Fire, no organised team-work; co-operation and "disciplined individuality" were preferred as more in keeping with the feminine temperament.[69] Though couched in anti-feminist terms, these ideas prefigure the view held by many feminists today that women's pacific, co-operative methods of organising are better than men's, as we have experienced them. Unlike the Girl Guides, Camp Fire could not be seen as a feminised (and implicitly inferior) form of a movement devised for boys; it had its own expressly feminine philosophy underpinning its esoteric symbolism, ceremony and organisation.

By 1925, Camp Fire had spread to 21 countries, and 600,000 girls had passed through its ranks. It had also spawned several sets of novels in the United States. In *Ven at Gregory's* (1925), Barbara declares: "I get every Camp Fire yarn I can get hold of, English or American."[70] Elinor Brent-Dyer, a keen fan of Elsie Oxenham's work, paid homage to Camp

Fire in the opening scene of *The Chalet School Wins the Trick* (1961), where Rosalie Dene surprises Audrey and her friends in the process of making a camp fire on the Chalet School's cricket pitch. We learn later that Audrey has always longed to be a Guide, but because the meetings take place on Friday nights after school and would involve a long walk home in the dark, her parents refuse to allow her to join. When an American mistress comes to the school on exchange, a Camp Fire is planned, with meetings on Saturday mornings which Audrey could attend; but "then we had to come to Switzerland because of Dad and I'm out of it all".

> She had read every book about Camp Fire on which she could lay hands, including some half-dozen of Elsie Oxenham's stories. She remembered that in one three girls had begun a private camp of their own, since there was not enough of them to form an official camp. She had decided to try to get up the same sort of thing out here . . . [71]

The book in question was evidently Oxenham's *The School Torment* (Chambers, 1920), which — given that it was 40 years old and long out of print — seems an unusual book for Audrey, a modern young woman, to have been reading.

Elsie Oxenham also wrote several books which focused on the Guides, notably the series about Jinty; and several about schools which had both Guides and Camp Fire, including *The School of Ups and Downs* (1918), *Patience Joan, Outsider* (1922) and *The Crisis in Camp Keema* (1928). The lengthy comparisons and rivalries indulged in by members of the respective organisations make these among the most interesting of her books. It's probably fair to say that, of the two, she was temperamentally most in sympathy with Camp Fire; but the argument as to their individual merits eventually runs out of steam when the reader grasps that all these organisations are essentially the same in their aims and their effects on girls. Guides, Camp Fire and Guildry were all amalgams of ideals both progressive and reactionary for women. Like the school stories in which they featured, they promoted an anti-feminist message about women's nature and role; yet, like the stories, they could also have a liberating effect.

A MIXED MESSAGE

Each of the crafts or skills or achievements for which awards were given in the various organisations can be interpreted as both good and bad for women. "Home Craft", for example, was expressed in terms which exemplified the general trend in society to extend domestic knowledge throughout the female population, equipping middle-class girls as well as their social inferiors with the necessary skills in the face of a declining servant population. In Guildry and Guides, girls won badges for every conceivable aspect of housework and childcare (for example, recognising three different sorts of baby's cry); Camp Fire gave beads for the same. Camp Fire's shameless glorification of the most tedious tasks was particularly insidious:

> The work of the home, if it be only the washing of dishes or the making of beds, is dignified and made interesting by being made worthy of recognition and praise when it is well done. The awarding of "honour" beads for doing these tasks well not only keeps them from becoming

humdrum and sordid, but it also clothes them in romance, and stimulates new interest.[72]

The effect was to school future wives and mothers in tasks which a patriarchal society wished to ensure they would continue to carry out in adulthood — but then, of course, without reward. In trying to make women's domestic role more attractive, all three movements were in tune with the anti-feminist drive to get women back into the home after the First World War. On the other hand, all three showed by rewarding it that women's work *is* work and deserves public recognition.

Health, too, another ideal common to all three, had its positive side: the prioritisation, at last, of girls' right to grow up as strong and fit and free as boys. But the negative side is not far to seek; the new science of eugenics, with its emphasis on the purity of the "race" and its need for healthy mothers to carry it on, underpinned all the strictures on exercise, diet and so on.

And if the idea of Guides and Camp Fire was to turn young women into good wives and mothers of men, the reality was to cement the bonds between women.

> As faggots are brought from the forest,
> Firmly held by the sinews which bind them,
> I will cleave to my Camp Fire Sisters,
> Wherever, whenever I find them.[73]

History has shown that girls and women have repeatedly taken control of movements intended to ensure their subordination and have been able to use them for their own ends. We all negotiate within the social, physical and practical constraints placed upon us. In contrast to the Victorian period, when young women were restricted to relationships within the patriarchal family, the Guildry Maids, Guides and Camp Fire girls of the first half of the 20th century enjoyed a sense of community and "sisterhood" outside the actual control of men, which allowed them to subvert the patriarchal ideology of the movements for their own ends.

Leadership was an important element in sisterhood. Torch Bearers in Camp Fire, Patrol Leaders in Guides, Maids in Waiting in Guildry existed not to rule over but to lead the way so that "your younger sisters may follow in your steps".[74] "The Guide movement was very popular with schools in the first half of the century as a method of teaching leadership," runs the caption to a photograph of "Early Girl Guides at St James's, West Malvern" in Gillian Avery's history of girls' independent schools, *The Best Type of Girl* (1991).[75] The stories of famous women served as models to those seeking to emulate them.

For single woman in particular — and there were more single women in Britain in 1921 than ever before[76] — the skills learnt and qualities developed in girls' schools and organisations fitted them excellently for participation in adult women's groups like the Women's Institutes and, in addition, for leadership of girls in schools, Guides, Guildry or Camp Fire. In Elsie Oxenham's Abbey books, the "Writing Person" confides to Joy and Jen about the women at the English Folk Dance Society's evening classes that:

> If you talk to them for long, you find they have "girls" in the background . . . Sometimes it's the children in their day-school classes; most of them are teachers, of course. But very often it's big girls, Guides, or a club, or Guildry, girls to whom

they're teaching folk-dancing in the evenings, mostly just for the love of it.[77]

Sisterhood also meant service. However condescending its expression, the reality of carrying out one's duty to those less fortunate than oneself brought many middle-class young ladies into contact with the way the rest of society lived, as they would perhaps never have done otherwise. The interwar years in Britain mark the move away from Victorian notions of philanthropy towards the principles of social welfare. That women played an important part in the shift may well have been due, in part, to the girls' movements and the ideas and practical experience that they gave their members.

Finally, "Love is comradeship".[78] All three movements fostered the ideal of friendship, the love of girls for their girl friends and of women for their women friends. Camp Fire with its greater tolerance of emotion provided most scope for the explicit expression of this. Here, for example, is Elsie Oxenham describing the Guardian's ceremonial dress in *The Crisis in Camp Keema* (1928):

> Across her forehead was a band of green beads, and woven into it was a white glittering pathway with little diamond designs, which stood for people, and which were in couples, as signs of friendship. In the front were two triangular Indian figures of women, hand in hand; a row of these, stencilled in various colours, encircled her skirt, all with joined hands.[79]

Here were the symbols of friendship, in pairs and rows, the true motivating force behind all the girls' organisations.

THE DECLINE AND THE ACHIEVEMENT

By 1954, when Elinor Brent-Dyer dropped Guides from her Chalet School stories, girls' organisations seemed to be in decline. In the late 1930s and during the war many countries replaced them with national youth organisations, and there was even talk of doing this in Britain. Camp Fire ceased altogether in Britain at about the same time (I do not know exactly when), though it still exists in the United States in an attenuated form, appealing to much younger girls.[80] Other movements began to lose their hold on older girls. As far as the Guides were concerned, membership levels did not really fall as much as one might have expected; the real problem was one of image.

> With the dawn of the 1960s a murmuring that had been heard for some time grew to a crescendo. The question was being asked loud and clear "Is the Movement out of date?" Statistics did not appear to support the view that Guiding was old-fashioned as numbers were creeping up year by year . . . The great British public, however, were slow to appreciate the fact that Guiding had been progressing steadily if unspectacularly for many years. "You don't mean to tell me the Guides are still going? How interesting! You tie knots, don't you?"[81]

What *is* very clear is that the move towards "social realism" in children's literature, which was anti-middle class and anti-single sex, led to fewer and fewer stories about girls' organisations being published after the Second World War, as a glance at the catalogues of second-hand dealers in children's literature will reveal.[82] Guildry's literary spokeswoman, Dorita Fairlie Bruce, gave up both her involvement in the movement and writing about it when she retired to Scotland in 1949.[83] Elsie Oxenham's interest in Guides and Camp Fire waned somewhat earlier when she married off her Abbey girls Joy (who previously, as a young widow, had been a Ranger Captain) and Maidlin (a Camp Fire Guardian).[84] Neither organisation features in the three books she published between 1954 and her death in 1959, though to be fair the action in the two last Abbey books focuses on her own fictional girls' association, the Hamlet Club.[85]

Guide stories endured longer than stories about any other girls' organisation. But while a number of novels with a Guiding theme appeared in the 1950s and 1960s (and stories with a Brownie theme into the late 1980s), together with annuals, magazines and diaries, still, the heyday of the genre had passed. Critics must agree that little of this postwar literature matches the classics of Dorothea Moore, May Wynne, Ethel Talbot, Christine Chaundler, Winifred Darch, Mrs Osborn Hann, Catherine Christian et al, dating from just before the First World War to just after the Second. A novel like Kevin McGarry's *Blue Goose East* (World Distributors, 1965), for example, one of a series about a "World Guide" called Marty who travels the world in company with her father, a Special Agent for the British government, is realms away from the Guide stories of Elinor Brent-Dyer and Elsie Oxenham. It's not a bad book, but not only is it apparently written by a man, it involves a lone girl, of necessity separated from her patrol, staying with three boy cousins (for whom she does all the cooking), while helping them to solve a thrilling mystery in Cape Cod. This kind of family-based, mixed-sex adventure tale (which Elinor Brent-Dyer herself tried her hand at, following the prevailing fashion, in her *Fardingales* and *Chudleigh Hold* series in the 1950s) illustrates the post-war reaction against the idea of a separate literature for girls; but it also represents a clear attempt to modernise the image of an organisation which was suffering from its single-sex status.

In recent times, the Guides have removed the word "Girl" from their title to try to attract more older young women and have modernised their uniform. In truth, the Guides remain strong, with three-quarters of a million members in January 1994 (down from 800,000 in 1975), surely because they still offer girls and young women something which is hard to find in other areas of their lives today.[86]

And what is that? The achievement of the girls' organisations lies in the fact that they offered girls an opportunity to undertake meaningful activity, chaperoned by responsible adults and in the apparent service of patriarchal ideals of women's role. So much was intended. What had not, perhaps, been foreseen was the degree of confidence girls gained simply from mastering the tasks set for them and from access to male preserves like camping, para-military uniforms and rituals and the acquisition of "masculine" skills. At the same time they laid claim to their own space, rules, symbols and ceremonies. The girls' organisations were very successful in helping to diminish what had hitherto been seen as "natural" differences between girls and boys in terms of strength, initiative, abilities and interests. They were radical in providing women with leadership roles, models and training.

In short, they gave girls self-assurance, independence and pride in their abilities, qualities which tended to conflict with the notion of women's subordinate role in society, led many to question it and helped some of them to challenge men's dominance. And as this was easier to do in a group than as individuals, the most significant aspect of the girls' organisations was surely the fact that they brought together so many girls and women and gave them a sense of sexual solidarity and common cause as well as an appreciation of and respect for women's nature, abilities and ways of doing things.

This threat to patriarchal society is of course removed when girls are absorbed into mixed organisations or, as is happening with the Scouts and the boys' schools, into boys' organisations on boys' terms. But the process began long ago, as far back as the 1950s and even earlier, when the attack on single-sex institutions began. Girls' schools, girls' clubs, girls' fiction were all called into question, and progressive thinking advocated replacing them with co-education, mixed clubs and so-called uni-sex (in which boys just happened to dominate) children's literature. Girls were encouraged to focus their attention on boys, rather than their girl chums, and friendships among women were subordinated to the higher priority of heterosexual love.

One could hardly claim that Elinor Brent-Dyer fell a total victim to this tendency, as the continued existence of the single-sex Chalet School till her death in 1969 demonstrates. Yet she was not immune to it. Len's mercifully understated love affair with Reg Entwistle and their precipitous engagement, while Len is still at school, may well be seen as a capitulation to the new heterosexual ideal.[87] I suppose it could also be read as a return to past values, since Len's mother married at a relatively young age herself; but Jo had at least seen something of the world and had established herself in a career by the time she decided to settle down with Jack Maynard. Nevertheless, the loss of all-girls' organisations like the Guides goes hand in hand with the greater emphasis on healthy friendships between boys and girls within the extended Maynard family that characterises so many of the Swiss books. The triplets who dress in shorts and wear their hair in pony-tails clearly have no time for old-fashioned pursuits like Guides. Whereas their mother left school and became Lieutenant to the Tiernsee 3rd,[88] Len, Con and Margot are headed for universities and careers. The chain of influence has been broken, as women, gaining greater access to men's world, abandon women's.

That Brent-Dyer valued women's friendships is not in question. When Jo moves to Switzerland she rejoices that she will thenceforth be closer to her three best friends, who live in France, Austria and Swizerland respectively: "they ought to be able to meet much more often now".[89] But the links are now firmly family-based, and the chain of influence, where it exists, lies not from Guider or Guardian to Guide, Guildry Maid or Camp Fire Girl, but from mother to daughter. After 1953, like many people of her time, Brent-Dyer ceased to regard organisations like the Guides as a significant factor in the socialisation of girls. From 1954, again like most people of her time, she came to rely on the family to perform this function, aided and abetted by the school itself — which, isolated in the Swiss Oberland, took on almost the character of an autonomous moral world, and no longer needed Guides.

NOTES

1. *Joey Goes to the Oberland* (1954), p.83.
2. *The Chalet School and Barbara* (1954), p.121.
3. *The School at the Chalet* (1925), p.235.
4. *Jo of the Chalet School* (1926), p.260.
5. Ibid., p.261.
6. Vronwyn M Thompson, *1910 . . . and then? A Brief History of the Girl Guides Association* (Girl Guides Association, 1990), p.12.
7. Helen McClelland, *Behind the Chalet School* (New Horizon, 1981), p.111.
8. Thompson, ibid., p.12.
9. *Friends of the Chalet School Newsletter 22* (Nov. 1993), p.3.
10. *The Princess of the Chalet School* (1927), pp.109-10.
11. Ibid., p.224.
12. *The Rivals of the Chalet School* (1929), p.134.
13. Ibid., pp.164-5.
14. *The Chalet School and Jo* (1931), p.69.
15. Ibid., p.248.
16. *The Rivals of the Chalet School*, p.111.
17. Ibid.
18. *Eustacia Goes to the Chalet School* (1930), p.165.
19. *The Chalet Girls in Camp* (1932), p.90.
20. *The Exploits of the Chalet Girls* (1933), p.273.
21. *The New House at the Chalet School* (1935), p.48.
22. *The New Chalet School* (1938), pp.303-4.
23. *The Chalet School in Exile* (1940), p.142.
24. *The Chalet School In Exile* (1940), pp.227, 286.
25. *The Chalet School Goes to It* (1941), p.75.
26. *Lavender Laughs in the Chalet School* (1943), p.153. "The Robins Make Good" is the title of a story by Elinor M. Brent-Dyer which appeared in *Girls' Own* Vol. 57 — another example of Brent-Dyer's life imitating her art.
27. McClelland, ibid., p.144.

28. *The Highland Twins at the Chalet School* (1942), p.185.
29. Ibid., p.143.
30. Ibid., p.111.
31. *Lavender Laughs in the Chalet School*, pp.57, 142.
32. *Gay from China at the Chalet School* (1944), p.71.
33. *Tom Tackles the Chalet School* (1955), p.30 (first published in *The Second Chalet Book for Girls*, 1947).
34. *The Wrong Chalet School* (1952), p.130.
35. Ibid., pp.129-37.
36. *Changes for the Chalet School* (1953), p.98.
37. McClelland, ibid., p.111.
38. *Challenge for the Chalet School* (1966), p.41.
39. For example, Dorothea Moore, *Terry, the Girl Guide* (Nisbet, 1912).
40. *The Highland Twins at the Chalet School*, p.106.
41. Dorita Fairlie Bruce, *Dimsie Intervenes* (Oxford University Press, 1937), pp.129-30. In this scene, the elderly Miss Carver speaks up for pacifism and internationalism, and against militarism, to be furiously rebuked by schoolgirl Dimsie who takes the jingoistic, pro-military line. Dimsie clearly represents Bruce's own views though, as Cadogan and Craig observe, "In a book written today, Miss Carver's standpoint would be Dimsie's, and vice versa (*You're a Brick, Angela!*, p.186). See also Mary Cadogan and Patricia Craig, *Women and Children First. The Fiction of Two World Wars* (Gollancz, 1978), pp.225-6,235-6.
42. *Jo of the Chalet School*, p.261.
43. In the first issue of *The Chaletian*, editor Daphne Paintin (now Barfoot) recalled (p.1) that when she first went to boarding-school in 1941 she was shocked that "Guide's honour" was even then not taken seriously. "The [Chalet School] books certainly gave me very high standards of honesty which I found, sadly, were not the norm." If Daphne was considered "very odd and rather priggish" for her views, then notions of "Guide's honour" may well have been considered hopelessly old-fashioned a decade and more later.
44. *History Notes* (Girl Guides Association, 1980), pp.27,7.

45. Thompson, ibid., pp.17, 19.
46. *The Rivals of the Chalet School*, p.132.
47. Jack Lambert in *A Leader in the Chalet School* (1961), p.89.
48. Rose Kerr, *The Story of the Girl Guides* (Girl Guides Association, rev.ed., 1937), p.29.
49. Ibid, p.30.
50. Kitty Barne, *Here Come the Girl Guides* (Girl Guides Association, 1946), p.24.
51. Kerr, ibid., p.243; Mary Cadogan and Patricia Craig, *You're a Brick, Angela! A New Look at Girls' Fiction 1839-1975* (Gollancz, 1976), p.155.
52. *The Chalet School and Jo*, p.63.
53. Marion Lochhead, *A Lamp was Lit. The Girls' Guildry through Fifty Years* (1949), p.28.
54. See, for example, the "Camp Fire Girls" books of Hildegard G. Frey, Margaret Love Sanderson and Jane Stewart.
55. *The Chalet Girls in Camp*, p.224.
56. Lochhead, ibid., p.25.
57. See Sheila Fletcher, *Women First. The Female Tradition in English Physical Education 1880-1980* (Athlone Press, 1984), Chap.1.
58. Eva Löfgren, *Schoolmates of the Long-Ago. Motifs and Archetypes in Dorita Fairlie Bruce's Boarding-School Stories* (Symposion Graduale, 1993), pp.96-7.
59. D. F. Bruce, "Adventures in Extension". *Lamp of the Girls' Guildry* (Oct. 1935), p.21.
60. *That Boarding School Girl* (1925), *The New Girl and Nancy* (1926), *Nancy to the Rescue* (1927), *The Best Bat in the School* (1931), *Nancy in the Sixth* (1935), all published by Oxford University Press.
61. D. F. Bruce, "London Extends". *Lamp of the Girls' Guildry* (May 1936), p.21.
62. D. F. Bruce, *Dimsie Intervenes*, p.14.
63. *British Camp Fire Girls Inc.*, (Birkenhead,1925) p.5.
64. Helen Buckler, Mary F. Fiedler and Martha F. Allen, eds., *Wo-He-Lo. The Story of Camp Fire Girls 1910-1960* (Camp Fire Girls, 1961), p.22.
65. Ibid., p.23.
66. Elsie J. Oxenham, *The Abbey Girls Play Up* (Collins,

1930), p.112.
67. *Wo-He-Lo*, p.23.
68. Ibid., pp.39, 37.
69. *British Camp Fire Girls*, p.11.
70. See *British Camp Fire Girls* and E. J. Oxenham, *Ven at Gregory's* (Chambers, 1925), p.191.
71. *The Chalet School Wins the Trick* (1961), pp.31-2.
72. *British Camp Fire Girls*, p.8.
73. *Wo-He-Lo*, p.54; also quoted in E. J. Oxenham, *A School Camp Fire* (Chambers, 1917), p.214, *The Junior Captain* (Chambers, 1923), p.300, and other novels.
74. E. J. Oxenham, *The School of Ups and Downs* (Chambers, 1918), p.172.
75. Gillian Avery, *The Best Type of Girl. A History of Girls' Independent Schools* (Andre Deutsch, 1991), illus. p.11.
76. Census of 1921. The First World War played a significant part in this, but there had been more women than men in Britain since the middle of the 19th century, and a growing reluctance to marry among both men and women as the century progressed. See Rosemary Auchmuty, "Victorian Spinsters" (unpublished Ph. D. thesis, Australian National University, 1975; in the Fawcett Library, London Guildhall University).
77. E. J. Oxenham, *The New Abbey Girls* (Collins, 1923), p.233.
78. E. J. Oxenham, *The Junior Captain*, p.301.
79. E. J. Oxenham, *The Crisis in Camp Keema* (Chambers, 1928), p.103.
80. In *The Abbey Chronicle No. 18* (September 1994), Olga Kendell recounts how, having advertised in her local (Croydon) paper for information about Camp Fire, she met two women who had belonged to a Camp Fire attached to a local Congregational Church until 1939. This, she says, "is the nearest to 'today' I have heard of". As far as American Camp Fire is concerned, I discovered on a visit to the US in 1990 that some of my American cousins had been Camp Fire girls in the 1960s and 1970s, but gave it up (as they claimed all girls did then) when they reached their teens.
81. Alix Liddell, *Story of the Girl Guides 1938-1975* (Girl

Guides Association, 1976), pp.9, 10, 64.
82. Gill Bilski is one dealer who specialises in Guide stories and ephemera.
83. Löfgren, ibid., p.109.
84. E. J. Oxenham, *The Abbey Girls Play Up*.
85. E. J. Oxenham, *Song of the Abbey* (Colllins, 1954) and *Two Queens at the Abbey* (Collins, 1959).
86. *Guardian* 5.1.94, p.2; Liddell, ibid., p.107; "Girl Scouts?" *Good Housekeeping* (Nov. 1990), p.125.
87. *Prefects of the Chalet School* (1970), pp.166-7. It's also possible that Brent-Dyer realised this was to be the last Chalet School book and wanted to settle the destinies of her favourite characters before she died.
88. *The New Chalet School*, p.303.
89. *Joey Goes to the Oberland*, p.62.

MY GOD, IT'S THE HEAD!

JUDITH HUMPHREY

AT the time when most school stories were written, Britain would have defined itself as a Christian country, with religious structures having a much greater cultural importance than is now the case. Religious training for the young was considered essential, chapel was (and is) an integral part of boarding-school life, so it is not surprising that some sort of religious experience is fundamental to many of the texts. This varies from an obligation to make the right noises to a faith which undergirds the whole of the author's life and, therefore, her work as well, and Elinor Brent-Dyer provides a striking example of the latter.

Typically for her time, Brent-Dyer was brought up to be a conscientious church-goer; this is made very clear in her biography, and we have evidence of her membership of the congregations of St Jude's in the Laygate, South Shields, the Church of St Bede's in the same town and of St Francis Xavier's Church in Hereford. However, the fact that her religion is much more than mere form is clear from its great importance in the texts, and Helen McClelland, Brent-Dyer's biographer, has even identified this as one of the reasons for the author's popularity: "the majority of Elinor's readers have quite evidently welcomed and appreciated this religious aspect of the stories".[1] Indeed, religion is present in Brent-Dyer's texts to an extent which has caused great irritation to critics unsympathetic to her beliefs; Mary Cadogan and Patricia Craig state, in their

1976 study of girls' fiction, *You're a Brick, Angela!*, that:

> a serious weakness of the Chalet School series is the religious sentimentality . . . this kind of simplistic Christianity was the logical outcome of the moral function which they [school-story writers] had assigned themselves . . . God, when properly appealed to, will not let anyone down.[2]

For Craig and Cadogan, the attitude to religion is an unforgivable attempt to mislead and delude impressionable readers, but this view is, itself, simplistic in the extreme, overlooking most of what is important about the treatment of religion in the texts. Brent-Dyer's use of religious elements in her writing springs from a deep personal faith, and is expressed with a breadth of view astonishing for her time.

By upbringing an Anglican, she entered the Roman Catholic Church in 1930, but no one reading her books could make even an approximate guess at the date of her conversion. McClelland suggests that contact with the deeply devout Tyrolese Catholics might have influenced Brent-Dyer's outlook and given her a breadth of vision unusual for her time. Whatever the reason, at a time when evangelical Christians regarded the Roman Catholic Church as the Anti-Christ (with the Church of England only one notch better off), and when Roman Catholics were strictly forbidden to join in the services of any other denomination, Brent-Dyer's priests and pastors were fraternising happily, and the vicar in *Fardingales* (1950) even shares his vicarage with a Presbyterian minister. The main characters of the Chalet series are fairly evenly divided between Anglicans and Catholics (for example, Miss

Annersley and Madge Bettany are Protestant, Miss Wilson and Jo are Catholic), and the books themselves range from the specifically evangelical trio *Nesta Steps Out* (1954), *Beechy of the Harbour School* (1955) and *Leader in Spite of Herself* (1956) to *The Little Marie-José* (1932), which, while being an historical novel, deals in very sympathetic terms with the Roman Catholic Church. None of this is surprising in our own ecumenical age, but for its time it was positively startling in its tolerance — and it is worth remembering, too, that while in our own secular philosophical climate tolerance is a virtue, it is frequently seen in church circles as lack of conviction and a tendency to condone sin. To write in this way in such a climate argues a robust courage which is far from sentimental, and the outworking of the religious beliefs of Brent-Dyer's characters is accomplished in terms of a rigorous analysis of faith which never shrinks from the difficult areas.

All this is crystal clear from the most cursory reading of the texts. Less obvious, but of crucial importance, is the way in which the combination of the woman-centred world of the school story and these strong religious elements culminates in perceptions of spiritual possibilities for women which are strikingly unusual and deeply empowering. Many of Brent-Dyer's readers are women of faith, and this is surely one of the reasons for our strong responses to the texts. In order to appreciate fully the function of religion in the work of Elinor Brent-Dyer, it is helpful to see her work in the context of her fellow-writers, for certain basic traits are common to all.

PRAYER IN DESPAIR

For almost every author of girls' school stories, religion is very definitely there; however unorthodox their personal beliefs, it was essential to make the right noises, and God is always in the background, there to help if needed. Angela Brazil, herself a conscientious if pantheistic Anglican, illustrates the principle in many of her books. Muriel and Patty, for example, are dramatically reminded of this background faith when they are threatened with death by drowning (*The Nicest Girl in the School*, 1909). Muriel questions Patty's lack of fear, is reminded by the other girl that God can look after them whatever the circumstances, and joins her in a familiar prayer:

> "Lighten our darkness, we beseech thee, O Lord, and by Thy great mercy defend us from all perils and dangers of this night."
> How often they had repeated the familiar collect in church or at evening prayers in the big schoolroom at The Priory, sometimes with little thought for its meaning; and how different it sounded now in the midst of the real peril and danger that surrounded them.[3]

Mary Louise Parker's Amy and her brother are in trouble of a different kind, but the remedy is the same:

> Judith and I have agreed to remember you and Robert in our prayers every night. You do, too, I expect, and you know there's a text in the Bible about people agreeing to pray about anything and Mummy says God gives us what we ask for if it is for our good. So don't worry, is what she would

say, just trust Him.[4]

For these authors, prayer is very much a last resort. They presumably meant what they said — it would be unwarrantable to suppose otherwise — but prayer is only a support in trouble. It is in no way integral to the life of the characters, and the deletion of the above passages would certainly make no difference to the rest of the book. Turning to God in desperation is neither an uncommon nor an unrealistic reaction — Elinor Brent-Dyer's Jo and Grizel also use the "Lighten Our Darkness" collect as they enter the caves where the madman has hidden Cornelia in *The Head Girl of the Chalet School* (1928) — but Dorita Fairlie Bruce, herself a devout and committed Christian, highlights in her books the lack of impact of this very formalised and peripheral religion. The younger girls at Jane's are only too eager to escape the chapel ritual; indeed Molly, plaiting her hair to make it curl, rejoices in the prospect that it might "frizz":

> "Perhaps she'll say it's so bad I musn't go to church," said Molly hopefully. "She might, you know. And I've got such a lovely book out of the Junior library."[5]

The same girls pray fervently during Dimsie's illness later in the book, but again this is little more than desperation. Indeed, in *Captain of Springdale* (1932), Peggy is bitterly attacked by her fellow-seniors for taking seriously Sunday's sermon and applying it to the very undesirable atmosphere in the school; her attempts to relate theology to everyday life are seen as embarrassing and almost shocking.

Church was church and school was school, and people didn't mix them — except the Head in her Scripture lessons, and even that was held by some to be taking an unfair advantage. To be kindly affectioned one to another didn't mean that you were not to criticize people's peculiarities, or try to find out what they'd done to be deprived of a prefectship.[6]

This attitude is very different from Elinor Brent-Dyer's. Certainly her girls find it difficult to talk to others about their deep faith. Mary-Lou, when called upon to justify her faith, "made a big effort... for she was speaking of things that lay deep down and she rarely talked of them, even to her nearest and dearest"[7], and Rosemary, in *Leader in Spite of Herself*, has to force herself to encourage younger girls to pray for an unpleasant classmate: "Rosemary flushed, but she knew now what she must say and though she found it hard, she spoke up sturdily".[8] When the girls do challenge their school fellows, however, there is always a positive response and a basic acceptance of their credo, which is not found in Dorita Fairlie Bruce's arguably more realistic approach. Very similar to Peggy's situation is Rosemary's attempt to impress on her juniors the link between their religious observance and the reality of their everyday lives:

Here you've just come from church. We had a sermon on love and on trying to imitate the way Christ was a Friend to all His friends, and you deliberately propose to treat another girl in the most unfriendly way anyone could imagine!

The reaction to this is not embarrassment or horror, but a schoolgirl equivalent of conviction and repentance — "she had given them plenty to think about. No more was ever heard of that wonderful plan".[9]

BORN AGAIN CHRISTIANS

Obviously if religion is to mean anything at all, it must be more than a socially acceptable external form, and the opposite extreme is provided by a group of authors of evangelical beliefs, with the emphasis on personal contact with God in repentance and conversion. This is certainly a much more fundamental and challenging human experience; unfortunately, however true the message, it is a sad fact that the vast majority of books of this type are unbelievably dreadful. They are written expressly to convert, and the message matters much more than the book, with the inevitable result that the plot is trivial and the characters incredible.

Elinor Brent-Dyer herself made at least token gestures in this direction. *Nesta Steps Out*, *Beechy of the Harbour School* and *Leader in Spite of Herself* were written for Oliphants, a religious press, and my own copies of *Nesta* and *Leader* were given respectively as prizes for Sunday School attendance and for gaining the highest number of points at a Girls' Brigade camp. The Sunday School in question was at the Glad Tidings Gospel Hall, an Assemblies of God Church in Hull, and certainly nothing which was not impeccably evangelical would have found its way into such an establishment. However, Brent-Dyer was incapable of producing a mere tract and, although the religious content of the books is certainly less diluted than in the Chalet series, it is expressed in very human terms of girls struggling for victory over their own negative characteristics. Nesta has to overcome a violent temper, Rosemary her diffidence and shyness, while Beechy has both to come to terms with the death of her mother and conquer her reluctance to own publicly her new-found faith. These can hardly be counted as Brent-Dyer's most successful books, yet she still keeps within the bounds of believable and involving characterisation.

In contrast, Dorothy Dennison, a fairly prolific author in this field, provides a graphic illustration of the principle that the worth of the book varies in direct proportion to its evangelistic message. Miss Dennison is a very competent writer, both humorous and realistic, and her *Rebellion of the Upper Fifth* (1919) is a delightful account of a mistress's battle with a form who idolised her predecessor and are unwilling to accept her. It is both funny and true, the situation is well-controlled and the characters live, but it is noticeable that the evangelistic content, though present, is very slight. Sliding down the scale a little is *Rival Schools at Trentham* (1923); the humour is still in evidence, and the girls' lofty ideals of social service are brought down to earth with a satisfying bump by aggresssive children and parents who grab all that they can get and then complain about it, leaving the girls in a "disturbed state of disillusionment". In this book, however, the message is more strongly given, and Marigold, the heroine, reaches the perfection seemingly inseparable from committed Christianity. Marvellously popular and sporting, Marigold has been at the school only a few weeks before she retrieves the fortunes of the netball team:

> For when the whistle sounded time, against the one goal scored by Ravenscourt, there were twenty-six scored by Tudor House. And of these, twenty had been scored by Marigold Marshall . . . By the time Marigold Marshall had been at Tudor

House a month, she was the most popular girl in the school . . . [She] was elected a member of the first netball team, and also showed signs of easily getting in the first hockey eleven.[10]

It is only fair to add that it is Marigold's insistence on attending a Bible Class with girls from the school which is Tudor House's bitter rival that almost shakes this happy state of affairs. She is even sent to Coventry for a while, but her Christian forbearance triumphs, and the episode ends in the wholesale conversion of the hockey team! For the most part, Marigold remains completely lifeless, a puppet of doctrine — and one does wonder whether it is absolutely necessary for every child who becomes a committed Christian to become an overseas missionary!

Miss Dennison's books are noticeably better the further away she strays from her message, but she is still amongst the best of the post-Victorian evangelical authors. Dennison was writing in the 1920s, and several of her Victorian predecessors show genuine and deep insight into the spiritual thought-processes of young girls[11], but by the 1950s the standard is consistently low, reaching rock-bottom in the books of Helen Humphries. The heroine of *Prudence Goes Too Far* (1966) declares:

> My Dad could not make me do what I did not want to do, and you are only a servant in my Grandfather's house. Ha, ha, wasn't it funny to hear Grandfather on the rampage about those hot water taps, and it was such an easy thing to do, mph, they are just made for japing . . .[12]

After nearly 130 pages in this vein, one feels that Prudence cannot go far enough.

It is ironic that authors who are attempting to give their readers something of fundamental and eternal importance cannot do so in terms of ordinary experience or even language. Humphries' Margaret (e.g. *Margaret the Rebel*, 1957) who also, inevitably, becomes a missionary, prays for help before an important hockey match: "ere the game started she lifted her heart to her Heavenly Father for His help and strength for this task now before her".[13] Praying for help in an everyday task is fair enough, but one doubts whether a 14-year-old is really likely to do so in Authorized Version English.

This removal of religious experience from the plane of everyday existence is inexcusable in authors who claim that such experience is the mainspring of life, and sadly must do much more harm than good to the message they are trying to convey. We have already seen that Brent-Dyer's specifically evangelical books do not evade reality in this way, but it is interesting that they, too, were published in the 1950s. All the texts give the impression of dating from an earlier period, and this was doubtless part of a rearguard action as children's literature became much more secular and as the country moved into the "permissive" and anti-church 1960s.

FAITH FOR LIVING

By far the most successful authors are those who can be classified as religious writers only in the sense that a relationship with God is so fundamental to their lives that it cannot avoid being reflected in their work, and who think, not in terms of theological formulae, but of a living relationship with a real person. Dorita Fairlie Bruce, Elsie Oxenham and Elinor Brent-Dyer all come into this category; none of these authors is writing solely to put forward a message, but their own deeply held convictions about the meaning of life are inevitably present in their books. The faith of all these women is certainly simple; simplistic, however, it is not, as religious concepts are rigorously analysed. There is also absolute commitment, and this is worked out in the texts in the reaction of the characters to difficult and distressing events in their own lives.

Elinor Brent-Dyer's Mary-Lou Trelawney is comforted after the death of her mother by the words of Job quoted by Miss Annersley, her former Headmistress: "though He slay me, yet will I trust Him"[14]; and several of the major characters symbolize their total self-giving concretely. Robin Humphries becomes a nun, Margot Maynard a medical missionary and when, in *The New House at the Chalet School* (1935), the girls hear that a former pupil, Luigia de Ferrara, has entered a convent, "it seemed to her [Jo] that if some of the elder ones had husbands and children, Luigia had taken an even greater step forward than they".[15] It might be noted that this taking of the veil in no way implies a sentimental retreat from life — Luigia eventually dies, with others of her order, in a Nazi concentration camp.

This deeply rooted faith is expressed very much in relation to the practicalities of everyday living. This is reflected even in fictional churches, for the ideal is always "a short service with plenty of hymns and a ten-minutes' sermon full of common sense"![16] Both Dorita Fairlie Bruce and Elinor Brent-Dyer speak of God, and relationships with him, in terms which, particularly for their generation, are startlingly down-to-earth. The former's Desda Blackett declares that:

There are occasions when a sense of common decency and good manners should drive one to church, if all higher motives are missing. The Lord puts us under such tremendous obligations that we have to do something in return, however small.[17]

God is a friend and should be treated with common courtesy, and Brent-Dyer frequently uses the concept of being "rude to God". When in *Joey and Co. in Tirol* (1960), Ruey Richardson attempts to go to bed after a day without saying her prayers, Len Maynard remarks:

as for prayers, you must please yourself, but I think you'll be jolly ungrateful if you don't even say a "Thank you" to God after the decent time you've had today. Rotten bad manners, I call it![18]

For these writers and their characters, religion is deeply related to ordinary life — God is not merely there to call on when balanced on a precipice or drowning in a cave. Because the books contain adventure elements, characters do land themselves in such predicaments, and certainly pray for help when in danger, but their faith is also very much involved in the fabric of everyday living. Miss Annersley, the Headmistress of Brent-Dyer's Chalet School, prays before tackling difficult pupils[19], and Mary-Lou Trelawney, soon to be Head Girl of the school, does likewise before trying to help Jessica, a younger girl, to face her stepsister's imminent death.[20] Even the treatment of erring pupils follows the theologically impeccable path of realisation of wrongdoing leading to repentance and ultimate forgiveness. Elsie Oxenham's Mary Devine struggles to bring her life into line with God's will[21], and Dorita Fairlie Bruce's Nancy discourses at some length on predestination and fatalism[22]; but these abstract theological problems, however fascinating to adults, are hardly likely to grip or inspire a child.

Brent-Dyer's strength in this area is that she can talk of profound subjects in concrete, illustrative terms which a child can appreciate. Jo Maynard, for example, encourages her stormy daughter, Margot, to fight her "devil" in terms of tennis practice:

> every time you give in to the devil, you're making it easier and easier for him to talk to you and coax you into doing things even when you know them to be wrong. It's like practising your tennis. When you first began, you couldn't get a ball over the net unless you stood quite close to it. But you worked at it and now you can get it over quite well, even from the back line. Do you see? . . . Whichever you practise hardest now, you'll go on doing when you're older.[23]

Again, when Mary-Lou is trying to explain to jealous Jessica that real love is willing to share, she uses very down-to-earth biblical examples, reminding the girl how the first reaction of the disciples to gaining the Lord's friendship was to go and tell their friends about him:

> when Christ made friends all round . . . did the Apostles go sulking round about it and say and think He ought to be satisfied with them? . . . they were maddest with the people who wouldn't have anything to do with Him — like those Samaritans that James and John wanted to call down fire from Heaven on.[24]

Because of their trust in a God who is involved in

every part of life, these authors can deal with difficult and sometimes untouchable subjects. Death, a difficult concept for post-Victorian children, is never ignored, but the attitude towards it is one of utmost confidence. Bruce's Triffeny refuses to go and look at her dead great-aunt:

> I'd hate you to think me unfeeling or anything but you see — I just don't believe in death — especially where Great-aunt is concerned. She was always so extremely alive, and she is still, only now she's quite well and happy and able for all the new experiences she has gone into. I can't help feeling that — that what's lying there is just the old clothes she's slipped out of . . . We care for them because she has worn them, but otherwise they are of no great importance now.[25]

Elinor Brent-Dyer even allows the occasional character to contemplate suicide — only to reject the idea firmly as cowardice. In the Chalet series, Grizel Cochrane is returning home from New Zealand deeply depressed, as the man she loves has married her best friend, and wanting only oblivion:

> "Oh, sometimes I wish I could just go to sleep and never wake up again!"
> Her lips thinned to a straight line and her eyes were very sombre. Then she relaxed, firmly pushing to the back of her mind the thoughts which had given rise to the wish. No help was to be found that way, and though she was bitterly unhappy just then, she would never have done anything to attain that rest. Grizel Cochrane had too much in her for that.[26]

The fact that suicide is a coward's way out is

emphasised by Godfrey's attitude when he is captured by natives in *The Condor Crags Adventure* (1954). He is allowed to contemplate making an escape attempt so that the natives will shoot him with their poisoned arrows, thus killing him more quickly (a "quick if agonizing death"!), but he will not consider suicide — 'I may be all sorts of a fool, but I'm not a funk!'"[27]

PROBLEMS OF FAITH

Very few problems of faith are ignored. Jo Maynard has to battle with the relationship between faith and healing when her youngest daughter is critically ill with polio, and the reality of grief and anxiety is acknowledged. When Miss Annersley tries to comfort Jo with the reminder, "Don't despair. Phil is in God's hands. She *could* not be safer," the distressed mother can only reply, "I know, but it's not a lot of comfort at this moment."[28]

Again it is Jo who has to try and reconcile human suffering with her belief in a loving God when she meets a woman of her own age who is in constant pain from acute rheumatism (*Jo to the Rescue*, 1945); and these are all questions to which there is no easy answer, nor is one suggested. The principle is always that of "going deep", of thinking through one's beliefs and working towards true understanding rather than superficial acceptance, and Brent-Dyer is certainly not alone in this, though the subjects she deals with are usually more profoundly disturbing than those of her fellow-writers.

In Kathleen McLeod's *Julia of Sherwood School* (1947), the girls are praying about the election of prefects:

Rhoda prayed very earnestly that Julia and Hilary might be chosen. She owned to the others that she had put the election in her prayers.

"It will be awkward if somebody else is asking God to let Addie Baron or someone else be chosen," said Sunny, trying to face a problem that has puzzled and distressed wiser folk than junior school-girls.[29]

The above-mentioned Triffeny finds the same problem when she prays to win a competition:

Up till that morning she had prayed for success, and then she had suddenly stopped, silenced by some vague confused idea that it wasn't, perhaps, quite playing the game to ask for special favours under the circumstances. Triffeny did not find prayer an easy matter; she felt it couldn't be if one thought about it at all.[30]

None of this can be classed as sentimental, and the analysis continues into areas of emotional difficulty. Forgiveness, for example, despite its cosy sound, is sometimes very difficult for human beings to achieve, and its treatment by Elinor Brent-Dyer is searching and austere. In *A Genius at the Chalet School* (1956), Nina Rutherford, a very talented and dedicated pianist, has her wrist injured because of the clumsiness and carelessness of another girl. Nina totally refuses to forgive the penitent Hilda, and is taken to task by her Headmistress:

[Nina] had no pity for Hilda's real unhappiness and all the Head could get out of her was a sullen, "It serves her right if she's miserable. She was warned and she didn't bother to remember. I can't practise and I couldn't have my lesson this morning."

"There are more important things than music, even," Miss Annersley said sternly — "I hope, until you feel differently about Hilda, you won't try to say Our Father, Nina. Have you ever thought what a terrible condemnation of yourself you are calling down if you ask to be forgiven your trespasses exactly as you forgive those of others? Think that over, please, and ask God to give you the grace of pity."[31]

Brent-Dyer's faith was too deep for her to be able to ignore its implications in any context and, on a rather lighter note, she is the only author to find a conflict between her beliefs and one of her plots. *The Highland Twins at the Chalet School* (1942) is set during the war, and, during the course of the book, Jo Maynard's husband is reported missing. Fiona, one of the twins of the title, has the Celtic power of second sight and suggests using this to bring Jo news of Jack. Brent-Dyer was no whit concerned with the credibility of this, but she was worried that it was wrong from a religious viewpoint. Ultimately she compromises by keeping the action going, but providing a touchstone in the person of Miss Wilson, the Deputy Head, who is disgusted by the whole proceeding:

> In a few words the Head explained, and "Bill's" face grew disapproving. "I don't like it, Hilda. It's meddling with powers best left alone."

Miss Annersley, with very uncharacteristic lack of logic, claims that she also disapproves, but is willing to try anything to bring comfort to Jo. Miss Wilson reluctantly agrees, but with caveats, which were designed to ensure that none of Brent-Dyer's impressionable readers rushed out to emulate the proceedings:

> Well, on your head be it, then. But I don't agree with it at all . . . you will forbid it for the future, won't you, Hilda? I do feel it's wrong . . . I've got a "free" for the next two periods, so I'll go to my room and say a rosary for Jo and Jack. And that's better than any amount of "seeing", even if it is second sight.[32]

FAITH IN A POST-CHRISTIAN SOCIETY

We now live in a post-Christian society, where church-going is no longer the acceptable social norm, where traditional moral values are not necessarily accepted and where Christianity is no longer the major cultural medium (many children are completely ignorant even of the basic Bible stories which their grandparents took for granted); and it is interesting to see how Elinor Brent-Dyer, the only author whose long writing life spanned the divide, adapts to this.

In the major part of the Chalet series, certainly before the 1950s, basic Christianity is the norm and is referred to only fleetingly, but as the social climate changes, the religious element in the books becomes much more specifically stated. By the 1960s several girls have arrived at the Chalet School with no religious background or interest, and they and the school regard each other with mutual incomprehension. The decision of Naomi Elton's aunt to let the girl decide on her own religious affiliations "caused a hubbub in the Staffroom, for such an arrangement had never before been heard of at the Chalet School"[33], and Mary-Lou has never before met an unbaptized person!

In 1960 Len Maynard is trying to persuade Ruey Richardson to say her prayers before going to bed, but Ruey, though ready enough to oblige, does not know how to pray.

> Religion had meant very little in her life so far. It had been rather a shock to her when she saw Len kneel down, night after night. It had been quite as much of a shock to Len to see Ruey tumble into bed without . . . Ruey mumbled the Lord's Prayer to herself and followed it up with a somewhat incoherent word or two of thanks for her new clothes and the new friends. That done, she remained kneeling, wondering what more she could say. She could find nothing, but she stayed there until Len got up. Then she rose too, and gave her friend a grin.
> "I hope you're satisfied now?" she remarked.[34]

Ruey needs very little persuasion to take her beliefs more seriously, but Naomi Elton (*Trials for the Chalet School*, 1959) has actively rejected God, after being lamed in a fire which also killed her parents, and the book is largely concerned with her journey back to faith. It is Mary-Lou Trelawney who has to cope with Naomi's "I don't believe in God. Or if He really is there, then He just doesn't care," and it is her staunch faith, even under difficult and dangerous circumstances, which impresses the other girl.

The thesis of the book is finally unconvincing, for Naomi makes a bargain with God — if she is healed, she will believe. New treatment does make it possible for her to receive medical help, but this is surely one of the worst bases for faith. Nevertheless, the attempt at grappling with lack of faith is an interesting one; it is unique even for Miss

Brent-Dyer, and would have been unthinkable earlier in the series.

Naomi's ultimate return to faith is inevitable, but this is not a facile bowing to the establishment. For the author and others like her, it was unthinkable that anyone should be left in the misery and loneliness of refusing to take the comfort and support offered by God. Mary-Lou takes charge on the basis of "how could anyone bearing the disabilities she [Naomi] did go through life without some help, and who could give it but God?", and this is very much the feeling of the author.[35]

IS GOD A MAN?

Whatever the attitude of individual authors, they unite in accepting the premise of a male God, male priests and a male-oriented theology, with apparently no awareness that this might pose any problem at all for women. Much work has been done by feminist theologians over the last century demonstrating the silencing and absorption of women even by the male language of theology as woman becomes "the silent Other of the symbolic order"[36], and there have been many attempts to cope with the difficulties.

Some, like Phyllis Trible and Mary Evans, have tried to reinterpret and reclaim biblical texts, emphasising the inadequacies of past translations and the woman-affirming structures within the texts.[37] Others, such as Elizabeth Cady Stanton, Rosemary Radford Ruether and Elisabeth Fiorenza, have espoused a more radical rereading, attempting to "bring to bear the whole force of the feminist critique upon biblical texts and religion" and to "denounce all texts and traditions that perpetrate and legitimate oppressive patriarchal structures and ideologies".[38] Some have found that the attempt leaves them outside the Church altogether; Mary Daly has rejected orthodox theology for a spirituality based on more ancient forms of women-centred worship[39], and for Daphne Hampson, "women are disrupted in their worship by the masculinity of the religion to the point that it ceases to be for them a vehicle through which they can love God".[40]

Men have been associated with that which is above, spiritual and like God, whereas women have been associated with that which is below, of the earth, sexual and unlike God, and this inferiority is the basis of difference and of the violently anti-woman premises of the early church fathers.

Woman is deprived of both Word and Image. In current theological debate Nonconformist churches are refusing to admit women to positions of teaching or leadership because of Paul's remarks in 1 Corinthians 14: 34-6 and 1 Timothy 2:8-15 about women being silent in church, while the resistance to the ordination of women as priests in the Anglican and Roman Catholic churches is justified by the perceived inability of women to be a true icon of the male Christ.women's submission to men was (and still is, in many circles) clearly taught as a divine imperative, valid in all contexts. Graham Leonard, until recently Bishop of London said:

> Headship and authority is [sic] symbolically and fundamentally associated with maleness . . . symbolically and fundamentally, the response of sacrificial self-giving is associated with femaleness . . . For a woman to represent the Headship of Christ and the Divine initiative would, unless her feminine gifts were obscured or minimised, evoke a different approach to God from those who worship.[41]

THE HEADMISTRESS : AN AUTHORITY FIGURE

With this theological background, it can be seen how vital and empowering an image is that of the authoritative woman, and here the school texts manage, in their treatment of the headmistresses, to circumvent traditional theology without anyone even noticing. It was, after all, inevitable that a girls' school should have a female Head and, despite the considerable personal qualities of these women both in fact and in fiction, they were rendered generally invisible by two factors. First, girls' schools had much less status than did boys' schools. One of the frustrations of trying to research the former is that so many have never been convinced enough of their own importance to keep their records, and it is clear from the statements of headmistresses involved in joint public school organisations that they felt themselves to be second-class citizens. The second is the perception of society in general (i.e. of men) of the Head herself.

It was at this time that ISIS (the Independent Schools' Information Service) was set up, and the idea met with initial resistance from school bursars (almost entirely male) and from the girls' schools who were doubtful about joining an organisation which they suspected would be dominated by headmasters and who feared that closer co-operation might encourage the transfer of girls to the sixth forms of boys' schools. Neither of these objections appears unreasonable, but both were dismissed by one headmaster (with the clear approval of John Rae) as "the long-felt complex shared by many headmistresses that they were second-class citizens".

Authority was conceived in male terms. So was

the faculty of rational thought, so that an intellectual woman in a position of authority was caught in a double bind. Either she was accused of having denied her femininity, or she was treated as a sex object anyway, whatever her position and qualifications. For Jonathan Gathorne-Hardy, writing in *The Public School Phenomenon* (1977), Mary Alice Douglas, Head of Godolphin School for over 30 years, was transformed into a pseudo-man by 29 years of "power and adulation", and he proves his point by comparing 2 photographs of the woman.

> In 1890, it is certainly a strong face, but it is a feminine one; she has long hair pulled back and piled up, a long skirt, fine bosom and a slender waist. In 1919 she is wearing collar and tie, a pinstripe coat, a waistcoat, a skirt (or are they trousers? It is impossible to see); she has the short-cut hair, greying at the temples, and the level gaze of a successful headmaster.[42]

Heads of schools in this country have traditionally enjoyed almost complete power and autonomy within their own domain. They can thus hardly avoid symbolising an ultimate authority, and while this is in itself an unusual enough position for a woman, it is further extended by the fact that temporal authority was seen very specifically as mirroring and representing the authority of God, to whom all earthly authorities were finally accountable. "It is not easy to place oneself under discipline when one believes one has outgrown such a necessity," declares the Headmistress in May Wynne's *Honour Of The School* (1926), "but the very effort will help you to understand that we are under discipline all our lives to a Higher Power."[43] It is very interesting, therefore, to see how this authority is presented in the books.

The vast majority of fictional headmistresses are extremely impressive women — as, indeed, were their actual counterparts; it was the exceptional characters who pioneered girls' education, as in all other fields. They combine absolute authority with large measures of understanding and loving-kindness and are, almost without exception, both adored and fervently respected by their pupils, "the terror and the adoration of the whole school".[44] In some of the earlier books these feelings are expressed in ways which are inevitably amusing to a modern reader. Angela Brazil's Miss Kaye is annually garlanded with roses on her birthday[45], and Kits Kerwayne kisses her Headmistress's hand in token of affection[46], but perhaps this kind of treatment is appropriate for ladies who attire themselves in "amethyst velvet and old lace", or who can be described as "a glittering vision in satin". Despite their gentility, however, there is no doubt at all about the autocracy of even the early heads. They are the supreme authority, and the most requisite characteristics of any such quasi-divinity are those of justice, mercy — and control.

Justice, with its implication of totally predictable right, goes hand in hand with dependability, and headmistresses are almost always bastions of serenity, reliability and security. Winifred Darch's Miss Eliot is respected by her pupils because, despite her strictness, "she was the most absolutely just person you could imagine and her word was to be depended upon utterly"[47], and in the beginning-of-term chaos at Dorita Fairlie Bruce's Maudsley Grammar School,

> nobody knew where to find anybody, and no-one was settled or tranquil, except the headmistress,

working steadily and quietly in her study, where she might be found by all who sought her, the one really abiding person in this upheaval of newness.[48]

The implementation of justice inevitably implies punishment, and few indeed are the Headmistresses who cannot reduce a schoolful of unruly girls to subjection by a mere glance from their chilly blue eyes. Their methods of control range from the remorseless wearing down of the culprit by calm, well-balanced arguments to the fury of Sybil Owsley's Miss Silverlock, who confronts her erring pupils in a blaze of confused metaphor: "Her white hair was hurled from her forehead. The deep pools of her eyes had changed to smouldering fires."[49]

Elinor Brent-Dyer's Miss Annersley can be as crushing as most, as evidenced in her reply to Len Maynard, who is blaming herself for the bad behaviour of some juniors:

> Go away, Len, and please try to overcome this absurd scrupulosity of yours. If it goes on, you will end up by becoming morbid. *No* blame attaches to you for whatever they are up to, and no blame is attributed to you. Now please go away. I have too much to do to be worried by the need to soothe your conscience.[50]

There is a fundamental dissatisfaction with heads who are weak and biased like Mrs Lane in May Wynne's *Playing the Game* (1947), who condemns pupils on the flimsiest of evidence and is totally unsympathetic to her girls. Even Antonia Forest's Miss Keith, the Headmistress of Kingscote eventually follows the pattern, despite being initially presented as a disaster. Miss Keith, vulgarized from the beginning of *Autumn Term* (1948) by her niece's irreverent appelation "me Auntie" is a silly woman, pompous, unsympathetic and addicted to psychological experiments rather than to common sense, but she is not ineffective. She can reduce sinners to pulp with the best of her forebears, and even manages eventually to imbue her irrepressible niece Tim with a modicum of respect for her position.[51]

THE HEADMISTRESS: A DIVINE FIGURE

Ultimately this supreme authority finds its natural expression in quite specific images of divinity. Elinor Brent-Dyer's Miss Annersley is referred to by her pupils as "the Abbess", though this is the image of the convent rather than the Church and is limited by the historical submission of female religious orders to the male church hierarchy. Nevertheless, it is an image of great dignity and authority, and Hilda Annersley can certainly be seen as the archetypal virgin goddess, self-contained, inviolate, totally controlled and totally controlling, yet doing so with justice tempered by mercy, humour and compassion. Ethel Talbot's Miss Graham takes the imagery further; she is presented as the High Priestess of the Rookery School, and is given divine attributes — her greeting to her excited and noisy girls is described, quite seriously, as "after the thunder, the still, small voice"[52], the phrase used to describe the appearance of God to Elijah (1 Kings 19:12).

Angela Brazil's Miss Cavendish rules St Chad's from a sanctum which bears a remarkable resemblance to a cathedral, including "a large, stained-glass window, filled with figures of saints, that faced the doorway".[53] The theme is continued even in Joanna Lloyd's much more light-hearted books, where the girls most sacrilegiously use the name of their Headmistress, Miss Atherton, as an oath in startling phrases like, "Did she, by Atherton", and "Good Atherton! What was Catherine doing now?"[54] It can even be argued that, together with omnipotence, these women take on within the books something of the divine quality of omnipresence. A recent article on Brent-Dyer's Hilda Annersley concludes:

> If I'd been asked I would have said that Hilda plays a large part in the majority of the books, but by doing the necessary re-reading for this article, I realised that this is not so — she invariably has only a small role: a welcoming speech at the beginning of term; a staff meeting; the chastising of a difficult pupil, and often little else. Yet the impression is there of her presence — the firm hand steering the characters through yet another turbulent term.[55]

THE HEADMISTRESS: A MOTHER FIGURE

However, it is possible to argue that the giving of power and authority to women in this way is itself problematical, merely replacing a male hierarchy with a female one, and posing no questions about power structures in personal relationships or in community — merely, in fact, changing pronouns. Mary Daly has pointed out that if the masculine character of God remains unchanged, the position for women is actually worsened as the God of the tradition, now female, absorbs women's reality into the tradition of western theological thought:

> The use of the feminine forms merely suggests that the christian divinity is so superior and

magnanimous that he can contain all female values . . . the christian god can arrogantly announce that he is also a "she" (during alternative services).[56]

The point is valid, but is avoided in school stories by combining the divine role with the strongly maternal function of both the Head herself and the school. The already quoted incident between Hilda Annersley and Len Maynard provides an illustration of the duality of the Head's role, for Miss Annersley is an old friend of Len's family and is actually very fond of the girl, to whom she is "Auntie Hilda" out of school hours.

For as well as administering justice, Heads must possess a world of experience and kindly wisdom; indeed the two are in many ways indivisible, as discipline is only justifiable and bearable in a context of love. It is deeply significant that this is mother love. Because our theology has perceived God as being exclusively male, and because our society has cast male and female human beings in different roles with different emotional responses, we have cut ourselves off from a vital aspect of God's love. The love of the father has to be earned and is dependent on good behaviour; that of the mother is eternal, unconditional and dependent only on relationship — we are loved because we are her children. The father is the judge, the punisher, the giver and upholder of the law, the one who gives us what we deserve; the mother is the refuge, the comforter, the one who accepts, upholds and gives, controlled by the impetus of her love, not our deserts.

However true or untrue this picture might be in relation to individual relationships, the social symbolism is immense and very deep-seated; thus if we perceive God only as Father, we are cosmically separated from the aspect of God's love which, perhaps, we most need. Thus, in the fusion of Godlike authority and maternal love, school fiction opens up to us fundamentally different possibilities of perceiving and relating to God.

ELINOR BRENT-DYER'S HEADMISTRESSES

All Brent-Dyer's headmistresses, even in her most lightweight books, show this fusion of authority and relationship in their interaction with their pupils. Miss Baynard, Head of Janeways, (*Caroline the Second*, 1937) has eyes which "could be very kind. But they could also be very piercing"; and when Philadelphia, the new Head Girl, complains because a friend who has returned to school unexpectedly early has not come to visit her, Gwen replies: "Dear idiot! I was the only one, and I've had Baynie to myself since four" — to which Philadelphia can only say "O-oh! You are lucky!"[57]

In *Leader in Spite of Herself*, Iris has behaved in a way which causes her to fear expulsion, and she is astonished when the Head, Miss Norris, treats her instead with kind and reasoned explanation of all that has gone wrong.[58] When Beechy goes to the Harbour School as a new pupil who has recently lost her mother, we are told that "for the first time since her mother's death Beechy felt that in Miss Eliot and Matron she had found two people who would stand by her" — and this despite the fact that she has been living with affectionate relatives.[59]

In the Chalet series, too, firebrand Cornelia, also motherless, is deeply upset by the serious illness of the Head, Mademoiselle Lepattre — "motherless from early babyhood, she had had most of her 'mothering' from Mademoiselle", and her cry of anguish is a broken, "'Guess I — feel 'sif — my mother —"[60]; and when, in an earlier book, Juliet Carrick is abandoned at school by her parents, Madge Bettany accepts her as her ward with remarkable calm.[61] It is significant that when, in *Gay from China at the Chalet School* (1944), the senior staff are injured in a car accident and Miss Bubb takes over as Head, she is a disaster, not because she is academically incompetent, but because she cannot understand or handle the relationship between staff and girls at the school.

Obviously it is the Heads of the Chalet School who are the most clearly realised, and this becomes more true as the series progresses. Madge Bettany marries early in the series, and is thus automatically excluded from the school community; this is presented as her decision, though an inevitable one, but married women were not, of course, allowed to continue in teaching until the 1950s. Therese Lepattre, initially Madge's partner and later Head of the school herself, is a less clearly realised character than her successors. She is shadowy enough for Brent-Dyer (who was, admittedly, notoriously careless in her writing) to change both her Christian name and the spelling of her surname between one book and another, and, as the younger women staff become the focus of the action, Mademoiselle is allowed to become seriously ill, to give up her job and, eventually, to die gently off stage.

The Heads who live in the memory are Miss Annersley and Miss Wilson and Nancy Wilmot, as she and Kathy Ferrars take over the roles of the now ageing Heads in the later books. We discover in *Three Go to the Chalet School* (1949) that Miss Wilson has become co-Head with Miss Annersley, and are left to assume that this is because of the latter's serious illness following the accident in *Gay from China* — the reason is never stated. The effect is clumsy, and in fact lasts only for five books. In *The Wrong Chalet School* (1952), Miss Wilson has been banished to the school's finishing branch in Switzerland. This is a pity; it breaks the strong relationship between the two women — and one wonders whatever possessed Brent-Dyer to cast the totally no-nonsense "Bill" as the Head of a finishing school!

The fact that Brent-Dyer was quite unconscious of the sort of woman she was creating and presenting as role model to her readers is, in fact, intriguingly illuminated by her treatment of the Annersley-Wilson duo and of Nancy Wilmot. All of these participate less in the maternal role than do many other fictional Heads because of the close connection with the school of Jo Maynard, who largely takes over the mothering function. Rosemary Auchmuty has pointed out the increasing masculinity of the originally plump and pretty Nancy Wilmot as she becomes a sturdy, lasso-throwing six-footer[62], and this seems to be connected both with her growing importance and authority within the texts and with her deepening relationship with Kathy Ferrars. It is tempting to speculate, too, that the creation of the dual Headship of Miss Annersley and Miss Wilson is an attempt to strengthen the Head's function by an injection of "manliness" in the person of Bill. The significant nickname and the fact that she is a teacher of science immediately put Miss Wilson on a masculine spectrum. She is a ferocious disciplinarian ("Best send Nell Wilson out to them . . . it needs someone like a sergeant-major"), and it is she who knows enough about electricity to cope with the failed lights in *The New Chalet School* (1938):

I know there's something wrong with the lights. . .
Miss Wilson will be along presently, and will see
what is wrong . . . someone has taken all the fuses
out of the fuse-box, and cut some wire or other.
Miss Wilson has put in new fuses, but the light is
still out.[63]

In *Tom Tackles the Chalet School* (1948) we find her
coming to "stand in a manly attitude before the
glowing fire"[64] but, despite the fact that Nell Wilson
must surely be one of Brent-Dyer's most delightful
characters, this does not work. The more obviously
feminine but deeply authoritative Miss Annersley
does not need shoring up in this way, and the
clumsiness and ultimate failure of the attempt illustrate both the strength of Brent-Dyer's female Head
and her own unconsciousness of the significance of
what she was writing.

SCHOOL ITSELF AS REFUGE

For Elinor Brent-Dyer, school is home for both staff
and pupils. When Matron Lloyd's sister dies, the
school staff are the only people left who know her
well enough to call her by her Christian name, and
they drop the nickname of years to do so, in a
commitment to her akin to that of a substitute
family.[65] For orphaned Biddy O'Ryan, adopted by the
school Guide Company and constantly connected
with it, first as a pupil and later as a teacher, "it's
the school that's really been home to her ever since
she was a kid"[66], and for old Herr Laubach, the
lonely, irascible art master, "the school is my whole
life now".[67] In terms of the books, this is a powerful
tribute to the school. In terms of Brent-Dyer's life, it
is indicative of the absorption into her fantasy world

which increasingly gave her the feelings of security and belonging missing in her actual life, and which gives to the books much of their addictive power.

For Helen McClelland's biography leaves us with the impression of a deeply lonely woman. Not only did Brent-Dyer lose her father at the age of three when he left her mother, she had to cope with the deaths of a close friend and an even closer brother within the same year when she was still only a teenager herself and, even more damagingly, all these traumas were ruthlessly repressed. It is difficult to believe that close friends in later years were unaware of the existence of either father or brother, but this seems to have been the case. Brent-Dyer did not marry and, whether or not this would have given her the emotional satisfaction she sought, she herself felt cheated. McClelland comments: "there seems little doubt that Elinor herself was never fully resigned to remaining unmarried . . . she thought of spinsterhood as second-best".[68] Ironically, the totally fulfilled spinsters in the books find their emotional fulfilment and love in other women, but Brent-Dyer herself never seems to have achieved this; friendships formed in a blaze of passion quickly died, and the deep and moving female bonding of Hilda Annersley and Nell Wilson or of Nancy Wilmot and Kathy Ferrars sadly seems to have evaded their creator.

That she took refuge in her fantasy world is clear from the way in which she patterned her real school in Hereford on the Chalet School to the point where the actual and fictional pupils wore identical uniform. This is the Word made Flesh with a vengeance, and it is a strange reversal of the more usual process of using elements of reality in a work of fiction. It is the strength of Brent-Dyer's own belief in her fictional characters, "this conviction that her characters were real people"[69], which caused her readers, too, to believe absolutely in them and forms much of the foundation of the addictive quality of her writing.

CONCLUSION

Because of the social climate in which they were written, school stories had to deal in some way with religion. While some writers were content to pay lip-service to established beliefs, others used their books purely as vehicles for their message, and attempted to convert their readers. Perhaps coincidentally, certainly fortunately, the writers of school-story books of quality were themselves deeply committed Christians, and were able to give their readers a profound and honest analysis of faith in ways which they could understand and identify with. This was clearly their conscious intention.

Elinor Brent-Dyer, speaking as Principal of the Margaret Roper School in Hereford on the school's ninth speech-day, said: "We are trying to train our girls . . . to become practising Christians . . . [which is] vital to our land and indeed to the whole Empire"[70]; and there can be no possible doubt that the same was true of her writing. Because of her constant wish to analyse and understand (a process she continually describes in the books as "going deep"), she was able to deal with theological subjects which her fellow-writers left untouched; and because of the phenomenal length of her writing life, she was forced to adapt her work to a society which no longer accepted her beliefs as axiomatic. This she achieved by means of apologetics, but achieve it she most certainly did.

The work of many authors, however, goes far

beyond their conscious intentions to provide images of omnipotent women which were, had they been heeded, deeply subversive of traditional theology. Because school stories are "only" children's books, and "only" girls' books at that, they were not heeded, and were left to make their impact, however subliminal, on the consciousness of their readers. We have seen that the texts present powerful images of women who are at once the total controllers of their universe, and deeply connected in love to the inhabitants of that world.

It has certainly been true for me that these images were imbibed at a subconscious level; it took an awareness of feminist reinterpretations of traditional male-centred theology to enable me to articulate what they had meant in my imaginative life. I suspect this is true of most readers — the unravelling of one's own emotional and intellectual baggage is a long and tortuous process. Yet the images are there, creating a fundamental disatisfaction with the partial vision of God which is so often all we are offered as women, pointing out how skewed is a theology which separates us from a full appreciation of God's love, and filling an emotional and spiritual void in a way not matched by any other literary genre.

I suspect that Elinor Brent-Dyer would have been shocked at some of the readings of her work contained in this analysis — I am sure that, at her point in time, she could have had no idea of what she was creating. I am also sure, however, that if she had had access to the theory which would have made sense of and allowed her to articulate her perceptions, she would herself have experienced the empowerment, the release and the fulfilment which she has offered to so many of her Christian readers in her re-vision of theology.

NOTES

1. Helen McClelland, *Behind the Chalet School* (New Horizon, 1981), p.179.
2. Mary Cadogan and Patricia Craig, *You're a Brick, Angela!* (Gollancz, 1976), p.204.
3. Angela Brazil, *The Nicest Girl in the School* (Blackie, 1910), p.235.
4. Mary Louise Parker, *Dormitory Wistaria* (Sampson Low, Marston, 1947), p.82.
5. Dorita Fairlie Bruce, *Dimsie Among the Prefects* (Oxford University Press, 1923), p.87.
6. Dorita Fairlie Bruce, *Captain of Springdale* (Oxford University Press, 1942), p.136.
7. Elinor Brent-Dyer, *Mary-Lou of the Chalet School* (1954), p.131.
8. Elinor Brent-Dyer, *Leader in Spite of Herself* (1956), p.45.
9. Ibid., p.86.
10. Dorothy Dennison, *Rival Schools at Trentham* (CSSM, 1923), pp.25, 27.
11. See Louisa Gray, *Nelly's Teachers . . . and What They Learned* (Nelson, 1882); *Ada and Gerty or, Hand in Hand Heavenward* (Nelson, 1875).
12. Helen S. Humphries, *Prudence Goes Too Far* (Pickering & Inglis, 1966), p.9.
13. Helen S. Humphries, *Margaret the Rebel* (Pickering & Inglis, 1957), p.110.
14. Elinor Brent-Dyer, *The Chalet School Reunion* (1963), p.77.
15. Elinor Brent-Dyer, *The New House at the Chalet School* (1935), p.96.
16. Elinor Brent-Dyer, *A Quintette in Queensland* (1951), p.275.
17. Dorita Fairlie Bruce, *Nancy Calls the Tune* (Oxford University Press, 1944), p.178.

18. Elinor Brent-Dyer, *Joey and Co. in Tirol* (1960), p.64.
19. Elinor Brent-Dyer, *Bride Leads the Chalet School* (1953), p.275.
20. Elinor Brent-Dyer, *The Coming of Age of the Chalet School* (1958), p.199.
21. Elsie J. Oxenham, *The Abbey Girls Again* (1924); *The Abbey Girls in Town* (1925); *Queen of the Abbey Girls* (1926), etc. All published by Collins.
22. Dorita Fairlie Bruce, *Nancy Calls the Tune*.
23. Elinor Brent-Dyer, *The Chalet School Does It Again* (1955), p.154.
24. Elinor Brent-Dyer, *Mary-Lou of the Chalet School*, p.131.
25. Dorita Fairlie Bruce, *Triffeny* (Oxford University Press, 1950), p.196.
26. Elinor Brent-Dyer, *The Chalet School Reunion*, pp.19-20.
27. Elinor Brent-Dyer, *The Condor Crags Adventure* (1954), pp.19, 27.
28. Elinor Brent-Dyer, *Two Sams at the Chalet School* (1967), p.179.
29. Kathleen M. McCleod, *Julia of Sherwood School* (Pickering & Inglis, 1947), p.110.
30. Dorita Fairlie Bruce, *Triffeny*, p.274.
31. Elinor Brent-Dyer, *A Genius at the Chalet School* (1956), pp.83-4.
32. Elinor Brent-Dyer, *The Highland Twins at the Chalet School* (1942), pp.244-5.
33. Elinor Brent-Dyer, *Trials for the Chalet School* (1959), p.32.
34. Elinor Brent-Dyer, *Joey and Co. in Tirol*, p.65.
35. Elinor Brent-Dyer, *Trials for the Chalet School*, p.104.
36. Julia Kristeva, "About Chinese Women:". In Toril Moi, ed. *The Kristeva Reader* (Blackwell, 1986), p.138.
37. Phyllis Trible, *God and the Rhetoric of Sexuality* (Fortress Press, 1978) and *Texts of Terror* (Fortress Press, 1984); Mary Evans, *Women in the Bible* (Paternoster Press, 1983).
38. Elizabeth Cady Stanton, *The Woman's Bible* (Polygon Books, 1985; first published New York: European

Publishing Company, Part I, 1895, Part II, 1898); Rosemary Radford Ruether, *Religion and Sexism* (Simon and Schuster, 1974) and *Sexism and God Talk : Toward a Feminist Theology* (Beacon Press, 1983); Elisabeth Fiorenza, *In Memory of Her: A Feminist Theological Reconstruction of Christian Origins* (Crossroad, 1983) and "The Will to Choose or to Reject: Continuing Our Critical Work". In Letty Russell, ed., *Feminist Interpretation of the Bible* (Blackwell, 1985), p.132.
39. Mary Daly, *Beyond God the Father* (Women's Press, 1986; first published 1973).
40. Daphne Hampson, *Theology and Feminism* (Blackwell, 1990), p.85.
41. Quoted in Hampson, ibid., p.66. Apart from any other considerations, the flaw in the argument which attaches "femaleness" to the sacrificial self-giving of which Christ must be the prime example, seems to have escaped the Bishop.
42. Jonathan Gathorne-Hardy, *The Public School Phenomenon 1597-1977* (Hodder & Stoughton, 1977), p.250.
43. May Wynne, *The Honour of the School* (Dean, 1926), p.28.
44. Edith Elias, *Elsie Lockhart: Third Form Girl* (Religious Tract Society, 1925), p.16.
45. Angela Brazil, *The Third Class At Miss Kaye's* (Blackie, 1908).
46. May Wynne, *Kits at Clinton Court School* (Warne, 1924).
47. Winifred Darch, *Alison Temple, Prefect* (Oxford University Press, 1938), p.29.
48. Dorita Fairlie Bruce, *Nancy to the Rescue* (Oxford University Press, 1929), p.22. Reprinted as *Alison in a Fix*, Spring Books, 1961.
49. Sibyl B. Owsley, *Dulcie Captains the School* (Sampson Low, Marston, 1928), p.133.
50. Elinor Brent-Dyer, *The Chalet School Triplets* (1963), p.93.
51. Antonia Forest, *Autumn Term* (Faber & Faber, 1948).
52. Ethel Talbot, *The Girls of the Rookery School* (Nelson, 1925), p.35.

53. Angela Brazil, *The New Girl at St Chad's* (Blackie, 1912), p.50.
54. Joanna Lloyd, *Jane Runs Away from School* (Blackie, 1955), p.79; first published 1946.
55. Sue Surman, *Friends of the Chalet School Newsletter 13*, Dec. 1991, p.12.
56. Mary Daly, *Pure Lust* (Women's Press, 1984), p.403.
57. Elinor Brent-Dyer, *Caroline the Second* (1937), pp.13, 18.
58. Elinor Brent-Dyer, *Leader in Spite of Herself*, p.67.
59. Elinor Brent-Dyer, *Beechy of the Harbour School* (1955), p.12.
60. Elinor Brent-Dyer, *The New Chalet School* (1938), pp.205-6.
61. Elinor Brent-Dyer, *The School at the Chalet* (1925).
62. Rosemary Auchmuty, *A World of Girls* (Women's Press, 1992), pp.130-1.
63. Elinor Brent-Dyer, *The New Chalet School*, pp.126, 135-7.
64. Elinor Brent-Dyer, *Tom Tackles the Chalet School* (1955), p.168.
65. Elinor Brent-Dyer, *Excitements at the Chalet School* (1957), p.86.
66. Elinor Brent-Dyer, *The New Mistress at the Chalet School* (1957), p.35.
67. Elinor Brent-Dyer, *Trials for the Chalet School*, p.54.
68. McClelland, *Behind the Chalet School*, p.157.
69. Ibid., p.178.
70. Ibid., p.144.

The Chalet School and Barbara (1954) and *The Chalet School Goes to It* (1941); first and paperback editions.

THE SERIES FACTOR

SUE SIMS

Let's begin by asking one question. In any medium which uses story as a device — literature, film, radio or television — which type of story attracts the greatest audience?

It doesn't take a Oxford English degree to provide the answer to that one. EastEnders and Coronation Street, The Archers — the soap opera pulls in by far the largest audiences for any regular television or radio programme. Film producers know that Back to the Future III or Rambo CCXVI will fill the cinemas far more reliably than most one-off movies.

Most people who read this book will have experienced a precisely similar situation in the literary world. The bestselling writers of our time do not always produce series — but quite often it's the series which first makes them bestsellers. One can look at many different genres and see this at work. Catherine Cookson tops the bestsellers league now, whatever she writes; but Tilly Trotter, Mary Ann and those unlucky Mallens helped to get her there. Terry Pratchett can now command hundreds of thousands of devoted readers for anything he produces, but he wouldn't have reached that pinnacle without *Discworld*.

And in the sphere of the thriller, I've just been reading an article on John Le Carré's George Smiley books, which comments:

> Although they are all thoroughly readable, it's fair to say that none of Le Carré's next three

books — *The Looking-Glass War, A Small Town in Germany* and *The Naive and Sentimental Lover* — quite lived up to *The Spy Who Came In From the Cold*. It was the relative failure of the last of these novels that prompted him to return to his greatest inspiration, George Smiley.[1]

It's interesting to note that the writer of this article assumes that the three non-Smiley novels were not as successful as their predecessors because Le Carré needed Smiley to inspire him. I would argue, as I hope to show in this essay, that what inspired Le Carré and drew in readers was not simply Smiley but the Series Factor.

Let's now leave Cookson, Pratchett and Le Carré, and become slightly more specific — and, if you will forgive me, personal. I've been collecting and reading girls' school stories ever since I stopped being a girl (about 23 years ago) and know by correspondence at least a hundred other collectors in the same field. By and large, all say the same — that the writers they collect most avidly (and, often, pay the most money for) are the writers of the series. Who are the names to conjure with in our world? Elsie J. Oxenham, Dorita Fairlie Bruce and — of course — Elinor M. Brent-Dyer. Slightly lower down the list (looking only at *numbers* of collectors — her fans would put her at the top) comes Antonia Forest with her Marlow stories. Outside the school story field, but collected by many of the same people, come L. M. Montgomery, Violet Needham, Lorna Hill, Monica Edwards — and Captain W.E.Johns' Biggles holds sway over many otherwise ladylike readers. Enid Blyton, who comes into almost every category, must also be on the list.

Clearly, the one thing all these writers have in common is that they have all produced series, often more than one. Other writers, often of great merit, or at least great prodigality of output, are read and enjoyed, collected by a select handful, but are not to be seen on every collector's wants list, or going for vast prices in bookshops. The most interesting example of this must be Angela Brazil. Here is a writer who is regarded by most historians of children's literature as being not only the first major writer of girls' school stories, but (judging by the amount of space they devote to other writers) practically the only one. The children's section of almost any second-hand bookshop will have several Brazil reprints (often marked — and priced — as firsts), even if it's lacking the most basic stock of other girls' school stories. And if one admits to reading and collecting school stories, the initial response will almost always be: "Oh, you mean Angela Brazil!" To the world at large, she is the archetypal girls' school-story writer.

Yet she is not collected. I don't mean, of course, that no one buys her books — many, including myself, do. There are even some well-heeled people who look out for first editions. But of the 50-odd wants lists in my filing cabinet, only one actually lists any Brazils — and then only first editions in dust wrappers. And of those who buy her, how many people read and reread her avidly, as Brent-Dyer or Bruce, Oxenham or Forest?

Is she, then, a poor writer? By no means. Her books, though often rather too whimsical and sentimental for modern tastes, are lively and amusing, with strong and sympathetic characters. She helped to establish a number of the more persistent school story clichés. But, foolish woman, she omitted to create a series. Almost all her books create a unique and disposable set of characters. Twice she provides a sequel to a book — *Monitress Merle* (1922) follows on from *A Fortunate Term* (1921) and the eponymous heroine of *At School with Rachel* (1928) is also at the centre of *St Catherine's College* (1929); but those are the only real sequels.[2] And thus the wants lists know her not.

I am not, of course, suggesting that non-series girls' school-story writers are not collected. Authors like Clare Mallory, Josephine Elder, Winifred Darch and Evelyn Smith have a devoted — and growing — following. But on analysis it will be found that those of us who collect these writers have almost invariably begun with one of the main series writers, and expanded to these lesser known practitioners. In other words, the Series Factor has given us a taste for school stories, and we feed where we can. After all, it's hard to explain otherwise why this quartet of writers are not better known. Darch, Elder, Mallory and Smith wrote excellent and thoughtful school stories, which depict the world of school as it really is (all but Elder were teachers) and are greatly loved by many. Objectively, many of us would admit (if only between consenting collectors in private) that they are better writers than their more famous sisters. But although they are collected, they are not "collectable". If one looks at only the financial aspect, one can buy most of their books without going out of single figures. And, given their quality, the most probable reason is their absent-mindedness in failing to produce some nice long series.

At this point, I can hear my more knowledgeable readers muttering: "Wait a bit. Most of those authors *did* create series. Why isn't this silly woman counting them as 'series authors'?" So I'll pause the argument here in order to define terms in proper scholarly fashion.

A series, then, in this essay, will be defined as any group of books by the same writer which uses the same group of characters sequentially for at least three books. This is a fairly arbitrary definition, and is made more on impressionistic than analytical grounds. We have a term for a single book which follows a predecessor — we call it a sequel. After that, English would seem to lack words for each individual follow-up, save the generic word "series". Furthermore, a group of school stories cannot qualify as a series simply by using the same school.

Josephine Elder's *Erica Wins Through* (1924) is set at the same school as her two *Scholarship Girl* books;[3] but we meet the characters in *Erica* only as remote and magisterial seniors in the two later books, and all the interest is refocused on to Monica and her friends. The first book has so little character connection that the first time I read *The Scholarship Girl* I didn't realise the schools and a handful of the characters were the same. Evelyn Smith uses the school she calls Myra Dakin's in *Val Forrest in the Fifth* (1925) and then again in *Milly in the Fifth* (1928); but in the latter, Val and her friends are sixth-formers and we hardly see them. Again, the two books are not in the least interdependent. Clearly, then, the use of the same school in three or more books isn't enough. We need to follow the same set of characters through — though if the series is long enough, the writer may gradually refocus the action on to a younger generation, while keeping the original protagonists as background.

So much for the series. What about the "series writer"? Of the four writers we've been discussing, all but Darch did actually create trilogies: the Farm School books by Josephine Elder,[4] Clare Mallory's Merry series,[5] and the Queen Anne's books of Evelyn Smith.[6] Are they then writers of series? I would argue that they aren't. In part, this is because the bulk of their work is not series-based. But there is a more subtle distinction. For collectors of the series writer, there is almost always an initial inclination to collect *only* the series — and often, only the major (i.e. the longest) one. Oxenham collectors generally start with the Abbey sequence, and only expand when they realise that many of the non-Abbey books are linked with the Abbey books by recurring characters. Bruce collectors will often begin by saying that they "just want Dimsies" or "only collect Springdales", before the virus spreads to adjacent collecting cells and they start demanding even *Mistress Mariner*, rarest and most expensive of Bruce's books. No one I know has ever said that they "only want the Queen Anne's books" or "just collect the Merry series". After all, they'd soon run out.

And, more importantly, one collects Abbey books or Dimsie books not pre-eminently because one enjoys the realism or the style of the writers (as is the case with Darch and these others), but because one has become so interested in the characters that one desperately needs to find out *what happens next*. When this happens, the books don't even need to be school stories to attract school story readers (Antonia Forest, who has only written four school stories in her total Marlow output of ten contemporary and two historical novels, is perhaps the best example of this). And of the major writers of schoolgirl stories mentioned, Elinor Brent-Dyer is probably the supreme example of the writer who pulls her readers in almost entirely by the Series Factor.

It is now to Brent-Dyer that we must turn; and first, we'd better list the series which she wrote. Within the definition I've given, the most famous is obviously the Chalet School series, 59 books, including *The Chalet School and Rosalie* (1951); three annuals — the three *Chalet Books for Girls* (1947-9); and one odd little extra, *The Chalet Girls' Cook Book* (1953). There is also a set of seven books, generically known as the La Rochelle series, which comprises *Gerry Goes to School* (1922) and *A Head Girl's Difficulties* (1923), which introduce the Atherton family; *The Maids of La Rochelle* (1924); where we meet the orphaned sisters Elizabeth, Anne and Janie Temple, who encounter the Athertons; *Seven Scamps* (1927), which introduces the Willoughbys and links them with the Athertons and the Temples; *Heather Leaves School* (1929), which centres on Heather Raphael, an unpleasant newcomer to the series, reformed mostly by the efforts of Janie Temple; and *Janie of La Rochelle* (1932) and *Janie Steps In* (1953), which follow through a number of threads already established. These are by no means as cohesive as the Chalet books, dealing as they do with three or four separate families whose fortunes and eventual marriages are interlinked; in these books Brent-Dyer has used the technique perfected by Elsie Oxenham, where groups of characters established separately are then brought together. There is a third sequence of rather bad thrillers: *Fardingales* (1950) and *The "Susannah" Adventure* (1953) focus on the Anthony family and their Roseveare cousins; *Chudleigh Hold* (1954) on the Chudleigh family; *The Condor Crags Adventure* (1954) links Humphrey Anthony with the Chudleighs; and *Top Secret* (1955) is another purely Chudleigh adventure. And for the sake of completeness, I should also mention here three sets of two books which, by my definition are not strictly series but bear witness to Brent-Dyer's love of continuations — *Lorna at Wynyards* (1947) and *Stepsisters for Lorna* (1948); *A Thrilling Term at Janeways*

(1927) and *Caroline the Second* (1928); *The School at Skelton Hall* (1962) and *Trouble at Skelton Hall* (1963).

But we can't stop here with a simple list of series. Two of the series listed above — Fardingales and Chudleigh Hold — and three individual books — *The School by the River* (1930), *Monica Turns Up Trumps* (1936) and *The Lost Staircase* (1946) — link up to some extent with the Chalet series, and thus become a sort of extension of the latter. The major characters in both *Monica* and *The Lost Staircase* turn up to finish their education at the Chalet School.[7] *The School by the River* introduces the Ecole des Musiciens in Mirania; Raphael Helston, morganatic grandson of the King of Mirania and created Duc di Mirolani in this novel, eventually marries the Belsornian Crown Princess Elisaveta[8] — a direct connection with the Chalet series. The heroine of *Chudleigh Hold* also turns up at the Chalet School[9] though Brent-Dyer has altered her surname from Chudleigh to Culver, and her Christian name from Arminel to Gillian (the Christian names of her family are left unchanged). Brent-Dyer's love of links can be seen further in that Gay Lambert and Gill Culver recount a précis of this adventure to the new Chalet School girl Jacynth Hardy, commenting, "Mrs Maynard's going to make it into a book some time, only changing the names, of course."[10] One presumes, therefore, that Joey Maynard did indeed write *Chudleigh Hold*, for some reason using the pen-name of Elinor Brent-Dyer . . . In precisely similar fashion, Jesanne Gellibrand relates the story of *The Lost Staircase*[11] (of which she is the heroine) to Jo; and we know from Brent-Dyer's manuscript notes that she did complete the story of Gay Lambert's adventures in China (referred to in *Gay From China at the Chalet*

School, 1944) though as far as we know the book was never published, and the manuscript is now lost.

But by far the most highly wrought link is that between the La Rochelle books and the Chalet School series; so much so that it would be possible to fill the rest of this essay with an exposition of all the connections. Space here, alas, permits only a very brief mention of the most important. They began in a small way with Gerry (of *Gerry Goes to School* and *A Head Girl's Difficulties*) visiting the Chalet School as Grizel's guest[12]; but the real forging of the links begins when the school is forced to flee the Tyrol in *The Chalet School in Exile* (1940) and Joey and Madge end up on Guernsey. It just so happens that the three sisters whom we first met in *The Maids of La Rochelle* live in Guernsey; and Joey and Janie (now married to Julian Lucy and mother of a promising family) become intimate friends.

What more natural than the presence of the second generation at the Chalet School when it restarts? And so we have Anne's daughters Beth, Nancy, Barbara and Janice Chester, Elizabeth's twins Nella and Vanna Ozanne, and Julie, Betsy, Vi and Katherine Lucy moving through the Chalet School, not infrequently as central characters. The second generation of Willoughbys (for the La Rochelle characters have intermarried with baffling frequency) present themselves in the pretty but feather-headed person of Blossom Willoughby and her sister Judy; these two are the offspring of Rosamund Atherton and Nigel Willoughby. We also meet Nita Eltringham, another Atherton-Willoughby sprog in that her mother is Cesca (Rosamund's mother's half-sister, but brought up as one of the Atherton children) and her father Mr Eltringham, the curate who acted as tutor to the

Willoughby boys. Yet another offshoot of the clan is Nan Blakeney to whose wedding (to David Willoughby!) the entire Chalet School is invited[13]; she is Rosamund's cousin, who goes after her mother's death to live with Janie Lucy.[14]

I remember when I first read the Chalet series at the age of ten or eleven being very puzzled by all these characters whose relationships I was clearly expected to know, even though they were never spelt out in the Chalet books. Why was Nancy so upset at Julie's peritonitis?[15] Who was this "Janie" whom Jo visited in Armiford, who had managed to get her large family dressed and out in the garden at the appalling hour of 7 a.m.?[16] And why was a certain Nigel Willoughby so willing to risk life and yacht to get Joey and her triplets over to England during wartime?[17] There was no way of finding out. At ten, one does not generally frequent second-hand bookshops, and the only references I'd come across to the La Rochelle series were by Brent-Dyer herself in *Chalet Club News Letters*[18] (I was, of course, a member). In answer to a query from a reader obviously as confused as myself, she had explained that these characters could all be found in the La Rochelle series, which had been out of print for a long time. So I gave up trying to understand — and only with adulthood, and the blessing of second-hand books, have I finally worked out the links.

So, then, in Elinor Brent-Dyer we have one of the best examples of a writer who not only creates a long series, but connects other books, both individual and sequential, to that series. And having established this fact, we have to ask — Why? What are the benefits of a long series? There is one obvious answer. Readers enjoy series — a point which I hope has been thoroughly illustrated in the first part of this essay. But so far we haven't tried to analyse this enjoyment any further. Nor have we asked what the benefits — and drawbacks — are for the writer. And since readers wouldn't exist without writers, with the writer we shall begin. What is it that leads a writer — and Brent-Dyer in particular — to create a series which lasts for 59 books plus extras and is written over 45 years?

Let's first get one simplistic answer out of the way. Writers do *not* create series just because their publishers ask them to. Clearly that may be a factor; but authors are not machines, and cannot necessarily produce a series to order if their inclinations don't already tend in that direction. If one takes three classic sets of children's books and compares their publishing history, this becomes obvious. Richmal Crompton, who wanted to abandon William after five short episodes, was encouraged by the editor of *Happy Mag.* to produce more William stories, and wrote a long series with no difficulty at all.[19] Tolkien, asked to produce a sequel to the mildly successful *Hobbit*, failed completely to produce another nice children's book about Bilbo Baggins, thought, wrote and revised for 14 years and finally came up with *Lord of the Rings*.[20] And C. S. Lewis, whose Narnia sequence might be considered a perfect example of publishers' persuasion, had actually written four of the seven books before *The Lion, the Witch and the Wardrobe* was published — because he wanted to finish the sequence he'd envisaged almost from the start.[21] Writers, in other words, are as individual as the books they produce, and will not write series unless they are already minded to do so.

What, then, makes a writer produce a series? I must confess that I've never actually produced one myself, so cannot analyse the desire from the inside, so to speak. But one can guess that it's partly a desire to be (in Tolkien's words)[22] a "sub-creator" — the creator of an entire universe which has a certain amount of connection with the world as we know it, but which is to a greater or lesser extent sufficient unto itself. Obviously any book may be an act of sub-creation, but there is a fascination in extending the bounds of one's empire — creating new characters, places, adventures, all inter-related and all clearly part of the same world. Psychologist and critic Nicholas Tucker, no fan of Brent-Dyer, described it as "the brick by brick assembling of a castle in the air."[23] The mind of the series writer takes pleasure in complexity, presenting characters who change (at least in age and status) and grow through experience. Any author knows the feeling of emptiness, almost of bereavement, on finishing the work in hand — if that author knows the imaginary world can be re-entered, it palliates the emptiness. There must be a great pleasure in creating new relationships between old characters, particularly when they are apparently far apart and have little obvious connection with one another. Len Maynard, Jo's eldest daughter, and Reg Entwistle, the half-educated and resentful adolescent from *Jo to the Rescue* (1945) are unlikely seeming mates; but this must make the challenge all the greater. ("I know — I'll have Len Maynard marry Reg Entwistle . . . now, how can I get a boy whom we haven't met since no. 19 in the series to marry Len in a few years' time? I know, bring him out to the San as a doctor!") Old characters can be reintroduced, a technique which is useful both for defining the imaginary world and (more pragmatically) for padding out an otherwise over-brief story — a technique which reaches its zenith (some would say its nadir) in *The Chalet School Reunion* (1963). The author of a long series need never lose sight of a beloved (or deliciously revolting) character, unless she is short-sighted enough to kill them off.

So the first factor which leads to the creation of the series must be the mind and personality of the writer. And once one has established the series, there are enormous advantages. But the advantages vary according to the creative process which the writer uses. Some, such as Enid Blyton[24] and C. S. Lewis[25], create by (as it appears to them) seeing pictures or watching their characters interact. For this type of writer, series are useful because, once the characters and background are established in their minds, they are able to see their puppets taking on a life of their own and almost creating their own plots. It is possible that this was Brent-Dyer's mode of working, but she seems to have belonged to the other school of writers — those who consciously devise events and relationships.

This is a somewhat dangerous statement, as I have Brent-Dyer herself against me. In the first *Chalet Club News Letter*, she writes: "So far as I am concerned, the people are there, just out of sight, but otherwise alive and panting to tell their stories. I am merely the loudspeaker through whom they broadcast . . ." We are also, I think, justified in using the evidence of her fictional Jo. Jo's character may bear little resemblance to the Elinor M. Brent-Dyer recreated by her biographer, Helen McClelland, but her writing parallels Brent-Dyer's in so many ways that we are surely entitled to assume Jo's methods are those of her creator. Indeed, McClelland quotes a friend of Brent-Dyer's who claimed that "Joey was Elinor herself as she would have liked to be".[26] How then, does Brent-Dyer, in her Jo persona, claim that she writes? Joey tells Robin that she too is merely "a loudspeaker"[27], creating characters who then take on a life of their own and broadcast their adventures to a waiting world without any conscious intervention of the writer — the Blyton technique, in fact.

The facts, though, do not match this claim. It's useful in this context to analyse Jo's first attempts to write a complete novel[28], as we are here given a very full picture of the process of creation. Jo, working on her first book, *Malvina Wins Through* (destined to meet a fiery fate) begins by listing some of the pranks which she and her chums played when middles; she then invents the Heroine, the Best Friend and the Bad Girl, whose motive for living is being nasty to the Heroine. Next she devises a series of discrete plot events, in each of which the Bad Girl tries to get the Heroine into trouble, but which don't seem otherwise to be causally linked. When this book is condemned by Matron ("Matey") as being "rubbish", Jo throws it in the furnace and begins a new story, *Cecily Holds the Fort*.

It's interesting that both this book and its abortive predecessor have titles which Jo chooses in advance, Brent-Dyer commenting that "It would not tie her down too much" — a clear indication that Jo's plots are worked out as she goes. *Cecily* is not dissimilar to *Malvina*, in that Jo begins with a character — Cecily; gives the latter an enemy (more convincingly this time in the person of a science mistress whom Cecily dislikes); and then creates a variety of incidents around these characters (p.71):

> With recollections of a certain fatal "experiment" of Evadne's, Jo provided a similar sensation for St Michael's High School, when Cecily nearly wrecked the laboratory in consequence of carelessness. Further memories helped her to add a few more pranks to her heroine's record. At the same time, the book contained nothing that might not have happened at the best regulated of

schools, though it must be admitted that most schools do not have quite such a spate of happenings all at once.

We can see Brent-Dyer working in exactly this way in her early books. If we look at her very first published novel, *Gerry Goes to School*, she creates her central character, Geraldine Challoner — a 12-year-old musical genius brought up by elderly great-aunts — and brings her into the large and lively Trevennor family, where she evokes the hostility of 14-year-old Jill. Part of the plot develops from Jill's enmity, but far more consists of unrelated incidents — a horse out of control, a fags' strike at St Peter's (a girls' school despite its name) — or simply of conversation between contemporaries, whether prefects, juniors or adults. The plot, in fact, could be described as rambling or realistic, depending on how organised you like your plots to be. And throughout her writing career, Brent-Dyer tended to follow this pattern.

Even when one of her books has a strong central theme, such as *The Lost Staircase*, much of the narrative is not related directly to that theme. Those of us who enjoy Brent-Dyer regard this as a potential strength, in that it reflects the disconnected nature of everyday life; but even so, we must admit that her non-admirers have a point when they accuse her of being unable to follow a plot through properly, and having an unstructured mind. Either way, it is undeniable that Brent-Dyer's strength does not lie in creating an organically connected plot.

What has all this to do with her use of the series? I would argue that the great advantage of this lengthy series is that the "plot" is ultimately the existence of the Chalet School itself, and its civilising influence on everyone (apart from Thekla von Stift and Betty Wynne-Davies) who goes there. Thus it doesn't really matter whether an individual book has a strong central character from whom all incidents arise (*Eustacia, Genius*) or is discursive and slightly disconnected (*Exploits, Changes*); everything that happens is automatically part of the central underlying theme. The Chalet School is the whole which is greater than the sum of its parts (which sounds a little like Joey's idea of maths). This releases Brent-Dyer to do what she most enjoys: making up stories as she goes; reproducing conversations which must, to the outsider, be at best puzzling and at worst utterly tedious; and providing us with incidents which could in theory, and sometimes in practice, be inserted into almost any book.

For instance, a brief mention in *A Head Girl's Difficulties* of some wild scamps at St Peter's who powder "the basins in the senior splasheries with some fizzy stuff" is reused at much greater length in *The School at the Chalet* (1925), where Bette and Bernhilda are convinced that witchcraft is causing the foaming basins. But, most of all, Brent-Dyer is creating for us an entire world where people can rub each other's corners off. That is the theme of *Gerry Goes to School*; and 45 years later, in *Prefects of the Chalet School* (1970), it remains a vital ingredient.

I doubt very much, however, whether any of this was consciously a motivation for creating so many Chalet books. There are other factors in creating a series of this type which she would have been quite aware of, and which she clearly enjoyed. Returning (if you will pardon the pun) to *Jo Returns to the Chalet School*, it may be recalled that Jo, much to her chagrin, has to rewrite an entire chapter of *Cecily Holds the Fort* because she has muddled up two of the prefects. She then concludes that the only way to avoid this problem is to create lists of the relevant characters, and becomes so absorbed in this exercise that "she finally made out the roll for the whole school, staff as well as girls. Then she put ticks by the side of all those who had appeared in the story so far." (p. 71).

This was certainly taken straight from Brent-Dyer's own experience. Helen McClelland has very kindly sent me copies of some of Brent-Dyer's working notes, including lists of the girls who comprised each form at the Chalet School, and she seems to have done this quite regularly. Certainly this is a sensible precaution against muddle (although it doesn't seem to have prevented her from other quite notorious confusions), but one cannot resist the idea that she enjoyed making lists and inventing names; enjoyed, in other words, all the paraphernalia of her imaginary school as much as actually telling the stories. Helen McClelland calls one of the chapters in *Behind the Chalet School* "Living in Chalet Lands"; and clearly Brent-Dyer revelled in her imaginary universe.

There are further advantages in the series for its creator. Once you've established the background, you don't continually have to stop to work out, say, the name of a form teacher, the games played by the school, the colour of the hatbands or the number and organisation of the houses. Since you and your readers already know all this, and are aware, too, of the personalities of many of the chief actors, you can concentrate on events which arise from those personalities — always the most fascinating — without having to spend chapters setting them up.

A good example of this can be seen in Grizel Cochrane. In *The School at the Chalet*, which isn't yet a series, we are shown how Grizel, cowed by her stepmother's mental cruelty, finds it hard to come to terms with the comparative freedom and atmosphere of approval of the newly formed Chalet School. Grizel gradually tests the limits of authority by a graded sequence of disobedience, culminating in an dangerous illegal expedition to the Tiernjoch; but Brent-Dyer delays this climax until Grizel has been up against authority enough times to demonstrate to the reader just what sort of person she is. By the time we reach the fourth of the series, *The Head Girl of the Chalet School* (1928), Brent-Dyer can make Grizel run off, equally illegally, to see the Falls of Rhine at the very beginning of the book and the reader simply nods. Yes, that's what Grizel is like. We know her now.

Obviously in the earlier books of any series the writer cannot take too much for granted, and Brent-Dyer gives us sometimes quite lengthy passages introducing the school and the major characters to novice readers. But eventually the series takes on such a momentum that the author can, if she so wishes, launch straight into the next book secure in the confidence that any new reader will either carry out her own research, hunting out the books which relate the previous history, or give up — and by this time there are so many readers that one less makes little difference. Perhaps I could give a personal example here. The first book I read was T*he Chalet School Wins the Trick* (1961) — no. 46 in the series — which begins (p.9):

> Rosalie Dene always vowed that it was she who had begun it, though she had certainly never intended it.
>
> Rosalie was one of the oldest of the Old Girls of the Chalet School, a fact of which she was privately very proud. She had also been school

secretary since she was twenty.[29]

As a result, there wasn't much about the school that she didn't know, to quote her old chum and schoolfellow, Joey Maynard.

Already there were mysteries. Why would a girls' school story begin its narrative with a grown-up like the school secretary? Who was this Joey Maynard? But so buoyant was the writer's self-confidence that I was carried along with the flow of the story, only resolving at the back of my mind to find out more about this girl and the school she belonged to. Paradoxically, the lack of background information is a positive advantage: just as a newcomer to a real school (or other institution) must make her way in this new world, aware that there are so many people, places and customs she has to discover, so the novice Chaletian is aware that there is an entire universe to be investigated, much of which is below the surface. The series, once established, carries its own authenticity within it.

And this brings us to the attraction of the series to the reader, rather than the writer. After all, a writer may create a series long enough to fill the entire British Library stack, but if no one reads it, it will stay there. What is so attractive about the series in general, and Brent-Dyer in particular?

Let's take the negative element first. It must be admitted that the series reader does not have to work so hard as the reader of a one-off novel. If one is lucky enough to get in at the beginning, so to speak, and start with *The School at the Chalet*, progressing through in the right order and taking in the various connecting books on the way, the whole thing is amazingly straightforward. But even for the majority who start in the middle and dart around as the books turn up, it's only the first plunge which is difficult. Once acclimatised, one can become involved with any new book immediately. In this sense, we series addicts are rather lazy. We know Jo and Madge, Mary-Lou and Verity; we recognise the Dripping Rock; and we could probably find our way quite easily from the Görnetz Platz down to Interlaken. There's no effort involved. It's what one might call the Warm Bath Effect — one simply sinks back into the bubbles and relaxes.

But of course, no reader would give laziness as a reason for loving these books. Far more potent is the relationship which we have with the characters. And here it must be admitted that a poor author is far more likely to get away with fuzzy or unrealistic characterisation in a series than in a single book. Familiarity may breed contempt, but it also breeds affection; and a character who might simply annoy or bore in one book, becomes part of the familiar and welcome landscape in a series. Rosemary Auchmuty comments: "As with real friends we tolerate all sorts of flaws and deviations for the sake of our shared past; we are invariably pleased to meet them again, to catch up on old times and find out what they're up to now."[30]

While I would not describe Brent-Dyer as a poor writer, she cannot be counted among the great ones of English Literature; she did not possess the skill to create many characters who would automatically linger in our memories after one meeting. But met in book after book, they don't merely linger, they take over. We care intensely what happens to them. This applies even to some of the minor characters. Who, reading *The Chalet School in Exile* (1940), can fail to identify with Maria Marani's numb terror for her father, taken to Buchenwald and then not heard from? But we care because we've known Maria since the very first book, and have met "Onkel Florian" many times. And the major characters are so well established that Brent-Dyer can take them far away from the Chalet School as such — can spend, indeed, entire books removing them from England to Switzerland or having holidays in Yorkshire or the Tyrol, confident that we will be just as interested in their out-of-school activities as ever we were in their school adventures. As Helen McClelland says:

> Elinor's principal achievement would seem to lie in having created at the beginning of her series a set of characters who gradually assumed an almost independent existence in her eyes and those of her readers. Then, by employing various devices, she was able to keep at least the most important of these characters on stage throughout the series. Later their multitudinous children were to follow in their footsteps at the school, often learning from the same teachers as had their parents. And what amounts to a personal relationship between reader and characters was slowly to be established.[31]

So important is this aspect of the Series Factor that it can carry the author through creative troughs which would destroy the non-series writer. I think that most lovers of the Chalet books would agree that, viewed overall, Brent-Dyer is at her strongest in the early books when the school is in Tyrol and the first fine careless (literally at times) rapture is still in full flow. Equally, most would agree that the books do not attract quite so much, taken individually, when the Chalet School moves out to the Oberland; and that the last dozen books are really quite poor. Sometimes, indeed, there are parts which are embarrassingly bad. One thinks, for instance, of the scene where Len finally accepts her destiny:

> Reg pulled her to him and Len sank down beside the bed. His arms went round her, then he held her from him and looked at her searchingly.
> "I take it we're engaged. Like it, darling?"
> Len chuckled. "So much I can't think why I didn't know it before. It all seems absolutely natural and *very* nice! Yes, of course we're engaged, only it *must* be kept dark until term ends."[32]

Nor is it merely individual scenes which fail to convince. From the early sixties onwards, many books are almost empty of any original incident or character, and rely on repetitions of earlier events with change of character and slight alterations in circumstance. The plot of *The Feud at the Chalet School* (1962) is that of *Rivals of the Chalet School* (1929), with the addition of proximity; *The Chalet School Wins the Trick* (1961) a re-working of *The New Chalet School* (1938), using a very similar set of enemy children. If the capacity to irritate of Val, Solange and their friends is less that that of the "Mystic M", that must point to the lower imaginative charge Brent-Dyer was able to put into the later book.

And by the time we have reached the last few books, the plots, such as they are, are mostly repetitions of the theme which was established way back in 1920 in *Gerry Goes to School*, and used many times since: new girl comes to school, finds another girl hostile (often because the new girl has become friendly with someone whose attention is coveted by her rival) and is finally reconciled with her enemy. In the earlier books, the theme is used sparingly: we can see it working in *Lavender Laughs at the Chalet School* (1943), for instance; and Barbara Chester confronts the same problem in *The Chalet School and Barbara* (1954).

As the series passes the two-thirds point, Brent-Dyer reverts to this plot more frequently: Margot resents Ted[33] as Francie resents Ruey[34] — and here the books are only three apart. And by the end, the heroines may be distinct, but the stories aren't. Jane, Flavia, Adrienne, Erica, Althea . . . all have to confront hostility and find eventual reconciliation. Brent-Dyer has succumbed to a formula.

Yet it cannot be denied that readers of the Chalet series search just as avidly for the last few books as for the Tyrol sequence — more avidly, indeed, as the later books (none of which were reprinted in hardback) are far rarer and more expensive to buy second-hand. Nor do these books, once acquired, sit on the shelf unread while their proud owner reads the first few over and over again. By existing as part of a series, they take on the positive attributes of the earlier books which they themselves lack, and are enjoyed as part of the sequence. For the reader as well as the writer, the Chalet School itself is the main plot. And since the Chalet School is central to *Althea and the Chalet School* (1965) or *Challenge for the Chalet School* (1967) just as much as *The Chalet School and Jo* (1931) or *The New Chalet School* (1938), readers are still faithful.

But we must now confront an apparent contradiction in the argument so far. I have suggested that the Chalet School is the major character in the series; but also, that the main reason we would give for enjoying the books is the relationship we have with the characters. How can both ideas be true? The seeming paradox can be resolved by looking more closely at what is meant by "the Chalet

School". If one thinks of it simply as an institution which exists independently of the people who teach and learn there, one has missed the whole point. Just as, in Christian circles, "the Church" means *not* the building in which people meet on a Sunday, but the entire body of believers, living and dead; so, in the Chalet series, "the Chalet School" means "the entire corpus of Chalet girls and staff" plus, indeed, a whole host of related individuals (Jack and Jem are disqualified by age and sex from ever attending the School as pupils, and will probably never teach there, but who would dare exclude them?).

This metaphysical concept of the School becomes clearer when one remembers its geographical and numerical vicissitudes. For 13 books it's in the Tyrol, growing from 3 pupils to about 300; the rise of Nazism seems to kill it, but it is reborn in Guernsey (with only 52 pupils) for half a book.[35] Fleeing again from the invading Nazis, it ends up in a village near Armiford[36] (Brent-Dyer's fictional version of Hereford) for 7 books, where it grows again; expelled by drains, it moves to an island off the Welsh coast[37], where it stays for seven books (making an preliminary excursion to the Oberland to establish a finishing branch[38]). It ends up on the Görnetz Platz[39] for the final 28 volumes, rising to "about four hundred [girls] . . . with the Kindergarten"[40], as well as "the English branch", about which we hear more or less nothing, though occasional girls come out from there to Switzerland. Clearly this school, which has occupied a minimum of 7 different buildings, cannot be regarded as a single physical entity.

Can it then be thought of as a purely theoretical idea — like that School Spirit headmistresses used to be so fond of quoting to us when we'd been spotted eating food in the street or losing more hockey matches than usual? This comes nearer the point, but still misses it. "School spirit", like peace, is something generally noticed when absent, and the Chalet School never loses it. No, the idea of the Chalet School is, very cleverly, projected on to certain characters, and continuity of character is at the core of the Chalet School.

In a very important sense, of course, continuity of character is the heart of any series. We have already seen that the use of the same school (as in Smith or Elder) is not sufficient; we need to follow the characters from book to book. This poses a problem for any children's writer who takes children as their main characters, whether in or out of school: eventually, our favourites become too old. One can use Malcolm Saville's expedient, and refuse to let them age (though even he had to allow a bit of maturity eventually[41]); but in a school setting, where progression through the school hierarchy is a fundamental part of the attraction, that won't work.

One can write a book for each year or each term, and then finish the series (Blyton's technique); or accept that school is no longer central but still follow the characters into adulthood, as Oxenham does. Brent-Dyer follows the natural sequence of events in letting her characters age and progress, and uses the technique of many non-series writers in allowing us to identify with a succession of new girls who are gradually moulded by the Chalet spirit; but with one significant addition. The Chalet spirit is actually represented by individuals who last far longer within the series than is usual in school stories.

Looking at the series overall, it is quite clear that there are three girls on to whom the Chalet spirit is projected: Jo, Mary-Lou and Jo's daughter Len. It would be interesting to discuss in some detail the precise qualities which are epitomised by these three characters, but space, alas, does not allow it. What must be said, though, is that Jo in particular symbolises the Chalet spirit. From p.15 of *The School at the Chalet* to p.166 of *Prefects of the Chalet School*, Jo is a continuous presence; there are even five books[42] where the school doesn't appear at all, but Jo is a key figure in all of them.

It may be significant that HarperCollins Armada, which has reprinted all the actual school stories, has until very recently seemed uninterested in four of these five (did the title give them the impression that *A Future Chalet School Girl* was a school story?). They presumably feel that there would not be a large enough market for books which focus largely on adults or are not set in a school. I think they are wrong: the school is there in the person of Jo — friendly, understanding, forgiving, loyal, humorous and tolerant.

The realisation of Jo's importance came to Brent-Dyer gradually. In *The Head Girl of the Chalet School* we are told that Jo is going to leave school at 17 to be lady-in-waiting to Elisaveta. By the time that point is reached, Brent-Dyer has begun to realise that it would be most unwise to remove her heroine from the Chalet School, and she is given another year as Head Girl. And when her time as a schoolgirl cannot be further prolonged, we are told that Jo can't think of going to Belsornia now, since Madge, with her own two children and her brother Dick's young family to care for, needs her badly.[43]

Actually, Madge, with Marie and Rosa to help her, is the envy of every reader with young children, and needs Jo about as much as she needs Rufus the dog; Jo herself recognises this.[44] No, it's a ploy chosen to keep Jo up at the Sanatorium (or, once Jem has bought the St Scholastika buildings for a summer home, down at the Tiernsee), and thus ensure that she can return to the Chalet School at every opportunity. It might not have lasted Brent-Dyer another 40 books, but marrying Jo off to a doctor at the Sanatorium was an even better idea. In other words, Jo's continued presence in or near the school is an essential ingredient in creating that sense of the Chalet School itself as the central character in the stories — because Jo *is* the Chalet School. She is the warp — the thread which forms the basis of the multi-coloured tapestry which is the Chalet School, and one of the major reasons why Brent-Dyer's "castle in the air" is still loved today.[45]

The Series Factor, then, allowed Brent-Dyer to create and revel in an entire world which expressed her values and ideals; and to communicate these through the creation of specific characters whom we follow throughout the series. It permits readers to enter this world and experience the characters as their friends. Without the Series Factor, Brent-Dyer would be of minor interest. With it, she will remain one of the most beloved writers for girls who "even if they live to be great-grandmothers, will be Chalet Girls to the end."[46]

NOTES

1. *Book and Magazine Collector* (October, 1993).
2. Occasionally a character from one book will reappear in a minor role in another: eg *A Patriotic Schoolgirl* (Blackie, 1918), *The School in the South* (Blackie, 1922) and *Joan's Best Chum* (Blackie, 1926).
3. *The Scholarship Girl* (Collins, 1925); *The Scholarship Girl at Cambridge* (Collins, 1926).
4. *Exile for Annis* (1938); *Cherry Tree Perch* (1939); *Strangers at the Farm School* (1940). All Collins.
5. *Merry Begins, Merry Again, Merry Marches On* (all Oxford University Press, 1947).
6. *Seven Sisters at Queen Anne's* (1924); *Septima at School* (1925); *Phyllida in Form III* (1927). All Blackie.
7. *The Chalet School Goes to It* (1941); *Gay From China at the Chalet School* (1944).
8. First met in *The Princess of the Chalet School* (1927); later adventures recounted in *Highland Twins at the Chalet School* (1942).
9. *Lavender Laughs at the Chalet School* (1943) et seq.
10. *Gay From China at the Chalet School*, pp.230-1.
11. *Lavender Laughs at the Chalet School*, pp. 104-6.
12. *Rivals of the Chalet School* (1929), chap. 17 et seq.
13. *Gay From China at the Chalet School*, esp. pp.105-7.
14. *Jane Steps In* (1953).
15. *Bride Leads the Chalet School* (1953), p.34 ff.
16. *Highland Twins at the Chalet School*, p.39.
17. *The Chalet School Goes To It*, p.39.
18. e.g. no.10, Nov.1963; no. 15, Sept.1966.
19. Mary Cadogan, *Richmal Crompton: The Woman Behind William* (Allen & Unwin, 1986), p.71.
20. Humphrey Carpenter, *J. R. R.Tolkien* (George Allen & Unwin, 1977), p.183 ff.
21. Roger Lancelyn Green & Walter Hooper, *C. S. Lewis* (Collins, 1974), p.236 ff.

22. "On Fairy Stories". In various collections, most accessibly *Tree and Leaf* (George Allen & Unwin, 1964).
23. *Times Educational Supplement*, 3 July 1970.
24. See e.g. Barbara Stoney, *Enid Blyton* (Hodder & Stoughton, 1976), p.206.
25. See e.g. "It All Began With a Picture". In various collections, e.g. *Of This And Other Worlds* (Collins 1982).
26. Helen McClelland,*Elinor M.Brent-Dyer's Chalet School* (Armada, 1989).
27. *Joey Goes to the Oberland* (1954), p.40.
28. *Jo Returns to the Chalet School* (1936).
29. Actually, she hadn't — she was initially Dr Jem's secretary at the Sanatorium. But Brent-Dyer clearly forgot this (one of the *disadvantages* of the series).
30. Rosemary Auchmuty, *A World of Girls* (Women's Press, 1992), p.87.
31. *Behind the Chalet School*, p.178.
32. *Prefects of the Chalet School* (1970), p.67.
33. *Theodora and the Chalet School* (1959).
34. *Ruey Richardson, Chaletian* (1960).
35. *The Chalet School in Exile* (1940).
36. *The Chalet School Goes to It* (1941) et seq.
37. *The Chalet School and the Island* (1950) et seq.
38. *The Chalet School in the Oberland* (1952).
39. *The Chalet School and Barbara* (1954) to end of series.
40. *Challenge for the Chalet School* (1966), p.19.
41. Malcom Saville, *Not Scarlet But Gold* (Newnes, 1962), Introduction, p.6.
42. *Jo to the Rescue* (1945), *Joey Goes to the Oberland* (1954), *Joey and Co. in Tirol* (1960), *A Future Chalet School Girl* (1962), *The Chalet School Reunion* ((1963).
43. *The New House at the Chalet School* (1935), pp.21-2.
44. Ibid., pp.250-1.
45. Even when she is in Canada, from *The Wrong Chalet School* (1952) to *Bride Leads the Chalet School* (1953), numerous references to her and letters from her keep her in mind.
46. *Prefects of the Chalet School* (with minor alterations!), p.38 — and many other places.

First and paperback editions of *The Coming of Age of the Chalet School*, *The Chalet School and Richenda*, *Trials for the Chalet School* and *Theodora and the Chalet School*.

CONFESSIONS OF
A CHALET SCHOOL COLLECTOR

GILL BILSKI

Do you remember those wonderful days when you could go into Foyles and see two whole shelves full of brightly jacketed titles by Elinor M. Brent-Dyer? And do you recall the nightmare of being able to afford only one? If only I had known!

Luckily my father was in the book trade and realised that once the books had gone out of print they were unlikely to be reprinted. Having decided that this was no "fly-by-night" passion, he bought up all the copies I did not yet possess. These were secreted in a cardboard box in the bottom of my mother's wardrobe, ready for use as birthday and Christmas presents. However, once I discovered this treasure trove, I would sneak in there when my parents were out and have an illicit read. Finally, I remember that my cousin was coming to stay and I owned up to knowing about the box. With a little persuasion I was allowed to have all of the books to put on my shelves to make a good show and, somehow, after she had gone home, there they remained.

I was always a great fan of school stories starting, as so many people do, with the Malory Towers and St Clare's stories by Enid Blyton. Such stories were far more abundant in the 1960s than they are today, and our library had a large selection which I borrowed regularly.

Although I had always known about the Chalet School series, for my mother had preserved a copy of

Eustacia Goes to the Chalet School (1930) from her own childhood, I avoided reading it. First, I thought the name Eustacia really odd and, second, my mother had recommended them — I was at an age when I automatically avoided anything recommended by my parents! Eventually, when I was about ten, I capitulated — mainly because I had read everything else that interested me in the local library. I started with *Trials for the Chalet School* (no. 41, 1959) which should have put me off them completely as there must have been so many things that did not make sense, since I had not read the previous ones. Happily it didn't, and I progressed to having a few copies of my own.

A little later, when helping at a jumble sale, I found a copy of *The Feud in the Fifth Remove* (1931) and was amazed to see that although by Elinor Brent-Dyer, this was not a Chalet School book. From this I discovered that she had written other books, and thought how I should love to read all of them.

At about this time I joined the original Chalet Club run by W. & R. Chambers (the publishers of the Chalet School series). This had been started in May 1959, and readers were invited to join for a small fee. In return they received newsletters written by Elinor Brent-Dyer about the books and how she wrote them, giving further news of characters who hadn't appeared recently, answering readers' queries and setting competitions. There was a membership badge of a small edelweiss on a pin and family trees of the Bettany family. There were also saving cards so that readers could save up for the new titles. In those days the majority of members were schoolgirls although, even then, there was an adult section with their own special competition. At its peak there were nearly 4,000 members from all over the world. The club ran until her death, when Chambers felt it could no longer be continued.

Although I joined only towards the end, I can still remember the thrill when the newsletters arrived, though sadly in later years they became fewer and further between. Elinor Brent-Dyer was very keen on giving advice on writing, but for me the interest was in her answers to readers' questions: finding out what had happened to old girls, and on whom the characters were based. I also loved the competitions but, sadly, did not win any of them.

Nowadays, if you were not lucky enough to have been a member, the newsletters are very difficult to find and, therefore, extremely collectable. The badge, too, is almost unheard of on the second-hand market. Unfortunately, being a pin, it tended to fall off clothes, and I certainly remember losing mine on a couple of occasions — though I found it again each time.

I was really pleased when Armada brought out the first four paperbacks in 1967. The first few were edited by Elinor Brent-Dyer herself to shorten and update them. I remember that one was *The Chalet School and Barbara* (1954), which delighted me as it filled in a large gap. I continued to read and reread them — I read the whole series from beginning to end for the first time when I got my last one, *Tom Tackles the Chalet School* (1955). Never mind that at the time I was supposed to be revising for my A-Levels! At this time I seemed to grow out of all my children's books, except for the Chalets. I have heard so many tales of how complete collections were consigned to jumble sales after the owner left home or "grew up". I am forever thankful that, although many of my books went this way, the Chalet School series stayed with me.

FROM FAN TO COLLECTOR

Shortly before this I had seen an advertisement in a periodical from Trisha Marshall, whom I subsequently discovered was an avid collector of Elinor Brent-Dyer, amongst other authors. She was actually asking for copies but my mother (who collects Elsie J. Oxenham, author of the Abbey girls series) wrote to her saying that we hadn't any to sell but we were collecting them too. This was my first contact with another collector, and I remember the wonderful feeling that I was not the only one. I had thought that I was the only person who loved the series so much and had never had anybody to talk to about the books.

Since then, I have had letters from many people who collect and love the books. So many of them have said that they had to keep their obsession quiet in case their friends and relations thought them odd. They felt that reading school stories in adulthood would not be considered normal, and they often express their relief at being able to talk about the books and admit to their secret passion.

Trisha put us in touch with other collectors and I visited them and saw their beautiful early illustrated editions and dust jackets, and thought that I would like those too. My first copies of the early stories had all been 1950s reprints without dust jackets or illustrations. It's difficult now, in retrospect, to imagine Jo, Robin or any of the others without seeing Nina K. Brisley's illustrations in my mind. Unusually, I remember no surprise or shock at her depiction of the characters, so I think she must have captured them as I had imagined them. More importantly, she evidently read the books as the characters and situations are "right". Although several other people illustrated subsequent editions and the later books, none of them seems right to me. To me her Jo *is* Jo. The dust jackets are important — most collectors prefer their books to have them. Our views of the artist's presentation of various characters may not always be the same, but as with the illustrations in the books, they add something to the story.

Having now been in contact with other collectors, I discovered the existence of "wants lists" and the necessity of making one to send around to other collectors who might have spare copies of books and, later on, to dealers. My first wants list contained only books by Elinor Brent-Dyer and was very long. However, now I was part of a network of collectors, books came thick and fast. I had had the natural assumption that if I did not have a book, it must be hard to find. I was soon disabused of this when I was sent multiple offers of the same title.

In the mean time, I was not sitting on my laurels. I visited jumble sales, picking up copies of *Bride Leads the Chalet School* (1953) and, more importantly, *The Chalet School and Rosalie* (1951). Again, at first, I did not realise how lucky I was. I thought that, since I had found it at a jumble sale, it must be common! I also haunted Charing Cross Road as, by this time, I had left school and was working in London. Sadly, I rarely found anything there, but was drawn by posters I saw in the shops to the Provincial Book Fairs Association's bookfairs in Russell Square. Again, there was little to buy, and dealers, when asked about Elinor Brent-Dyer, either gave me blank looks or expressed astonishment that anyone would collect that sort of book. I had to bite my tongue on several occasions! This was, of course, long before the days of dealers specialising in girls' fiction.

Undaunted, I went to second-hand bookhops and,

just occasionally, there was a title I wanted. There is a heart-stopping moment for collectors when this occurs. I recall that on one of my forays to Cecil Court (off Charing Cross Road) I saw the words *Elizabeth the Gallant* (1935) on a book on the 10p shelves outside a shop. By this time I knew that it was a very rare Brent-Dyer, but I remember closing my eyes and counting to five before I dared to look at it again. It was literally a case of not believing my eyes. Once I opened them again and saw that it really was what I thought, I grabbed it and shot straight into the shop to pay for it before they changed their minds. Some 15 years later I can still remember that moment of disbelief at what I was seeing.

Thus my mishmash of reprints and paperbacks, plus the last ten or so books bought new, gradually became my collection as it is today — all first editions with dust jackets (although I must admit that some of the jackets on the first 11 are from similarly sized reprints; I suppose this is cheating a bit, but I like the way they look and I can always hope for first edition dustjackets to turn up). It's taken a very long time — over 25 years — and I only got my last original jacket to replace a photocopy (*The Exploits of the Chalet Girls*, 1933) in 1992. I also got my last two Brent-Dyers that year, so now have a copy of some sort of everything she wrote.

My collecting also led to my moment of fame. Andy Warhol said that everyone is famous for 15 minutes — in my case I think it was 10, but fame none the less. Martin Spence, another avid Brent-Dyer collector, was asked to appear on *Woman's Hour* to talk about the Chalet School series and why they still appeal today. He was also asked to find another collector and picked me. We went to Broadcasting House and recorded an interview. It was really fascinating, and lasted for well over half an hour. Sadly, when it was actually broadcast, on 23 March 1987, it had been drastically cut down to ten minutes. I am sure that all my best bits were lost, but it was fun and I was delighted to be able to speak about my passion to a bigger audience than I am usually able to command!

BOOK SELLING

In the mean time, I had got married and then left work to have my children. This meant that I no longer had my own money to buy books. Unfortunately my husband is not a bibliophile, and he objected to the housekeeping money disappearing just because I had seen a dust jacket for *Peggy of the Chalet School* (1950) that was marginally nicer than mine. Something had to be done. Since having been in contact with other collectors, I had sold odd spares that were on other people's wants lists. Now, I thought, I probably knew enough to gather a few books together and produce a list. I did have an inbuilt advantage in that my mother had been producing sales lists for some time. This meant that I had access to her mailing list and, at the beginning, I was able to send out my list with hers, thus saving the postage. I compiled my first children's list in March 1983 — three sides of A4 paper. I sold a few — at that stage, I thought I would sell all of them. Another misapprehension.

In the past, when ordering from dealers' catalogues, I had often found that the particular books I wanted had already gone. Logically, I suppose, I assumed that dealers sold virtually all their books. I was surprised and disappointed to find that from the eighty or so books I had lovingly gathered together, I sold only twenty. These twenty were divided between only seven customers, and only one book was wanted by more than one. Looking at that list today, I only wish I had a few of the books that were so easily disregarded then. For example, out of the five Brent-Dyers on the list, only one was sold. *Carnation of the Upper Fourth* (1934) in a first edition was unsold at £1.75. Incidentally, of those seven initial customers, I am still in contact with four who buy regularly. By my second list, I was evidently a little more in tune with what people wanted as I sold fifty of ninety books, including all the Brent-Dyers!

Why did I choose to sell children's books? Basically because children's books were what I knew about. Not only was I a Brent-Dyer collector, but by this time I was collecting quite a few girls' authors, not to mention Biggles. I knew about these and, from reading other dealers' catalogues when hunting for my own books, I had found out about other authors and who was collectable.

From there it grew. I learnt from my mistakes; if all the dealers receiving my lists pounced on one particular title, it was guaranteed that I had badly underpriced it, but each time I was caught like this I remembered and knew for the next time. Sometimes I was stuck with books that I had paid a lot for, thinking them collectable, only to find that they did not sell — again, I did not get caught twice — or not with the same book, anyway!

Originally the lists were produced on stencils as my mother had a duplicator, but these were difficult to read so I bought an electric typewriter and had the lists properly printed as booklets. However, I used to dread the time when I knew I had to sit down and type the lists from my handwritten scrawl. Finally I bought a word processor. Now I could enter books as I bought them and when it was time to print the pages off, all I had to do was to number the books and make sure that the lists agreed with the actual books on the shelves. With the extra time that this allowed me, I started to give short descriptions of the books, as I felt that customers would be more likely to try new authors if they knew a bit about the story. By advertising in various book magazines, my mailing list grew, and I now produce catalogues of 40+ pages about 6 times a year.

A friend of mine who is a Biggles collector asked me about three years ago whether I wanted to share his stall at a local book fair. Book fairs are similar to antique fairs, in that many dealers attend with their own stands and they give a chance for those without shops to reach the general public. I had attended them since early in my collecting career, and had vaguely thought that one day I might have a go at selling at one. His offer decided me, and I spent hours pricing all the books that I thought I should take and putting them into boxes.

The first attempt at Bushey in Hertfordshire did not go particularly well. I sold very few books and decided that if I was going to do this properly I would have to get some folding shelves to display the books so customers could actually see them. Slowly I began to realise which books sold well at the fairs and got to know many of the regular customers and which sort of books they wanted. I started exhibiting at a couple of other fairs as well, and now attend at least one a month, sometimes more.

There are a lot of disadvantages to book fairs. First, having to get up really early on a Saturday morning has never been one of my favourite activities. There is also the lugging of boxes of books and folding shelves out of the car boot and into the hall and back again, without much difference in weight at the end of the day! The final problem is the total unpredictability of numbers attending. Despite all the organiser's best efforts at advertising, bad weather, very good weather or a major sporting event on television can cut numbers drastically. Luckily there are advantages, too, in that they enable me to find new customers and to meet others whom I have known for years.

The money was, of course, useful as it enabled me to buy books that I could never have considered before, and also paid for extras such as holidays and Christmas presents. Now it is essential, as our main income has decreased so much owing to the recession that the money goes on necessities such as food and clothes for the children.

However, most of all, selling books is fun. I love books. I love searching for them, finding those that collectors want, talking to people about them and — the most important — reading them. How could I have dreamt when I found that copy of *Trials* in the library that it would lead to this?

THE COLLECTOR/DEALER NETWORK

There are only a few major specialist children's dealers — probably no more than ten. Many of them started as collectors themselves, following the maxim to deal in what you know. Most serious collectors are in contact with some or all of them, sending them wants lists and receiving their catalogues. Prices from these dealers are necessarily higher as they are specialist and frequently need to use their expertise. Additionally, they tend to have to pay more for their books as they are known to be specialists.

There are other smaller children's dealers who

generally specialise in one or two areas such as Biggles, William, school stories, Blyton or similar subjects or authors. There are also general dealers and bookshops who have a children's section. These are the places where bargains may occasionally be found, as such dealers cannot be conversant with current prices in all subjects. We all have our favourites — and I have no intention of divulging mine here!

Many collectors become dealers to a lesser or greater extent because they have spare books that they do not want to give away to jumble sales or charity shops when there could be a fellow collector somewhere who is desperate for them. Most just sell them to other, larger, dealers who can pass them on, but there are the few such as myself who don't stop there and go on to produce catalogues and, eventually, let it take over their lives!

Dealers' attitudes to their own collections are also interesting. Until recently I assumed that all dealers put their collections first and that dealing was firmly in second place. If I get a better copy of a book in my collection, I keep it without a second thought and sell the copy which isn't so good, hoping to recoup some of the outlay on the new copy. However, I have heard that some dealers steadily downgrade their collections, believing that the condition of their own books doesn't matter and they prefer to sell the better copies. I find this a very strange way of going about things and cannot, personally, imagine putting my dealing before my collecting.

Dealers' reactions to the request for Brent-Dyers are interesting. Nowadays, at least, there is generally an admission that they have heard of her, unlike when I was first collecting, when the invariable reply was "Who?" Quite a few of the general dealers do not understand that Chalet School books do not all have the same value, and have a habit of putting out copies of *The School at the Chalet* and *The Chalet School Reunion* at the same price, which is wonderful if you happen to be there at the right time! They also realise that they are much sought after nowadays and tend to make that price quite high.

COLLECTORS

I know many collectors from all over the world, most of whom I consider to be friends. Those first lonely days after giving up work were filled with the fun of building up a business and being in contact with so many other like-minded people. But what are these other Brent-Dyer collectors like? It is impossible to generalise. Although there is not a typical Brent-Dyer collector, they do all share one thing: a love of books in general and her books in particular.

Whilst I know seven or eight male collectors, the vast majority are women. They range in age from seven to over eighty. They live all over the world. Most are naturally English-speaking, from the UK, Australia, New Zealand and Canada, although two are Swedish. It is very hard to keep up correspondence with so many of them, with other calls on my time, but rarely a day goes by without my receiving a letter from one of my "book friends", as I call them.

The vast majority discovered the Chalet School when they were round about ten years old. They read and collect assiduously. At the age of about fifteen, a break often came. In the past, many collectors have told me that they had to move to the adult library at about this and were no longer allowed to borrow their favourites from the children's library. Nowadays, it is more likely to be outside interests such as boys, or teasing and mocking from their contemporaries, that stop them reading the books. Those who decide that they want to stay with them are likely to keep their love of the books very quiet, feeling embarrassment at keeping them. They often have their break a little later, when they leave home and do not have the space to keep all their childhood favourites. So many people have told me that at some stage or other they had all or most of the Chalet School series, including all the later difficult titles, but gave them away or, worse still, found that they had been given away by parents whilst they had been living away from home.

Many of these collectors have a nostalgic urge to replace their collection and, perhaps, recapture some of their childhood. They may see one in a shop and suddenly remember their love of the books in their younger days and, having read one, the memories come flooding back and they feel they must read them all. A recent collector, a lady in her 70s, had thought that the series ended with the war as that was when she had stopped reading them. One can only imagine her feelings when she discovered that there were 44 more books that she didn't know about!

There are a few collectors who did not read the Chalet books in childhood. Some have discovered them through their children reading them, and they are usually new to book collecting in any form. Some are collectors of other girls' stories such as the Abbey books by Elsie Oxenham or the several school series by Dorita Fairlie Bruce. They graduate to the Chalet School for one of two reasons. Either they have got as far as they can go easily with their current collections and want another series to collect or else they bow to friends' pressure and try one. Of course, having tried one, they are hooked.

Chalet collectors also have widely differing ideas as to the form their collections should take. Some collectors are anxious to read and have the text in any form, even paperback, and either don't know or don't care that these are edited and cut. They are rarely interested in her other books, though very occasionally they will branch out into the connecting stories. These are stories such as the La Rochelle series of seven books and *Monica Turns Up Trumps* (1936), which tie into the Chalet School series at various points when characters from them appear in Chalet books.

Some collectors have budget limits. They decide how much they can aford to spend on their books and try to stick to this figure rigidly. This is useful for the dealer, as she does not waste time or money offering a book that is outside their price range. The problem here is that some of the rarer books are always outside the limit, in whatever condition they are.

Others are keen to have beautiful first editions in dust jackets, although they are happy to have any complete edition of the book to start with, just to read the story. They will then upgrade their copies as and when possible. They are completists in the true sense. They are determined to get all the books Brent-Dyer wrote, including the elusive school geography readers and the awful religious "Sunday School Prize" stories. Some collect ancillary items, such as postcards of the Achensee where the first few books are set. I expect that you have realised by now that this is a pretty good description of me!

There are a very few who will pass by a book they have not read because it does not have a dust jacket. I can see the logic behind this as it means there is no need to upgrade, less money is spent in the long run and the collector has definitely no chance of becoming a dealer because she has so many cast-off upgraded copies to sell. A very few collect only Brent-Dyer; the majority collect other similar authors. Many (though not myself) collect Elsie Oxenham as well, but, if they do, virtually all have a decided preference for one or the other.

Some go further and make lists of the characters and try to fit the correct time-scales to the series. This is not an easy thing to do. I myself am attempting this, as it's a long-held ambition to have my own personal encyclopaedia of the Chalet School. It is driving me mad, as names change, ages change, and some things are just totally illogical! These collectors have also been known to continue the stories beyond *Prefects at the Chalet School* (1970, the last book of the series) in their own minds. Recently in the *Friends of the Chalet School Newsletter* members have been writing about how they thought Brent-Dyer would have continued the series and whether they felt she would have brought events up to date into the 1970s. Despite my own opinion that she realised that *Prefects* would be the last book in the series, many collectors find themselves having withdrawal symptoms when they reach the end and feel they must know what happens to the characters, even if they have to write the story themselves.

THE PART COLLECTING PLAYS IN PEOPLE'S LIVES

Most Chalet collectors share an objective view of the books, unlike some collectors of other authors. They know about the faults and illogicalities and enjoy discussing them. They know the stories are not perfect, but accept them just the same.

Just as the collectors are all different, so is the

part that collecting plays in their lives. For some it is a very minor part. If a book happens to be on a shelf right in front of them, or someone writes to offer them a book from their wants list, they are pleased to have it. They wouldn't go out of their way to look for it, however. At the other end of the scale, there are those who would drive 50 miles out of their way because they have heard a vague rumour that there might be a second-hand bookshop. They send for every children's catalogue they see advertised and put a lot of effort into finding the books they want.

Many collectors produce a wants list that they send round to dealers. These range from half a page with a few titles to 20-plus handwritten foolscap pages (yes, I do know a collector who has one that long). Some send updated lists every time they write — this is very useful for the dealer, because it means that she doesn't get stuck with books she buys for a specific person, only to find that they have already got them. Yes, we all get caught that way! This doesn't matter so much for a rare Brent-Dyer title, but some obscure books are not wanted by other people.

Once a collector produces a wants list, she is well on the way to ruin. What started as a harmless pastime is beginning to become an all-consuming passion. She has admitted on paper that she is truly a collector. She is no longer reliant on being the first to ring for that elusive title in a catalogue, only to be told that it went at 6.30 a.m. She has put herself in the hands of the dealers, and has to trust that it is to her that they offer that elusive title that appears on 60 other wants lists.

Reactions to being offered that elusive title are very different. From some you receive a dull acknowledgement letter — please send the book, followed by a cheque in an envelope with no letter at all. From others you receive an effusive letter saying how delighted they are, and a lovely letter of thanks when they pay. These are the people I prefer to find books for and I feel that their gratitude and pleasure make it all worthwhile. I know from personal experience the pleasure when a letter or phone call comes offering a book that I really want, and so cannot understand those collectors who do not seem bothered, or even do not reply at all.

Once the collector has most of the books in some edition or other, there is a void in her life. She knows that the last few books she wants will be hard to find and needs to have some purpose when she visits her accustomed bookshops or book fairs. She begins to think it might be nice to have hardback editions of all of them, then perhaps dust jackets would be a good idea; they will brighten up the shelves. Finally she gets this inexplicable urge to have first editions — the first printed form in which the book appeared. She is getting a collection together.

Eventually it can become an obsession. I know of a few collectors who have become obsessive about their collections. They ring dealers almost weekly, phone for books from catalogues at 7 a.m. (how do they get their post so early?) and plague the life out of dealers at book fairs by telling them of all their new acquisitions and asking why the dealer hasn't found them a new title recently. I must admit that I tend to hide when I see them coming! I should also add that I don't know any Brent-Dyer collectors who have reached this stage of obsession (yet).

These extremists are also obsessive about the condition of the books. I think that possibly they are treating their books as objects. They tell anyone who will listen about the value of the books and how little money they have had to spend. Mind you, their idea of little money and mine are not the same. They are willing to pay any price to get the books they want and have been known to offer a dealer more money when they are told that a book from a catalogue has been sold. These people are not good for book collecting. They push up the prices for other collectors and the only hope is that when they have completed their collections they will be happy and stop spoiling the fun of collecting for others.

SOCIETIES

In 1994, the centenary of Elinor Brent-Dyer's birth, reading and collecting her books have never been more popular. In one of my recent catalogues, all the Brent-Dyers sold almost immediately — a total of 34. Several of the titles, none of which was rare, attracted 10 or more people. Prices for the rarer titles are probably at their peak for a while, as the collectors prepared to pay the very high prices of recent years have completed their collections, but there is a very large demand for the cheaper, commoner titles. In future years, the prices will almost certainly rise still further once these new collectors have found all the easy titles.

Whilst a tatty reprint of *The School at the Chalet* will probably fetch no more than £2 or £3, a copy of *The Chalet School Reunion* in its dust jacket could well set you back £100 or more. I saw a copy of *The Chalet School in Exile* (1940) in its almost impossible to find withdrawn dust jacket a couple of years ago for about £150. Moving briefly from the Chalet School series, I have never seen Brent-Dyer's two rarest books — *The School by the River* (1930) and *The Little Marie-José* (1932) — in a catalogue, so if a copy did turn up, the price can only be imagined.

In recent times, several popular children's authors have had societies and magazines devoted to them. Some had regular meetings, and it was felt by Brent-Dyer collectors that something similar should happen for their favourite author, as nothing had been done since the demise of the original Chalet Club. After all, many of the others, such as Elsie Oxenham and Violet Needham, had been out of print for years, whereas the Chalet School stories were still being published in paperback and bought. However, no one was willing to take it on. It fell to Ann Mackie-Hunter in Australia to do what we had seemed unable to do in the UK.

Ann was a member of the Abbey Girls of Australia, but was also a keen Brent-Dyer collector. One cold, wet Sunday afternoon in 1989 she had some time on her hands and decided to practise her typing and, rather than straight and boring copy-typing, she decided to create a mock Chalet newsletter. That evening, a friend of hers (the founder of the Abbey Girls of Australia, Val Shelley) rang, and, when Ann told her what she'd been doing, Val said she should start a new club. Ann was somewhat dubious about the idea, but, before she could say a definite no, Val collected subscriptions from some Brisbane Abbey Club members who were also Brent-Dyer readers at their meeting the next morning. Faced with a *fait accompli* that evening, Ann ran off some copies the next day and posted them. Australian Friends of the Chalet School was born.

Two of the Oxenham newsletters, the *Abbey Guardian* and the *Abbey Chronicle*, advertised FOCS and the membership grew, mainly from Australia but a handful from the UK, New Zealand and Canada. An advertisement in the *Australian Women's Weekly* and the *Bookseller and Publisher* in

Australia brought in more new members. I joined, somewhat belatedly, at the end of 1989, as it was so expensive to get cheques in foreign currency, and I suggested that it might be easier if someone in the UK could collect subscriptions to save everyone having to purchase the cheques individually. Just like Ann, I really could not have imagined what this little suggestion would lead to. At the same time the society dropped its Australian prefix and became just Friends of the Chalet School as we wanted to stress that the society was international — just like the Chalet School.

In the middle of 1991, Ann had another of her bright ideas. As so many new members were joining from the UK, wouldn't it be nice to have a UK corner in each newsletter? I agreed prematurely, realising too late that what Ann really meant was that it would be nice if I wrote a UK corner. As I couldn't think of any convincing reason why I shouldn't do it, the UK corner first appeared in *Newsletter 12*.

Membership all over the world has grown and is now over 800, with members living in Austria, Australia, Canada, the Channel Islands, Eire, France, Germany, Japan, New Zealand, Singapore, South Africa, Sweden, Switzerland, Zimbabwe, the USA and the UK, predominantly female, but with twenty-plus male members. Ages range from seven to over eighty. The general feeling from new members is that they are delighted to find that there is such a society, and relieved that they are not the only adults addicted to school stories! In mid-1993, Ann decided that producing four newsletters a year virtually single-handed was getting too much, and thought that it would be better to have an editorial committee of four, each producing one newsletter a year. Once again I agreed that it was a good idea, and immediately found myself on the committee together with Clarissa Cridland and Polly Goerres, two UK members who had already become involved by volunteering to organise events for Brent-Dyer's centenary in 1994. The first result of this was *Newsletter 21*, edited by all four of us.

To give you an idea of how on earth we can fill four newsletters a year, this issue contained comments from members on previous articles including paperbacks, matters medical, music and what happened next; whatever happened to . . . ? (a regular feature picking out characters who seemed just to disappear); potted autobiographies of members; a report on arrangements for the centenary events; reports on meetings in Scotland, Nottingham and Somerset; a report on the lending library (we are trying to collect copies of all her books which are lent to members for a small fee); a résumé of *Joey and Co in Tirol* (1960); and ten articles on various subjects such as how one member started collecting, Elinor and Miss Le Poidevin (her friend from Guernsey), memories of Herefordshire and the historical background to *The Chalet School in Exile*. There were also items for sale and wanted and a couple of puzzles.

Meanwhile, in mid-1991, Daphne Paintin (now Barfoot) from Bideford in Devon thought that there ought to be a newsletter produced in the UK and so wrote to various people that she thought might be interested. Thus was born *The Chaletian*, a similar newsletter, with many of the same subscribers. Once the *Friends of the Chalet School Newsletter* started being produced in Britain, and owing to changes in her personal circumstances, Daphne decided to close *The Chaletian* in July 1994, after nine issues had appeared.

The aim of Friends of the Chalet School is to bring

together people from all over the world who enjoy Elinor Brent-Dyer's books. We do that through the newsletters, which are written by the members, and also through local meetings, where devotees can get together to talk about their passion (and all kinds of other things as well!). We are called *Friends* of the Chalet School because, despite the large membership, we like to consider ourselves as friends, bound in friendship by a common love of Elinor Brent-Dyer's books.

WHY PEOPLE COLLECT THE CHALET SCHOOL BOOKS

There is a basic human instinct to hoard or collect things — usually things that interest us — and books are a very popular form of collecting. Books are not holy relics, but should be looked after, especially in our field, in that there are a limited number of them about, and if all the copies were destroyed (as nearly happened to Elinor Brent-Dyer's two rarest books, *The School by the River* and *The Little Marie-José*), then they are lost for ever. In the majority of cases, collectors do not revere their books, but they do appreciate them and understand their rarity.

We do pay high prices for particular volumes when cheap paperback editions are available, but is there a good reason for this? Collecting hardbacks rather than paperbacks is logical as they are more durable, especially when read many times, and often contain the full text which has been abridged and edited in the paperbacks. As for collecting first editions, this is more problematic. I have never been able to pin down a good reason for wanting a first rather than an early reprint when the text (and often the binding) are identical. I myself am afflicted with this collecting malady as well, and it is, to my rational mind, illogical; but who said book collectors have to be logical? Maybe a very few collectors regard books as objects, but surely the majority collect only books that they are interested in and wish to read.

However, I need to be more specific. Why collect girls' school stories and why, in particular, collect Elinor Brent-Dyer? Apart from the very few modern writers who still write school stories, the majority, and almost all of the best ones, were written before the Second World War. In those days it was possible to open a small private school with almost no qualifications, as is described in Gillian Avery's *The Best Type of Girl* (Andre Deutsch, 1991), an excellent history of girls' independent schools. All that was needed was a large house and a few wealthy families, so many impoverished spinster ladies opened such schools with the idea of improving their financial position. There were also many expatriate children, especially from India, were sent back "home" for their education and upbringing, who were in the sole charge of these schools. Of course, many of the schools did not survive the death of the principal; others closed as a result of the Second World War. Finally, the Education Act of 1944 sounded the death knell for most of the remainder, since the small private schools could not compete with the publicly funded sector.

The 1920s and 1930s were the heyday of these schools, and many of the school stories of the time were written about them, rather than the large public schools. They were read by the pupils themselves and by the many children at council schools who could only dream about attending such places. This is, of course, not restricted to those years. My own daughter, who attends a state village school, plays a very long and complicated boarding-school game based on her reading of the Malory Towers and St Clare's books by Enid Blyton.

Some of these stories, such as those by Josephine Elder, Evelyn Smith and, to a lesser extent, Winifred Darch (most of whose stories were about high schools), were realistic and showed the schools as they really were; while some, such as those by Dorothea Moore, were wildly exaggerated in order (presumably) to produce a more exciting story. In most cases it was the adventures and activities of the girls out of lesson time that predominated. I can only assume that this was because they were read by schoolgirls at the time. It was felt that they would not want to read about the mundane day-to-day things that took place in their own school lives and about relationships between characters, but needed a little excitement and adventure to spice up the story.

But why do people today still read and enjoy these books? Part of the answer lies in the fact that many girls' stories on whatever subject were set within a school background, so if you read girls' stories of any sort from that time it is almost inevitable that they will be school stories. The other major reason is nostalgia. Some of today's collectors went to school then, and those who didn't probably know enough about the 1920s and 1930s from television and films to be able to imagine what it was like. The books give a rose-tinted view of the times; the majority are about upper middle-class children at upper middle-class boarding schools.

After the Second World War, things changed. The small schools no longer existed and people could not take things for granted any more. Their homes and families had been violated by Nazi bombs and the feelings of comfort and safety were no longer there.

Girls and women were far more emancipated, and stories no longer needed to be set in the cosy pre-war school world.

In addition to the more unlikely tales, there was a small nucleus of writers who brought in real events. May Baldwin was one of the first, setting school stories in France during the German occupation of Alsace (*The Follies of Fifi*, W. & R. Chambers, 1907), and during the separation of Church and State (*Peg's Adventures in Paris*, W. & R. Chambers, 1906), amongst many other current events. She even covered such subjects as child abuse and racism in books published in the first 30 years of this century, such as *The School in the Wilds* (W. & R. Chambers, 1925) and *Hilda's Experiences* (W. & R. Chambers, 1913). Others followed, including, notably, Olive Dougan, who wrote *The Schoolgirl Refugee* (Blackie) in 1940 about a half-German girl who had to come to England as her friends were Jewish and her brother was in hiding from the Nazis.

This subject leads us on to Elinor Brent-Dyer and what I consider to be her finest book: *The Chalet School in Exile*. Like Olive Dougan, Brent-Dyer was ahead of her time in depicting what was really happening in Germany, so much so that the original dust jacket was withdrawn shortly after publication as the picture of a Nazi officer was considered either too frightening for children or not conducive to high sales.

I think this realism is one of the things that draws collectors to the Chalet School series. Although the later books in the series degenerated into standard formula school stories, often repeating earlier plots, the first ones showed clearly what life was like in Austria, Guernsey and England. They did not gloss over unpleasant detail; readers feel that the Chalet School was a real place full of real people who had their faults as well as their good qualities.

I found this whilst rereading the series yet again recently. There is the feeling of comfort, that I know these people and that they are real to me. I found myself really looking forward to the times when I could sit down and read about them. Often I remember the major events of the book and think to myself "Not Eustacia's accident again" or "Not the rivalry with the Saints"; but although these are important happenings, it is the normal things that stand out now. Despite the floods and snowstorms, not to mention a Ruritanian princess — probably necessary to sell the books at the time — there is what seems to be a real school set in a real time and place.

Once the earlier stories have been read, the lure of the series beckons. The characters grow older and develop, and we need to know what happens to them next. When I pick up a Chalet School book, I know that although I may not remember the plot I will remember the characters. We all have our favourites and there are those we loathe, but we know that it will all come out all right in the end. The books are both addictive and satisfying. .

Brent-Dyer fans collect the books because they enjoy the contents — whether contained in a tatty paperback or a fine first edition in dust jacket. Most collectors like nice copies, but only because they enjoy the books. There is no point in having beautiful copies of books that remain unread. I am proud of my Brent-Dyer collection. They do look nice on the shelves, but if I did not read and enjoy them there would be no reason to have them, and I'm sure that the vast majority of collectors feel exactly the same.

IMAGES OF THE CHALET SCHOOL DUSTWRAPPERS, COVERS AND ILLUSTRATIONS

CLARISSA CRIDLAND

THIS chapter looks at the dustwrappers, covers and illustrations used for the Chalet School series, published by W. & R. Chambers and HarperCollins Armada in the UK, Dymocks in Australia and Latina in Portugal. I first wrote about this subject in *Friends of the Chalet School Newsletter 14*, published in February 1992. Looking back, I realise how little I knew then, and how much more I still have to discover. At the time, I did not even own a full set of books (the article dealt only with the Chambers and Dymocks titles) and relied on other Friends to provide me with the missing information. As well as writing the article, I produced a chart which briefly described the fronts, backs, spines and flaps of the dust wrappers of every edition of the books and which also listed the various inside illustrations: not possessing all the books myself this was inevitably full of inaccuracies.

However, the obsession which gripped me when preparing the article has not abated, and I am now collecting every edition of every book Elinor M. Brent-Dyer ever wrote. I am also planning to publish a book which will cover the illustrations from all her books, and which will, where possible, give biographical information about the artists concerned. Tracking down the various artists is proving extremely difficult, even though I have been working in publishing for 18 years and have numerous contacts: publishers do not always keep records. I am at the time of writing (mid-October 1994) about a quarter of the way through the process and hope to be able to publish the book towards the end of 1995. What is it, though, that has fuelled my obsession this far?

Chambers published 58 titles in the main Chalet School series and five extras — the three *Chalet Books for Girls*, *The Chalet School and Rosalie* and *The Chalet School Cook Book*. There were five named artists for the series as published by Chambers — Nina K. Brisley, Mackay, W. Spence, D. Brook and Balmer. In addition, there were various unnamed artists, some of whom illustrated just one dust wrapper and a couple who did several. Into this last category has to come the artist who did the illustrations for the three *Chalet Books for Girls* and the first dustwrapper for *Three Go To The Chalet School*, whose signature appears only on *The Third Chalet Book for Girls* where it is almost illegible — the closest I and other Friends have been able to get is "Terre Tomilton".

Dymocks in Australia published the first six books in the series in the early 1950s using two further artists, one unnamed and the other Alan P. Rigby. The two titles so far discovered in Portuguese (*The School at the Chalet* and *Jo of the Chalet School*) were produced with the Mackay and Brook illustrations already used by Chambers. In 1967 Collins started to issue the series under the Armada imprint: unfortunately they have not credited any of the artists who have done the covers and some of these are still unnamed — it is not even clear how many there have been. Two of them, however, are Gerry Haylock, who drew some of the covers in the 1970s, and Gwyn Jones, who has done all the covers since the early 1980s.

Nina K. Brisley illustrated the early dust wrappers of the Chambers editions of the first 19 books, as well as those for nos. 21-5 and 27. It is probable that she also did the first dust wrapper for *The Chalet School in the Oberland* (no. 26) since she certainly did the frontispiece, but there is no signature. It is probably partly because she was the main artist for the Chalet School series over a period of 21 years that Nina K. Brisley is acknowledged as the "true" Chalet School illustrator; however, the charm of her paintings must also have something to do with this. The illustrations have a delightful period feel and they are also extremely accurate in what they portray.

Why Chambers should have used other artists is still a mystery, since Nina K. Brisley did not die until 1978. Nina Kennard Brisley was the sister of Joyce Lankester Brisley (of Milly-Molly-Mandy fame). They had another sister, Ethel, who specialised in miniatures and portraits. It was Ethel who introduced her sisters to Lord Northcliffe, who in turn introduced them to the editor of *Home Chat*. For years they produced illustrations and occasional verses for the paper, while building up their contacts with other papers and magazines.

Ethel moved into fashion illustration, but she did also produce one book of her own and one with Nina, as well as having a few drawings in annuals. For her book illustrations she used the pen name of Tony Brisley. Nina herself went on to illustrate not only a number of Elinor Brent-Dyer's non Chalet titles, as well as the Chalets, but also several of Elsie J. Oxenham's books among others.

The first title to be illustrated by an artist other than Nina K. Brisley was *The Chalet School in Exile*. Brisley did indeed do the original dust wrapper (depicting a Nazi standing in a threatening attitude over Joey and the Robin) but, possibly because there were complaints about this choice of subject, a second dustwrapper was commissioned. This shows the girls in hiding from the Nazis (to my mind no less frightening a subject) on the front and Cornelia Flower running towards the burning plane (in Guernsey) on the spine. The first edition of the book is to be found with both wrappers, although the early one is far more rare. It is probable that when the second dust wrapper was printed, the copies of the first one were stripped off the books and destroyed. To the best of my knowledge, the book was not reprinted until 1950 and it was then reprinted a further three times, the second dust wrapper being used in all printings.

In the late 1940s John Mackay, an Edinburgh artist who did a lot of work for Chambers, was asked to illustrate new wrappers for *The School at the Chalet*, *The Exploits of the Chalet Girls*, *The Chalet School and the Lintons* and *The New House at the Chalet School*. He had already done *The Little Missus*, one of Elinor Brent-Dyer's non-Chalet titles which was published in 1942, and he was to go on to draw the covers for the four Geography Readers in 1951. Mr Mackay cannot now remember why he was asked to illustrate the Chalet titles since they were not his normal type of book, but he thinks that it was because the "usual Chalet School artist" was "no longer available".

Why the books should have been reillustrated at all is a mystery, although the war may have had something to do with it. There were no Chalet School reprints (so far as I have been able to trace) between 1942-7, with the exception of *Jo to the Rescue* which was reprinted in 1946 (the first edition having been printed in 1945). The last printings of the four titles reillustrated by Mackay were in 1941 and it is possible that the original plates were lost either by the publishers or by the printers during the war years. However, this is not a very likely theory since, for example, both *Princess* and *Head Girl* were also reprinted in 1941, and when they were reprinted after the war in 1949 it was with the original Nina K. Brisley illustrations. Chambers no longer have any records and it seems likely that we shall never know why these titles were reillustrated.

Between 1947 and 1949 Chambers published the three *Chalet Books for Girls* and *Three Go to the Chalet School*, illustrated, as I have mentioned above, by an artist whose signature is not legible. It seems odd that Chambers should not have asked John Mackay to do these as well, or alternatively that they should not have asked this artist to do the Mackay reprints mentioned above. The three *Chalet Books for Girls* not only had full colour covers (or a dust wrapper in the case of the third book), but also full colour frontispieces and several black and white line drawings: it is thus a great pity that the artist did not apparently read the stories, since the girls are depicted in incorrect stripy blazers and navy blue tunics.

It is interesting to note that in 1970 at least two books were produced by Murrays' (*My Treasure Hour Bumper Annual* and *My Treasure Hour Playtime Annual*) which contain large chunks of *The Chalet Book for Girls* and the *Third Chalet Book for Girls,* in which the black-and-white illustrations from the 1940s are redrawn in the style of 1970! To date, I have not found a third volume, but it would seem only logical that *The Second Chalet Book for Girls* was treated in a similar style.

Chambers had a number of other Chalet titles reillustrated, although it is difficult to understand why they did some and not others and why the new illustrations were commissioned at different times. After Mackay, the next artist to reillustrate the books was W. Spence, who did *Princess* and *Rivals* in 1955, *Eustacia* in 1956 and *Head Girl* in 1960, as well as doing the dust wrapper for *Joey Goes to the Oberland* in 1954. So far, I know nothing about W. Spence, except that he or she illustrated a number of other children's titles during this era, including Elinor Brent-Dyer's *Chudleigh Hold*. Most Chalet fans would agree that the W. Spence illustrations probably fall into the middle of the best-to-worst scale of accuracy and charm.

D. Brook, who illustrated most of the later Chalet School titles, also reillustrated some of the earlier titles: *The Chalet School in the Oberland* in 1958, *Jo of the Chalet School*, *The Chalet School and Jo* and *Jo Returns to the Chalet School* in 1960, and *The Chalet School and the Lintons* in 1964. This last title was the only hardback to have three different illustrators in the UK, although four of the early titles were reillustrated by artists in Australia.

Why *The Chalet School in the Oberland* (and also *Shocks for the Chalet School* which was probably drawn by D. Brook) should have been reillustrated so soon after the first editions were printed is a puzzle. The original illustrations in both cases (*Shocks* by Nina K. Brisley and *Oberland* probably so) are charming and could not possibly have dated within four years. It is possible that there was an objection to the smoking on the spine of *Oberland*, but this alone would surely not have justified having the whole wrapper reillustrated.

In the early 1950s Dymocks in Australia published the first six titles under their own imprint. They used the original Nina K. Brisley illustrations for *Princess* and *Rivals*, but had the other four titles reillustrated. The new illustrations for *Jo of the Chalet School* and *Head Girl* depict the same subjects as those by Brisley and have a charm all of their own; unfortunately the artist is not credited. Alan P. Rigby, about whom I know nothing, was commissioned to do the dustwrappers for *The School at the Chalet* and *Eustacia*. These have to be two of the most inaccurate illustrations in the whole series, and for this reason alone are well worth collecting!

The 1950s saw Chambers experiment with a number of different artists, who have not signed their work and whose identities remain a mystery. In 1951 Chambers published an original paperback, *The Chalet School and Rosalie*, which had a cover by an unknown artist. Several people have suggested that the style is similar to that of Nina K. Brisley, but there is no signature to prove this and to my eye it isn't close enough. Other unknown artists drew the dust wrappers for *Changes for the Chalet School* in 1953 (although the spine uses the Mackay illustration from *Exploits*), the 1955 edition of *Tom Tackles the Chalet School*, the 1955 reprint of *Three Go to the Chalet School*, and the 1958 reprint of *Shocks for the Chalet School*, although it's possible that *Tom* and *Shocks* were drawn by D. Brook since they are very much in the same style.

To the best of my knowledge, there was no second dustwrapper for *The New Chalet School* (although the spine illustration was changed). If anyone should find one (the original portrays Joey with Maria Balbini sitting on a bed), then I should be delighted to hear about it. It is possible that Chambers planned to have the dust wrapper reillustrated and then did not do so — this seems to have been the case with *Joey Goes to the Oberland,* for in the *Chalet Club News Letter* of November 1963 it was announced that this title would be reissued with a new dust jacket, and to the best of my knowledge this never happened.

The publication of the Chambers edition of *The Chalet School and Barbara* saw a new departure, not only in that the school was now set in Switzerland, but also in that all the dust wrappers were illustrated by D. Brook and that none of these was reillustrated. There are some dust wrappers which are not actually signed by the artist, but since they are very much in the same style and in all cases except one (*A Future Chalet School Girl*) the books have frontispieces signed "D. Brook", it seems probable that D. Brook did all the illustrations for the later titles.

I am at the moment still trying to gather information on D. Brook. It has been suggested that her name was Daphne Brook and it has also been suggested that she is a relation of George Brook who illustrated some of Enid Blyton's Secret Seven series, since the illustrations look so alike. I personally cannot see any likeness and Hodder & Stoughton, who publish the Secret Seven books and who *do* keep records, have no address for George Brook.

There was one further artist used by Chambers during Elinor Brent Dyer's lifetime, and this was Balmer who drew the dust wrapper and presumably the woodcut used on the spine and title page for *The Chalet School Cook Book*. The *Cook Book* is a fascinating book in its own right, being a collection of recipes linked with conversations between Joey Bettany, Simone Lecoutier, Frieda Mensch and Marie von Eschenau, set in Tyrol after the four have left school and before Marie's wedding, although it wasn't published until 1953. To today's reader, used to a more healthy way of eating, the recipes make interesting reading, with large amounts of lard etc being used, and the book is eagerly sought after by cookbook collectors as well as Elinor Brent-Dyer's fans. The dust wrapper is rare and really only worth paying for if you are a completist, since it competes with those by Alan P. Rigby for being the most inaccurate in the series. I still have no leads on who Balmer might be.

In 1988 Chambers reprinted the first four Chalet titles as "facsimiles", using the original Nina K. Brisley dust wrappers, but dropping the original inside plates and commissioning some new illustrations in the style of woodcuts by Janet MacKay. For most collectors these completely spoilt the books, and they were not a success commercially. They can still be found fairly easily in remainder bookshops.

Most of the Chambers books had some inside illustrations. The first twelve books each had four black-and-white plates by Nina K. Brisley — a frontispiece and three others. In the early titles, these were kept for the second printing and sometimes the third, although the order of the plates was sometimes changed. Reprints in the second half of the 1930s usually kept just one of the plates as a frontispiece. *The New Chalet School* had only a frontispiece and once the war started the black-and-white plates were dropped. Most of these early titles did not have new frontispieces when they were reillustrated. From *The Chalet School in Exile* onwards, black-and-white line drawings or ink drawings (sometimes reproduced in a colour such as dark green and sometimes reproduced in black and white) were used.

The exception was *The Chalet School Reunion* (the fiftieth book in the series) which was illustrated with four three-colour illustrations as well as a colour frontispiece. The dust wrapper for this, too, was different in that it wrapped right round the book, rather than having one picture on the front and a different one on the spine with a plain (or textual) back. The Brisley plates for the early books are delightful and they really do add to the enjoyment of reading the books. They are incredibly accurate in their portrayal of the various scenes shown — unlike most of today's artists Nina K. Brisley certainly read what she illustrated. The black-and-white line and the ink drawings inevitably do not reveal as much as the plates, but they still add to the books' appeal. To the best of my knowledge, the only book which had a new frontispiece when the dust wrapper was reillustrated was *The Chalet School and Jo*.

The spines of the books are usually what one sees first in a bookcase, and most of the spines of the dust wrappers of the Chalet School series are extremely attractive. Nina K. Brisley's spines are particularly charming — perhaps because many of the early ones were designed to be at least an inch-and-a-half thick and so she could portray an actual scene from a book. The illustrations on the spines for the middle books vary in that some, for instance, show simply a head and shoulders portrait of Joey or girls skiing, and others show an identifiable scene from part of the book — e.g. Elma Conroy sitting by a window smoking and reading Stuart Raynor's letter in the original *Chalet School in the Oberland*.

Titles from *The Chalet School and Barbara* onwards all had more detailed spines, although it isn't always easy to identify the scenes; however one can probably assume that they feature the heroine of the particular book. In 1951-2 Chambers issued reprints of most titles with a blue spine. Why, it is hard to conjecture, although possibly to give the books a "series" look. The idea was obviously not a success, since by the mid-1950s all titles once again had illustrations on their spines. (It is amazing how many of those blue spines feature on sales lists!) However, it is possible that Chambers had either lost or destroyed the films for some of the spine illustrations.

The 1956 reprint of *Jo of the Chalet School* had the original spine illustration from *The New Chalet School,* and the reprint of the same year for *The New Chalet School* had the original spine illustration from *Princess*, which by that stage had a new dust wrapper. For some extraordinary reason, when Dymocks issued their editions of nos. 2-4 in 1952, they also used blue spines. Their edition of *The School at the Chalet* had a magenta spine (even worse!), whereas *Eustacia* had a wrap round illustration.

One point of interest is that all the artists who portrayed the adult Joey did so in a way that is instantly recognisable. Four examples by different artists are the spine of *Jo Returns to the Chalet School* (Nina K. Brisley), the illustration opposite p.16 in *The Second Chalet Book for Girls* (unknown), the spine of *Joey Goes to the Oberland* (W. Spence) and the final plate in *The Chalet School Reunion* (D. Brook). In each case one can say instantly "that is Joey". Her dark hair with its whorls of plaits over each ear and her slim figure, clearly seen even in a head-and-shoulders portrait, are unmistakable.

There are four different styles of paperback illustration. The first, used from 1967-70, is easily identifiable since above the lettering on the front covers there are two lines in an upside down V, made to look like the eves of a chalet roof. The second, used from 1970 to about 1984, can be recognised by the somewhat gothic type of lettering. The third style is the pointillist artwork used from 1984 onwards, and what I term the fourth style is actually the same artwork but with the box for the titles, used from about 1989.

As I said at the beginning of this chapter, HarperCollins do not credit their artists, and neither do they hold any records, having moved twice over the last decade. It was, of course, easy to get in touch with the current artist, Gwyn Jones, who has been responsible for the third and fourth styles, but tracking down the artists of the previous two styles has been more problematical. Fortunately, I know well Marion Lloyd, who was Editor of Armada from the mid-1970s to the mid-1980s, and she gave me Gerry Haylock's name.

When I wrote to him, however, giving him details of the second style covers, he replied saying that he had certainly done some of them, but he was fairly sure that others — and especially *Exile* (showing the girls crawling out of the cave) — were the work of another artist. I have yet to find out any information on this second artist — and indeed it is possible that there may have been more than one other.

The artist who did the covers between 1967 and 1970 has also proved a problem to identify. Marian and various others have suggested that Betty Maxey may have drawn the covers, but so far I have been unable to trace her. More recently, an FOCS member, Richard Macfarlane, has suggested that Sheila Rose was the artist. I am hopeful that he may be right and think I can probably find her.

The accuracy of the paperback illustrations often leaves much to be desired. Most artists these days do not read the books they illustrate, but simply work from an editor's brief of often only a few lines. This may explain the inaccuracies of the incorrect uniform colours (the uniform from *The Chalet School and Barbara* onwards changed from the original brown and flame to a bright gentian blue with touches of crimson) and there were even scenes illustrated which had been cut from the paperbacks. The early paperback illustrations now have a certain nostalgic charm of their own — and for someone of my age (I was born in 1955) the sight of Eustacia in baby doll pyjamas brings back definite memories! The first and second styled books not only had front cover illustrations, but also had smaller illustrations on the back cover.

Having read through what I have written for this chapter, I am not sure that I have answered the question I asked — "what is it, though, that has fuelled my obsession thus far?" — and I'm not sure that I can put this into words. The charm of Nina K. Brisley's illustrations has to play a large part, but cannot alone be responsible. Perhaps it is the fun of finding out more, or the fun of buying or being given a book I don't have. Probably, though, it is what links all of us who are Friends of the Chalet School — the friendships I have made in my researches. Whenever I ask for help, I receive replies to my queries. Sometimes I already know the answers and sometimes they set me leaping for joy and off on another tack. Whichever it is, it doesn't matter. It is the spirit of friendship in which those letters were written which is important and which gives me the encouragement to go on with my research.

This chapter has been written at an interim stage and doubtless I shall get letters as a result. Some may point out mistakes, others will fill in further clues. I look forward to them all.

First, subsequent and paperback editions of *Three Go to the Chalet School* (1949) and *The Chalet School and the Island* (1950).

BOOKS BY ELINOR M. BRENT-DYER

LA ROCHELLE SERIES

(published by W. & R. Chambers, Edinburgh)

1. *Gerry Goes to School* (1922)
2. *A Head Girl's Difficulties* (1923)
3. *The Maids of La Rochelle* (1924)
4. *Seven Scamps* (1927)
5. *Heather Leaves School* (1929)
6. *Janie of La Rochelle* (1932)
7. *Janie Steps In* (1953)

CHALET SCHOOL SERIES

(published by W. & R. Chambers, Edinburgh)

1. *The School at the Chalet* (1925)
2. *Jo of the Chalet School* (1926)
3. *The Princess of the Chalet School* (1927)
4. *The Head Girl of the Chalet School* (1928)
5. *The Rivals of the Chalet School* (1929)
6. *Eustacia Goes to the Chalet School* (1930)
7. *The Chalet School and Jo* (1931)
8. *The Chalet Girls in Camp* (1932)
9. *The Exploits of the Chalet Girls* (1933)
10. *The Chalet School and the Lintons* (1934)
11. *The New House at the Chalet School* (1935)
12. *Jo Returns to the Chalet School* (1936)
13. *The New Chalet School* (1938)
14. *The Chalet School in Exile* (1940)
15. *The Chalet School Goes to It* (1941)

16. *The Highland Twins at the Chalet School* (1942)
17. *Lavender Laughs in the Chalet School* (1943)
18. *Gay From China at the Chalet School* (1944)
19. *Jo to the Rescue* (1945)
    The Chalet Book for Girls (1947)
    The Second Chalet Book for Girls (1948)
    The Third Chalet Book for Girls (1949)
31. *Tom Tackles the Chalet School* (1955)
(first published in *The Second Chalet Book for Girls* and *The Third Chalet Book for Girls*)
    The Chalet School and Rosalie (1951)
20. *Three Go to the Chalet School* (1949)
21. *The Chalet School and the Island* (1950)
22. *Peggy of the Chalet School* (1950)
23. *Carola Storms the Chalet School* (1951)
24. *The Wrong Chalet School* (1952)
25. *Shocks for the Chalet School* (1952)
26. *The Chalet School in the Oberland* (1952)
    The Chalet School Cook Book (1953)
27. *Bride Leads the Chalet School* (1953)
28. *Changes for the Chalet School* (1953)
29. *Joey Goes to the Oberland* (1954)
30. *The Chalet School and Barbara* (1954)
32. *The Chalet School Does It Again* (1955)
33. *A Chalet Girl from Kenya* (1955)
34. *Mary-Lou of the Chalet School* (1956)
35. *A Genius at the Chalet School* (1956)
36. *A Problem for the Chalet School* (1956)
37. *The New Mistress at the Chalet School* (1957)
38. *Excitements at the Chalet School* (1957)
39. *The Coming of Age of the Chalet School* (1958)
40. *The Chalet School and Richenda* (1958)
41. *Trials for the Chalet School* (1959)
42. *Theodora and the Chalet School* (1959)
43. *Joey and Co. in Tirol* (1960)
44. *Ruey Richardson — Chaletian* (1960)
45. *A Leader in the Chalet School* (1961)

46. *The Chalet School Wins the Trick* (1961)
47. *A Future Chalet School Girl* (1962)
48. *The Feud in the Chalet School* (1962)
49. *The Chalet School Triplets* (1963)
50. *The Chalet School Reunion* (1963)
51. *Jane and the Chalet School* (1964)
52. *Redheads at the Chalet School* (1964)
53. *Adrienne and the Chalet School* (1965)
54. *Summer Term at the Chalet School* (1965)
55. *Challenge for the Chalet School* (1966)
56. *Two Sams at the Chalet School* (1967)
57. *Althea Joins the Chalet School* (1969)
58. *Prefects of the Chalet School* (1970)

JANEWAYS BOOKS

A Thrilling Term at Janeways (Thomas Nelson, 1927)
Caroline the Second (Girls' Own Paper, 1937)

LORNA BOOKS

Lorna at Wynyards (Lutterworth Press, 1947)
Stepsisters for Lorna (C. & J. Temple, 1948)

ADVENTURE BOOKS

Fardingales (Latimer House, 1950)
The "Susannah" Adventure (W. & R. Chambers, 1953)
Chudleigh Hold (W. & R. Chambers, 1954)
The Condor Crags Adventure (W. & R. Chambers, 1954)
Top Secret (W. & R. Chambers, 1955)

SCHOOLGIRLS ABROAD

(A series of geography readers published by W. & R. Chambers, 1951)

1. *Verena Visits New Zealand*
2. *Bess on her Own in Canada*
3. *A Quintette in Queensland*
4. *Sharlie's Kenya Diary*

SKELTON HALL BOOKS

The School at Skelton Hall (Max Parrish, 1962)
Trouble at Skelton Hall (Max Parrish, 1963)

OTHERS

Judy the Guide (Thomas Nelson, 1928)
The New House Mistress (Thomas Nelson, 1928)
The School by the River (Burns, Oates & Washbourne, 1930)
The Feud in the Fifth Remove (Girls' Own Paper, 1931)
The Little Marie-José (Burns, Oates & Washbourne, 1932)
Carnation of the Upper Fourth (Girls' Own Paper, 1934)
Elizabeth the Gallant (Thornton Butterworth, 1935)
Monica Turns Up Trumps (Girls' Own Paper, 1936)
They Both Liked Dogs (Girls' Own Paper, 1938)
The Little Missus (W. & R. Chambers, 1942)
The Lost Staircase (W. & R. Chambers, 1946)
Kennelmaid Nan (Lutterworth Press, 1954
Nesta Steps Out (Oliphants, 1954)
Beechy of the Harbour School (Oliphants, 1955)
Leader in Spite of Herself (Oliphants, 1956)

PRICE GUIDE TO BOOKS BY ELINOR M BRENT-DYER

GILL BILSKI

The prices given below are all for the cheapest readable edition available, that is, reprints without illustrations for the early titles and first editions for the later titles (which were not reprinted), both without dust jackets. The numbers used for the Chalet books are the hardback numbers (see Bibliography). These are the prices you could expect to pay when buying from specialist second-hand children's book dealers. It's quite possible to find them at considerably higher prices — or, of course, to find one cheap in a charity shop!

£5 or less: Chalets 1-7, 10-12. *The New House Mistress.*

£10 or less: Chalets 8-9, 13-16. The first six *La Rochelle* books.

£15 or less: Chalets 17-18, 20-23, 25, 30. *The Feud in the Fifth Remove, Monica Turns Up Trumps, Janie Steps In, Carnation of the Upper Fourth* (RTS edition — the 1958 Lutterworth Press edition is abridged), *A Thrilling Term at Janeways, The "Susannah" Adventure, Chudleigh Hold, The Condor Crags Adventure, Top Secret.*

£20 or less: Chalets 19, 24, 26, 31, 34-6. *Judy the Guide.*

£25 or less: Chalets 27-9, 32-3, 37-42, 44-6, 48-9, 51-5. *The Lost Staircase.*

£30 or less: Chalets 56-8. *The Chalet Book for Girls, The Third Chalet Book for Girls, Lorna at Wynyards, Fardingales, Kennelmaid Nan.*

£40 or less: Chalets 43, 47, 50. *The Second Chalet Book for Girls, Stepsisters for Lorna.*

£50 or less: *The Chalet School and Rosalie, The Little Missus, Nesta Steps Out, Beechy of the Harbour School, Leader in Spite of Herself,* both Skelton Hall books.

£60 or less: *The Chalet School Cook Book.*

£75 or less: *Caroline the Second, Elizabeth the Gallant, They Both Liked Dogs,* the four geography readers.

Unknown: *The School by the River, The Little Marie-José.*